Language and Social Disadvantage

Language and Social Disadvantage

THEORY INTO PRACTICE

Edited by
JUDY CLEGG

JANE GINSBORG

John Wiley & Sons, Ltd

Other Wiley Editorial Offices

John Wiley & Sons Inc., 111 River Street, Hoboken, NJ 07030, USA

Jossey-Bass, 989 Market Street, San Francisco, CA 94103-1741, USA

Wiley-VCH Verlag GmbH, Boschstr. 12, D-69469 Weinheim, Germany

John Wiley & Sons Australia Ltd, 42 McDougall Street, Milton, Queensland 4064, Australia

John Wiley & Sons (Asia) Pte Ltd, 2 Clementi Loop #02-01, Jin Xing Distripark,
Singapore 129809

John Wiley & Sons Canada Ltd, 6045 Freemont Blvd, Mississauga, ONT, L5R 4J3

Wiley also publishes its books in a variety of electronic formats. Some content that appears in print
may not be available in electronic books.

Library of Congress Cataloging in Publication Data

Language and social disadvantage : theory into practice / edited by Judy Clegg, Jane Ginsborg.
   p.   cm.
  Includes bibliographical references and index.
  ISBN-13: 978-0-470-01975-7 (pbk. : alk. paper)
  ISBN-10: 0-470-01975-1 (pbk. : alk. paper)
  1. Language acquisition.   2. Children with social disabilities.   I. Clegg, Judy.   II. Ginsborg,
Jane.
  P118.L5738 2006
  401′.93—dc22   2006008773

British Library Cataloguing in Publication Data

ISBN-13: 978-0-470-01975-7
ISBN-10: 0-470-01975-1

Typeset in 10/12pt Times by Integra Software Services Pvt. Ltd, Pondicherry, India
Printed and bound in Great Britain by TJ International Ltd, Padstow, Cornwall
This book is printed on acid-free paper responsibly manufactured from sustainable forestry in which at
least two trees are planted for each one used for paper production.

Contents

List of Contributors

Judy Clegg, Human Communication Sciences, University of Sheffield

Jane Ginsborg, Royal Northern College of Music

Nicola Botting, School of Psychological Sciences, University of Manchester

Monica Bray, Speech and Language Therapy Group, Leeds Metropolitan University

Julie E. Dockrell, Psychology and Human Development, Institute of Education, University of London

Ivy Doherty, School of Allied Health Professions, Leeds Metropolitan University

Marion Farmer, Division of Psychology, School of Psychology and Sport Sciences, University of Northumbria

Fleur Griffiths, Educational Consultant, Hartlepool Local Educational Authority

Frances Harris, Sure Start Speech and Language Development Project, City University

Linda Hobbs, East Riding of Yorkshire Council, Children, Family and Adult Services

Victoria Joffe, Department of Language and Communication Science, City University

Diane King, Psychology and Human Development, Institute of Education, University of London

Jenny Landells, School of Allied Health Professions, Leeds Metropolitan University

James Law, Centre for Integrated Healthcare Research, Queen Margaret University

Jenny Leyden, Human Communications Sciences, University of Sheffield

Ann Locke, Education and Language Consultant

Caroline Pickstone, Institute of General Practice, University of Sheffield

Helen Stringer, School of Education, Communication and Language Sciences, University of Newcastle upon Tyne; Newcastle upon Tyne Hospitals NHS Trust

Marcin Szczerbinski, Human Communications Sciences, University of Sheffield

Morag Stuart, Psychology and Human Development, Institute of Education, University of London

Introduction

THE ORIGINS OF THE BOOK

This book derives from research originally carried out by Ann Locke, Jane Ginsborg and some of their colleagues in the Department of Human Communication Sciences at the University of Sheffield. The research focused on the language and cognitive development of socially disadvantaged young children at nursery and primary schools (Locke, Ginsborg & Peers, 2002). A large proportion of children tested for the purposes of the research were found to be entering nursery school with delayed language skills, according to clinical definitions, which impacted on their subsequent development, including their educational attainment. The results of a series of research projects carried out in collaboration with local educational services suggest that language delay needs to be addressed not only by teachers and other professionals in primary schools, but even in secondary schools.

There is a growing body of research into the relationship between language and social disadvantage. The purpose of this book is to show how current theories, supported by educational, health and psychological research, inform interventions designed to enhance children's understanding and use of language.

WHY A BOOK DEVOTED TO LANGUAGE AND SOCIAL DISADVANTAGE?

The development and particularly the educational attainment of children in areas of socio-economic deprivation are of national concern. Programmes such as Sure Start and other government-funded initiatives aim to improve social and educational outcomes for disadvantaged children. The promotion of child development, generally, is central to these initiatives, but, increasingly, speech and language development is also becoming a priority.

In recent years, more emphasis has been placed on the association between children's early speech and language development and their educational attainment.

Language and Social Disadvantage: Theory into Practice Edited by J. Clegg and J. Ginsborg
© 2006 John Wiley & Sons, Ltd

There is increasing evidence to show that early speech and language skills are fundamental to literacy development: for example, 'Speaking and Listening' now forms part of the National Curriculum. Yet many nursery and primary schools in areas of socio-economic deprivation report that the speech and language skills of very young children are inadequate for the Early Years curriculum, and as a result these children start their school careers already at a disadvantage. It remains to be seen whether the language delays identified by Locke et al. (2002) and other researchers resolve over time or if they persist; furthermore, we do not know the long-term consequences of persisting language delay.

WHAT IS SOCIAL DISADVANTAGE?

There are, of course, conflicting perspectives on and accounts of social disadvantage. These are reflected – and indeed reflected on – by the contributors to this book. Different criteria are used to define social disadvantage, with socio-economic status being perhaps the measure used most often. However, factors such as family status, type of housing and level of maternal education can also be used to identify social disadvantage. Research suggests that it is often associated with high levels of unemployment, poor health, short life expectancy, high rates of offending behaviour and increased use of mental health and social services. There are multiple and interrelated reasons, at genetic, biological and social levels, which may explain these findings. Delayed or disordered language development in childhood may constitute just one more of a range of possible causes. However, it is imperative to note that in many studies the outcomes and attainments of children from socially disadvantaged backgrounds are compared with 'norms' that do not necessarily reflect their own expectations or aspirations.

HOW DOES THIS BOOK WORK?

Theory and practice are the two key topics of this book. It is therefore divided into two parts. The first part addresses the complex theoretical interrelationships between language and social disadvantage. Cognition, literacy, behaviour, learning and socio-emotional development are considered in depth, together with the outcomes of different types of intervention. The second part of the book looks at the practical applications of theory, reporting and evaluating recent interventions designed to promote language development in nurseries, schools and other contexts. These reports highlight the innovative nature of many such interventions – typical of current practice – but do not flinch from reflecting on some of the difficulties involved.

The contributors are leaders in their fields and together combine perspectives from education, speech and language therapy and psychology. This interdisciplinary, collaborative approach to the study of language and social disadvantage reflects the integrative nature of the work of professionals with different theoretical orientations involved in the education and care of socially disadvantaged children.

EMERGING THEMES

Three major themes are explored in the book. The first is the impact of social disadvantage on language development. Jane Ginsborg (Chapter 1) critically discusses the effects of social disadvantage on children's language acquisition and use. Complex issues are tackled, including the theories proposed to explain language delay in socially disadvantaged children. Concepts of difference and deficit, and their implications for education and academic achievement, are challenged. The distinction is drawn between language difficulties resulting from the environmental impact of social disadvantage, and language difficulties resulting from cognitive or other biological deficits. Both, however, may underlie cognitive, educational and psychosocial outcomes.

The second theme is the socially disadvantaging impact of speech and language difficulties (SLD) on children. Nicola Botting (Chapter 2) examines the interplay between language and cognition in typical and atypical development. Sociocognitive responsiveness and information processing are highlighted as two aspects of cognition particularly relevant to language development. Here, the relationship between cognition and language development in Specific Language Impairment (SLI) is discussed, emphasising the fluctuating trajectories of cognitive development in children with SLI and how this may impact on language development over time. These points are then explored further in relation to language and social disadvantage, particularly focusing on ways in which delayed cognitive and language skills can lead to persisting social disadvantage. The role of language in the development of literacy and numeracy is examined by Ivy Doherty and Jenny Landells (Chapter 3), who show that children with delayed language are at increased risk of experiencing difficulties with the development of literacy and numeracy. Judy Clegg (Chapter 4) stresses the importance of considering the long-term trajectories of and outcomes for children with SLD, whether or not they are from socially disadvantaged backgrounds. She argues that risk and resilience factors should be identified, even though changes do occur over time; long-term outcomes for communication, cognition, educational attainment and psychosocial functioning are all described in detail. Psychosocial aspects of development are explored further by Marion Farmer (Chapter 5). She discusses the role of language in the development of social and emotional understanding, and highlights the centrality of language to the development of the self, self-concept, emotional understanding and social cognition. Early conversation enables children to develop self-awareness and emotional self-regulation, but language delay can impact severely on opportunities for conversation; this in turn affects opportunities for effective social interaction in subsequent years. Helen Stringer and Judy Clegg (Chapter 6) discuss the relationships between language, behaviour and social disadvantage, specifically focusing on the higher rates of SLD and educational and behavioural difficulties (EBD) observed in socially disadvantaged children. They discuss a range of explanations for the co-morbidity of SLD and EBD, advocating collaboration between speech and language therapy and child and adolescent mental health services. Monica Bray (Chapter 7) presents an alternative perspective on social disadvantage, showing that social exclusion and therefore social disadvantage can result from the language and communication difficulties experienced by people with learning difficulties. Bray argues that social inclusion is to a great extent dependent on language and communication skills.

At the end of the first part of the book, we focus on the third theme: intervention. James Law and Frances Harris (Chapter 8) take a critical stance, questioning the role of intervention and at the same time asking how it can be most effective in improving the speech and language abilities of socially disadvantaged children. They distinguish between large-scale and more specifically focused intervention programmes. The former aim to alleviate the effects of social disadvantage, in the long term; communication may be just one of many targets. The latter aim simply to facilitate speech and language development, and usually involve intense activity only in the short term. The notion of 'good outcomes' for children exposed to both types of intervention is challenged.

James Law also provides an introduction to the research reports in the second part of the book, showing how current theories underlie recent, and often innovative, intervention programmes. He highlights, in particular, the challenges of delivering specific programmes and evaluating their effectiveness in everyday, real-life situations. Caroline Pickstone describes and evaluates a language-screening project in a Sure Start area, designed to determine if it is possible to identify preschool children with clinical language delay at risk of long-term language difficulties. Linda Hobbs describes a practitioner-led project aimed at enhancing the understanding and use of language in groups of children at the Foundation Stage. Marion Farmer and Fleur Griffiths highlight the value of promoting conversation in preschool and primary settings in order to facilitate language development. Julie Dockrell, Morag Stuart and Diane King present a rigorous assessment of the impact of an intervention programme designed to promote vocabulary, narrative and inference drawing in preschool children. Jenny Leyden and Marcin Sczcerbinski report on a project involving collaboration between speech and language therapists and nursery staff to improve young children's spoken language and thereby their subsequent literacy and educational attainment. Helen Stringer provides a more holistic approach to intervention, describing a programme designed to improve narrative ability and social skills in secondary school-aged pupils with both SLD and EBD. Finally, Victoria Joffe evaluates an intervention promoting language understanding and use by secondary school-aged pupils; unlike many interventions this programme is fully integrated with and delivered through the educational curriculum.

In the Afterword, Ann Locke carefully considers the current situation and draws attention to three important and interrelated issues. The first is the necessity for policy makers and politicians to recognise the importance of language development.

The second is the urgent need for more research to be carried out with the aim of determining long-term social and educational outcomes for children with delayed and disordered language. Finally, she argues that large-scale interventions should be designed and delivered on the basis of robust evidence. Only such interventions are likely to be effective in promoting young children's language development and improving their life chances in the long term.

REFERENCE

Locke, A., Ginsborg, J. & Peers, I. (2002). Development and disadvantage: implications for the early years and beyond. *International Journal of Language and Communication Disorders*, **37**(1), 3–15.

I Language and Social Disadvantage: Current Understanding

1 The Effects of Socio-economic Status on Children's Language Acquisition and Use

JANE GINSBORG
Royal Northern College of Music

INTRODUCTION

OUTLINE OF CHAPTER

In the first part of this chapter, social disadvantage is defined in terms of socio-economic status (SES). Evidence that children from low-SES backgrounds are more likely to experience language delay than children from high-SES backgrounds will be presented. Environmental explanations, suggesting that children from high- and low-SES backgrounds experience different kinds of language environment, which influence both the rate of language acquisition and language competence on starting school, will be discussed. The second part of the chapter considers the extent to which the differences that have been found represent deficits. Given the importance of oracy and literacy in education, and the links between them, it is clear that children from low-SES backgrounds are more likely to be disadvantaged academically than those from high-SES backgrounds, thus renewing the cycle of social disadvantage.

DEFINITIONS OF SOCIAL DISADVANTAGE

Social disadvantage is defined in a number of ways. Research into the association between social disadvantage and developmental outcomes frequently measures SES in terms of level of parental education (usually maternal), or occupation (usually parental) (e.g. Bee, Van Egeren, Streissguth, Nyman & Leckie, 1969; Bernstein, 1962a, 1962b; Hart & Risley, 1995; Tizard & Hughes, 1984; Tough, 1977). Alternatively, social disadvantage is represented by economic deprivation: for example, low family income (Adams & Ramey, 1980), poverty (e.g. Brooks-Gunn, Klebanov, &

Language and Social Disadvantage: Theory into Practice Edited by J. Clegg and J. Ginsborg
© 2006 John Wiley & Sons, Ltd

Duncan, 1996; Patterson, Kupersmidt & Vaden, 1990), or income-to-needs ratio (Raviv, Kessenich & Morrison, 2004). Defining social disadvantage in different ways is problematic. Correlations found between parental education and occupation, and measures of income, are not high; the duration and timing of poverty varies from one family to another, and has different effects on developmental outcomes; even if the family itself is not economically-deprived, living in a poor neighbourhood can affect development (Duncan, Brooks-Gunn & Klebanov, 1994). In recent years, researchers have attempted to distinguish between poverty status and SES (see McLoyd, 1998, for a review). In this chapter, however, I define social disadvantage, generally, as 'low SES'.

EVIDENCE FOR DIFFERENCES IN THE LANGUAGE COMPETENCE

There has long been concern that children from low-SES backgrounds underachieve academically in comparison with more privileged children. Academic underachievement has often been attributed to language skills inadequate for accessing the curriculum. Early evidence for differences in the language competence of children from high- and low-SES backgrounds was proposed in the UK by Bernstein (e.g. 1958, 1962a, 1962b, 1973), Tough (1977, 2000) and Tizard and Hughes (1984); in the USA (where low SES is often associated with minority ethnic background), similar evidence was put forward by Bereiter and Engelmann (1966), Stewart (1970), Baratz (1970) and Labov (1969). More recently, the results of a large-scale longitudinal, observational study of the development of spoken language in young children from high-, mid- and low-SES backgrounds (Hart & Risley, 1995, 1999; Walker, Greenwood, Hart & Carta, 1994) suggest that children in lower-SES environments have slower rates of vocabulary growth associated with lower IQ when they are three years old, and poorer educational achievement when they are nine or ten. Similar studies have confirmed these findings (Arriaga, Fenson, Cronan & Pethick, 1998; Fish & Pinkerman, 2003; Hoff, 2003). Peers, Lloyd, and Foster (2000) carried out a survey of children's language skills as part of the standardization process for the Clinical Evaluation of Language Fundamentals Preschool (CELF-Preschool[UK]). This suggested that UK children from low-SES backgrounds are almost twice as likely to experience receptive language delay than children from mid- and high-SES backgrounds; moderate or severe expressive language delay is more than five times as likely in children from low-SES backgrounds.

In this chapter, I will be focusing on environmental explanations for the differences in language competence and use that have been observed in children from different backgrounds. I will attempt to consider in turn – given the high correlations between these factors – the effects of low SES, generally, on cognitive and language development; the level of parental education; home environment; the relationship between principal caregiver and child; the nature of the interaction between mother and child, including the quantity of speech addressed to the child and the nature of the child-directed speech, and the language environment experienced by the child, more generally.

ENVIRONMENTAL EXPLANATIONS FOR DIFFERENCES IN LANGUAGE COMPETENCE

THE EFFECTS OF POVERTY ON COGNITIVE AND LANGUAGE DEVELOPMENT

Poverty affects children psychologically (see Bradley & Corwyn, 2002, for a review). It can also affect them psychosocially and physically (Brooks-Gunn, et al., 1996; Evans, 2004). For example, family income is a better predictor of non-verbal and verbal IQ measured at five years of age than ethnicity, maternal education and single motherhood (Duncan et al., 1994). In terms of the physical effects of poverty, poor health – particularly in the perinatal period for infants who were born prematurely (Siegel, 1982) – and nutrition (Smith, Brooks-Gunn, & Klebanov, 1997) can give rise to physiological or neurological deficits, as can exposure to environmental pollutants (Klebanov, Brooks-Gunn, McCarton & McCormick, 1998; McLoyd, 1998; Needleman, Schell, Bellinger, Leviton & Allred, 1990).

LEVEL OF MATERNAL EDUCATION

Even though, as we have seen, family income has been shown to be a more effective predictor of developmental outcomes than maternal education, it has been argued that it is worth studying the relationship between maternal education and cognitive development simply because it is a more stable measure than family poverty (Duncan et al., 1994; Huston, McLoyd & Garcia Coll, 1994). It is usually correlated with paternal education (Entwisle & Astone, 1994) and many low-income families are headed by single parents, usually the mother (Hernandez, 1997). Adams and Ramey (1980), for example, undertook a longitudinal study of low-SES infants at risk of 'mild mental retardation'. The higher the level of risk, the lower the level of maternal education and IQ.

Why should this be? Belsky (1984) and Wells (1986) take an ecological approach, suggesting that parenting is influenced by parents' own personality and developmental history as well as the child's temperament. Such an emphasis on the wider social context of the family is supported by Parks and Smeriglio (1986), who link parental education to knowledge about parenting, child development and the level of stimulation provided in the home, where such factors influence children's cognitive development. While some aspects of language development, such as the appropriate use of tense, seem to be acquired irrespective of level of maternal education (Rice, Wexler & Hershberger, 1998), others have been shown to be related to maternal education. Dollaghan, Campbell, Paradise et al. (1999) studied interactions between mothers and their infants. The mothers were categorised as black or white, with one of four levels of education, from college graduates to those who had not graduated from high school. The researchers found significant correlations between level of maternal education and 3-year-old children's receptive and productive language. Measures of productive language included mean length of utterance in morphemes

(MLUm) (Walker et al., 1994), number of different words and total number of words. Analysis showed that there were significant differences between the three groups on all the measures, such that the children of college graduates had higher scores than both the other groups, and for receptive language, the children of high-school graduates had higher scores than the children whose mothers had not graduated from high school.

Finally, in a recent investigation of risk factors underlying speech delay in 3-year-old children, Campbell, Dollaghan, Rockette, et al. (2003) calculated the odds ratios for seven variables thought to be linked to speech delay. The highest risk factors were the mother not having completed high school and the child being male; odds ratios were high, too, for a family history of developmental communication disorder and Medicaid health insurance (representing low SES, but highly correlated with low level of maternal education).

HOME ENVIRONMENT

As we have seen, the home environment is very important for developmental outcomes (Belsky, 1984; Bradley & Caldwell, 1984; Brooks-Gunn et al., 1996; Snow, Barnes, Chandler, Goodman & Hemphill, 1991). However, the kind of home environment experienced by children is not necessarily affected by SES. Olson, Bates and Kaskie (1992) measured interactions between mothers from different SES backgrounds and their children, when the children were 6, 13, and 24 months old, and then followed them up when they were 6 years old. The results suggest that – over and above the effects of SES – differences in language competence at the age of 6 years were attributable to two aspects of mother–child interaction at the age of 2 years: the mother's non-restrictiveness of the child, and the amount of verbal stimulation she provided.

On the other hand, a potential link between SES, home environment and language is illustrated in a study carried out by Lawrence and Shipley (1996), who examined black working- and middle-class, and white working- and middle-class parents' use of language with their 3–5-year-old children. Differences between the language used by parents in the four groups were discovered. Given that the black parents differed from the white parents in the same way that working-class parents differed from middle-class parents, the researchers postulate a single underlying factor: 'distance from mainstream culture' (Labov & Harris, 1986).

NATURE OF INTERACTION BETWEEN MOTHER AND CHILD

'Interactional style' was identified long ago as a predictor of children's cognitive development (Bee et al., 1969; Hess & Shipman, 1967). Interactional style comprises factors such as attachment, the child's temperament and quality of interaction (Fish & Pinkerman, 2003; Murray & Hornbaker, 1997); it can predict childhood language skills (Bee, Barnard, Eyres et al., 1982). Other features of interaction that are considered to facilitate language acquisition include joint attention

(Harris, Jones, Brookes & Grant, 1986; Tomasello & Todd, 1983) and mothers' verbal responsiveness to early infant vocalisations (Tamis-LeMonda, Bornstein, Baumwell & Damast, 1996).

Given that features of mother–child interaction can differ, does this have implications for the interaction of mothers and children from high- and low-SES backgrounds? Low-SES mothers may have less time or energy for playing or engaging in conversation with their children (Farran & Haskins, 1980; Snow, Dubber & de Blauw, 1982), display more restrictive and authoritarian parenting (Hashima & Amato, 1994) and talk less to their children, using a more directive than facilitative manner (Hoff, 2003).

There is thus much evidence to show that the nature of mother–child interaction plays a part in language development. However, the crucial aspects of mother–child interaction have yet to be identified. While in some cases interactional differences have been attributed to SES, other studies have shown that effective mother–child interaction can enhance the language skills of low-SES children. We turn now to examine children's language environments more closely in an attempt to explain differences in the language competence and use of children from high- and low-SES backgrounds, starting with evidence that the sheer quantity of speech addressed to children has a vital role to play (Huttenlocher, Haight, Bryk, Seltzer & Lyons, 1991).

QUANTITY OF CHILD-DIRECTED SPEECH

Hoff and Naigles (2002), in their review of the literature pertaining to children's lexical development, point out that there are two views of language input. The social-pragmatic view focuses on the interaction between caregiver and child. The alternative view, put forward by Hoff and Naigles, is 'that language acquisition is a data-crunching process and conversation is a delivery mechanism whose value lies, to a substantial degree, in the nature of the data that it delivers' (p. 422). Hoff and Naigles cite Schwartz and Terrell (1983) and Smith (1999), who showed empirically that words are learned faster by children the more often they are heard. Thus, the words that children produce first when they begin to speak are likely to be those that their parents say most often (Naigles & Hoff-Ginsberg, 1998). Bornstein, Haynes and Painter (1998) showed that the size of children's comprehension and production vocabularies was related to the number of word types used by their mothers when talking to them as well as their MLU. Vocabulary size is not the only measure of language competence, of course: Hoff-Ginsberg (1997; 1998) investigated the effects of birth order as well as SES on the development of syntactic skills and argued that firstborns develop the ability to understand and use syntax faster than do their younger siblings because more speech is addressed to them.

Meanwhile, the findings of Hart and Risley (1992, 1995, 1999), who carried out a longitudinal, naturalistic, observational study of 42 children and their families, illustrate SES-related differences in the quantity of language to which young children are exposed, and their potential long-term consequences. Thirteen families were defined as 'professional/managerial'; 23 were defined as working class (equivalent to 'blue-collar workers' in the UK), and six were living on welfare benefits (equivalent, arguably, to 'working-class' in the UK). Each family was visited once a month, from when the child was 8 months old until their third birthday, and everything that was said to the child, by the child or around the child, for an hour, was documented. At the end of the study each child's vocabulary growth rate, use of vocabulary and IQ were measured. When the children were 9–10 years old, a follow-up study was carried out, involving 29 of the 42 children.

The most striking differences in the language experiences of children in the three types of family related to utterances – measured as the average numbers of words per hour – that were addressed to them. A total of 600 words per hour were addressed to children in the welfare families, 1200 in the working-class families and 2100 in the professional families. In terms of time spent interacting with their children, adults in the professional families spent twice as long as the adults in the welfare families. However, there were differences in the nature of the language used, too. The average numbers of adult utterances per hour representing affirmative feedback and prohibitions to their children were calculated for each group. In professional families affirmative feedback was offered more than 30 times. In working-class families, affirmative feedback was offered 15 times. However, in welfare families, affirmative feedback was offered only six times per hour, and children were twice as likely to hear a prohibition.

As might be expected, the children's vocabulary growth rate and use were reflected by the amount of language they had experienced; so were their IQ scores. There were also significant positive correlations between their test performance on the vocabulary measures at the age of 3 years and at the age of 9–10. Hart and Risley conclude that 'the most important difference among families was not the relative advantages conferred by education and income but the amount of talking the parents did with their children' (1999, p. 181).

NATURE OF CHILD-DIRECTED SPEECH AND THE LANGUAGE ENVIRONMENT MORE GENERALLY

Although quantity of child-directed speech is crucial, then, Hart and Risley's study illustrates the importance, too, of the nature of child-directed speech, and the language environment more generally. At the beginning of this chapter, Bernstein's evidence for differences attributed to SES was cited. In order to examine this in more detail, we need to take a step back, as it were, from young children's language acquisition and development, and look at the theory underlying so much subsequent research, before returning to specific aspects of child-directed speech and how these may influence language outcomes.

Basil Bernstein (1924–2000) was the British sociologist who put forward the verbal deprivation hypothesis – one of the most influential and controversial explanations for educational underachievement. This hypothesis arises from the theory of socio-linguistic codes, whereby it is argued that language can be used in different ways in different social contexts. These different ways of using language are known as codes, or sets of principles that underlie shared systems of meaning. Thus, language is used not only to communicate information but also to establish position in social relationships – within the family, at school, at work – and, more broadly, within the class structure of our society. Elaborated codes are relatively context-free; they enable language users to call on universalistic meanings, to be reflexive, and thus to manipulate ideas. Restricted codes, meanwhile, limit language users to their immediate, specific, context.

Bernstein and his colleagues carried out empirical research from the late 1950s into the 1970s, the findings of which support his argument that the middle classes use elaborated codes, while the working classes are more likely to use restricted codes (Bernstein, 1996). For example, in one early study Bernstein (1958) found that a group of working-class youths aged 15–18 gained higher scores on non-verbal than verbal IQ tests. In a follow-up study (Bernstein, 1960), a group of middle-class youths, also aged 15–18, scored equally well on the same tests, while a second sample of working-class youths, like the group from the earlier study, also scored higher on the non-verbal than the verbal IQ tests. A third study (Bernstein, 1962a, 1962b) compared the spontaneous use of language in the context of small-group discussions held by working-class and middle-class youths. The former was described as 'restricted': in comparison with middle-class youths, the working-class youths used shorter words, longer phrases and were less likely to pause when speaking; they also used more personal pronouns. The language used by the middle-class group was described as 'elaborated' . The youths used longer words, shorter phrases and paused more often. They also used more 'uncommon' adverbs and adjectives, subordinate clauses and passive verbs.

Subsequent research confirms that mothers from low-SES backgrounds use more directive speech and prohibitions than do mothers from high-SES backgrounds (Bee et al., 1969; Hart & Risley, 1992; Hoff, 2003; Lawrence & Shipley, 1996). Although directive speech, in the form of imperatives, has been associated with poorer outcomes (e.g. Adams & Ramey, 1980; Hart & Risley, 1995, 1999), this is not to say that directive speech is necessarily less helpful than facilitative speech to language development (Murray & Hornbaker, 1997); Barnes, Gutfreund, Satterly and Wells (1983), for example, argue that it is useful where it contributes to reciprocal interaction.

In contrast to research on parents' child-directed speech, the British educational psychologist Joan Tough carried out a longitudinal study to investigate the nature of the language used by 12 'disadvantaged' children, whose parents had left school at the minimum age and were in unskilled or semi-skilled employment, and 12 'advantaged' children, with highly-educated parents in 'professional' careers (Tough, 1977). Observations and recordings were made of each child talking on three occasions when they were 3½, 5½ and 7½ years old.

According to Tough's analysis of the transcripts of the children's talk, at the age of 3 years, the disadvantaged children were less likely than the advantaged children to: talk or reason about their experiences, past or present; talk or speculate about future events, and to make plans for themselves or other people; recognise or solve problems; project themselves into other people's thoughts and feelings; or engage in imaginative 'pretend' play. Two years and four years later, the children were observed engaging in activities designed to encourage them to use talk for the purposes identified in the first part of the study. However, once again Tough found differences between the advantaged and disadvantaged children. The latter produced shorter answers to questions and Tough inferred from their talk that their thinking was 'less complex'; they did what was required of them, and no more (Tough, 1977, pp. 169–70). In Tough's view, academic underachievement can be explained in terms of verbal deprivation causing social and cognitive disadvantage. Shortly before she died, she summarised her findings from this, and subsequent research, thus: 'What is clear is that the character of talk used persistently in particular kinds of situation will play a part in how, and for what purposes children learn to use language, and in the development of attitudes and thinking skills. It is the way in which parents and others draw young children into their ways of thinking that determines the kind of skills, concepts and attitudes children will have established by the age of three and which may continue to affect them throughout their lives' (Tough, 2000).

Meanwhile Tizard and Hughes (1984) compared the conversations of 30 four-year-old girls, half from working-class and half from middle-class families, with their mothers. Middle-class mothers and children discussed a wider range of topics, used complex language more often than working-class mothers and children, and used a wider vocabulary. Furthermore, middle-class children asked more questions than working-class children, and their mothers answered more questions adequately than working-class mothers, who were more likely to ignore their children's questions. While Tizard and Hughes's findings supported those of Tough (1977), they disagreed with her conclusions; as we shall see, their focus was on individual differences, and the differences between the interactions of the two groups of girls at nursery school.

The effects of class on conversations between mothers and children aged between 1½ and 2½ years, but at similar levels of language development, were investigated by Hoff-Ginsberg (1991). Once again, the focus was on adults' language. Video-recordings of interactions between 30 working-class and 33 upper-middle-class dyads in four different contexts were analysed. Mothers were interviewed to assess their attitudes towards and beliefs about their children, and to assess mothers' adult-directed speech. Measures were taken of maternal speech rate, total number of word roots used, MLUm, directive speech, conversation-eliciting utterances and topic-continuing responses. In support of earlier findings (e.g. Bee et al., 1969), upper-middle-class mothers' speech was more contingent on their children's, and less directive; as we have already seen, this was found to be related to general conversational style rather than attitudes towards children as conversational partners or beliefs regarding children's language abilities. Differences were found between the language used in different contexts but there were no other significant differences between the two social groups on any of the other measures.

The work of Lawrence and Shipley (1996) has been mentioned, briefly, in the context of class- and race-related differences in the home environment. The principal findings of their research were that black mothers and working-class mothers talk less to their children than do white mothers and middle-class mothers. Significant main effects of class and race, and a significant interaction between class and setting were identified.

We now return to the relationship between adults' language use and outcomes for children. Bornstein et al. (1998) investigated the determinants of vocabulary competence in children aged about 20 months and found that children's vocabulary competence is directly related to their social competence and their mothers' vocabulary and attitudes towards parenting. As we have seen, it is indirectly predicted by maternal vocabulary, which is in turn predicted by SES, verbal intelligence and knowledge of child development. Thus, mothers from higher-SES backgrounds with high levels of intelligence, who knew more about child development, were more likely to make longer utterances to their children, using a wider vocabulary.

In addition to vocabulary, the development of syntax as a measure of language competence should also be discussed. Analysis of syntax in the conversation of young children from mid- and low-SES backgrounds shows that children's syntax development is influenced by parental input but SES does not specifically predict the frequency of complex speech independently of parental input and teacher input (Huttenlocher, Vasilyeva, Cymerman & Levine, 2002).

We have seen, then, that language environment associated with SES has been put forward as an explanation for differences in adults' and therefore children's understanding and use of language; we have also explored the nature of those differences. We must now discuss the extent to which they are considered to represent deficits requiring intervention.

DIFFERENCE OR DEFICIT?

NO DIFFERENCE: A METHODOLOGICAL PROBLEM

It is sometimes argued that differences between the language competence of children from low- and high-SES backgrounds are exaggerated. If the standardisation of norm-referenced language measures is not carried out using genuinely representative samples of the population, rather than just the children of well-educated, middle-class parents, the performance of children from low-SES and/or ethnic minority backgrounds is likely to appear lower than it really is (Dollaghan et al., 1999). Findings based on parental reports, such as the Communication Development Inventory (CDI), are also likely to be affected (Arriaga et al., 1998). Cultural bias in tests, and even in the variables that are coded in observational research, is perceived as a problem (Campbell, Dollaghan, Needleman & Janosky, 1997).

NO DIFFERENCE: INDIVIDUAL VARIATION

Research focusing on differences between groups sometimes fails to recognise the similarities between them. Although Tizard and Hughes (1984) found differences between working-class and middle-class children's use of language, as we have seen, they argue that these differences are small; there was considerable variation within the groups and overlap between them. Important similarities between the groups included the frequency of conversations held between mothers and children, the length of conversations, the number of words uttered in each 'turn' and the amount of time mothers and children spent playing together.

Language development is also affected by children's sex, intelligence and personality, as well as their upbringing and relationship with their parents. Individual variation may explain many differences. An early proponent of this view, Wells (1986) directed a longitudinal study of 128 UK children aged 1–10 years, which involved recording and analysing samples of their interactions with parents, peers and teachers as well as taking more formal measures of children's talk. The results of the study in relation to social background showed no differences in how often, or in what contexts children talked, or the pragmatic functions of their speech. Wells did observe certain differences between the groups in the number of auxiliary verbs used by children by the age of 3½ years, MLU and oral comprehension, but he minimises these: again, the differences are small; performance, rather than competence, was being measured; MLU may be affected by use of dialect; some children may have scored worse on the oral comprehension scale as a result of being in a test situation.

Since the mid-1980s, however, a large number of studies has been carried out to explore the effects of multiple factors; in this chapter alone we have considered research of this nature by Parks and Smeriglio (1986), Hart and Risley (1992, 1995, 1999); Walker et al. (1994), Duncan et al. (1994), Brooks-Gunn et al. (1996), Bornstein et al. (1998); Dollaghan et al. (1999), Campbell et al. (2003), Fish and Pinkerman (2003), and Raviv et al. (2004).

DIFFERENCE BUT NOT DEFICIT

The verbal deprivation hypothesis was put forward by Bernstein in response to concern in the UK that many children from working-class backgrounds were not achieving their full educational potential. This concern was echoed in the USA in President L. B. Johnson's 'War Against Poverty', which sought to redress the linguistic and cultural deprivation from which poor, and particularly black, children were thought to suffer. Initiatives such as Project Head Start – the forerunner of Sure Start in the UK – were the result.

The research outlined in this chapter focuses on the identification of factors that influence the development of language and cognition. Some of these factors have been shown to differ in families from different social backgrounds; children from different social backgrounds have different levels of language competence, which may in turn affect their subsequent academic progress. Given these findings, it is easy to assume that children from low-SES backgrounds are exposed to inadequate language environments and are therefore deficient in their language acquisition and use – particularly when, for example, distinctions are made between the use of 'simple' and 'complex' language (Huttenlocher et al., 2002; Tough, 1977).

The American sociologist, William Labov, was one of the first researchers to be highly critical of this assumption. He argues that the language of the black urban ghetto children whom he observed inside and outside the classroom is highly skilled, imaginative and communicative, when they speak to each other. These characteristics are much less in evidence, however, when they speak to adults. If their poor academic achievement is to be ascribed to their use of language, it must result from the asymmetry of interactions between children and adults, whether teachers or researchers (Labov, 1969/1979). Tizard and Hughes also reject the notion of 'working-class language deficit' (Tizard & Hughes, 1984, p. 159), and suggest, rather, that their findings reveal 'a difference in language *style*, related to a difference in [mothers'] underlying values and attitudes... [that] obviously make sense in terms of the different educational and occupational careers of the two groups of women' (p. 159). Meanwhile, contemporary researchers in the USA are unhappy with the interpretation of the findings of many studies that appear to reinforce the notion that privileged children's language is the norm and that of low-SES/ethnic minority children is inadequate in comparison (Garcia Coll, Lamberty, Jenkins et al., 1996); worse, that this is so because of deficiencies in their environment or genetic inheritance (Herrnstein & Murray, 1996; Jensen, 1969).

Labov argues that children use different registers at home and school. Similarly, conversational settings at home or at school can also influence the language used by adults and children, attenuating the effects attributed to SES. Thus, middle-class mothers are perceived as interacting with their children in more 'working-class' ways when they are helping them manipulate toys (Brophy, 1970) or trying to control their non-verbal behaviour (Wooton, 1974); working-class mothers interact with their children in more 'middle-class' ways when they are reading books together (Dunn, Wooding & Herman, 1977; Snow, Arlman-Rupp, Hassing et al., 1976). More recently, Hoff-Ginsberg studied working-class and upper-middle-class mother–child interactions in different communicative settings: at mealtime, while dressing, reading books and playing with toys. In the four settings, 'reading stood out as the most different... mothers' child-directed speech had the greatest lexical diversity, the greatest syntactic complexity, and the highest rate of topic-continuing replies. [It] was also among the two highest settings in terms of the overall rate of maternal speech. These findings support the widespread notion that book reading is particularly conducive to a supportive style of mother–child conversation' (Hoff-Ginsberg, 1991, p. 792). While book reading is clearly an effective context in which parents can talk with their young children, another implication of these findings – as Hoff-Ginsberg observes – is that it may be unwise to draw general conclusions from studies of adult–child interactions in this setting.

DEFICIT: IMPLICATIONS OF DIFFERENCE FOR EDUCATION

We have considered the possibility that differences in children's language competence, occurring for whatever reason, are simply a matter of register, or style. As we have seen, however (Hart & Risley, 1995, 1999), they have implications for educational achievement, and these in turn have implications for the kinds of intervention that are devised and implemented (see Part II of this volume).

To return to the verbal deprivation hypothesis, Bernstein himself was at pains to make it clear that he did not see children themselves as deficient. Language codes, he argues, reflect the division of labour, and therefore the balance of power, in society: context-dependent, restricted codes are needed for the production of goods, while elaborated codes are used for the reproduction of ideas. Ideas are communicated principally through education, which is controlled by the middle classes; they determine the purposes of education and the curriculum. The values of our education system are such that children are required to use elaborated codes in order to achieve academic success.

This is illustrated in Tizard and Hughes's (1984) comparison of children's language at home and at nursery school. While they underplay the differences they observed between working- and middle-class interactions at home, they report striking disparities at school. These arise, they suggest, from school routines, and the need for children to conform to rules, whether implicit or explicit. Interactions between members of staff and groups of children are quite different from the one-to-one interactions of a mother and child; they often involve a teacher asking questions and the child answering – briefly – so the next child can be questioned. Above all, interactions at nursery school are decontextualised; staff relationships with children are professional, rather than emotional, and it is likely that when children do have the opportunity to talk about the things that interest them, nursery staff do not possess the relevant knowledge to encourage them appropriately. Tizard and Hughes found that the working-class children in their sample were particularly affected by the nursery school setting; they were more subdued, passive and more dependent than at home. The staff, in turn, were more likely to pitch their talk at a 'lower' level to the working-class children, suggesting that they had lesser expectations and standards for this group of children. In other words, they were *socially* – and potentially academically – disadvantaged as the result of perceived differences in their behaviour, including language competence.

More recently, Wood (1998) discusses (and dismisses) this 'self-fulfilling prophecy' (Rosenthal & Jacobson, 1968). He considers the possibility that some children underachieve at school because of a clash between their family values and those of school, but points out that this is difficult to address without asking more basic questions, such as 'what is education for?'. Finally, he suggests that 'language and cognition are fused in verbal reasoning. Comprehension problems . . . act as a barrier to learning and understanding. Lacking expertise in the processes of creating coherent, "disembedded" or "decontextualized" accounts of what they know and understand, children may appear intellectually incompetent when, in reality, they are still grappling with the problem of making sense to other people' (Wood, 1998, p. 180).

Children's use of spoken language, then, may influence the way they are taught at school, and the way they learn. However, it is also crucial to the development of literacy (Shankweiler, Lundquist, Dreyer & Dickinson, 1996; Snow, Burns & Griffin, 1998). Phonological awareness is predicted by spoken language measures (Cooper, Roth, Speece & Schatschneider, 2002); phonological (Bryant, MacLean & Bradley, 1990) and metalinguistic awareness (Chaney, 1992, 1994, 2000; Griffin, Hemphill & Camp, 2004), and narrative ability (Roth, Speece, Cooper & De La Paz, 1996) have all been linked to successful early reading, as have vocabulary (Dickinson, McCabe, Anastasopoulos, Peisner-Feinberg & Poe, 2003), semantic knowledge and metasemantic skills (Roth, Speece & Cooper, 2002).

The NICHD Early Child Care Research Network (2005) reports the most recent findings from a longitudinal study of reading development involving more than a thousand children. The aim was to determine the roles played by comprehensive oral ability and phonological awareness (measured when the children were 3 years old), and vocabulary comprehension and performance (measured using when the children were 4½ years, and in first grade, at 6 or 7 years). Reading was measured via decoding skills and word recognition at 4½ years and in first grade, and comprehension in third grade, when the children were 8 or 9 years. Comprehensive oral ability at 3 years predicted oral ability and vocabulary development at 4½ years, but more importantly, the decoding component of reading at 4½ years. Meanwhile, word recognition in first grade and reading comprehension in third grade were predicted by oral ability at 4½ years.

There were only two findings specifically related to SES. The relationship between oral ability when the children were 3 and 4½ was even stronger in low- than high-SES children, as was the relationship between decoding skills in first grade and reading comprehension in third grade. The authors suggest that these relationships are even more critical for children who may experience home language environments in which they are unlikely to learn letter-sound correspondences (Senechal & LeFevre, 2002). These findings confirm Snow's (2001) proposal that the language environment at home predicts not only language competence at school but also the development of reading skills and subsequent reading comprehension.

IMPLICATIONS FOR INTERVENTION

Interventions such as Project Head Start in the USA, and Sure Start in the UK, are designed to address many of the issues discussed in this chapter relating to the potential effects of social disadvantage. They begin early; they involve whole families, within communities; they aim to improve children's health, well-being, and readiness for education. It should be noted, however, that there is little evidence yet as to the kinds of intervention that are most successful, given the huge differences in the language environments to which children are exposed before the age of 3 years (Dollaghan et al., 1999). Hart and Risley (1995) argue, for example, that 41 hours of high-quality intervention would be needed, each week, merely for the lowest-SES children in their sample to hear the same number of utterances addressed to them as the highest-SES children. In contrast, Huttenlocher and her colleagues claim, on the basis of their findings, that 'children from low-SES families, whose syntactic level is quite low at the beginning of the year, may grow as much or more than children from higher-SES families, if their teachers provide input comparable to or greater than the input in the higher-SES preschools' (Huttenlocher et al., 2002, p. 366). We explore this debate further in Part II of this volume, where we report a series of current interventions to enhance young children's spoken language.

SUMMARY AND CONCLUSION

In this chapter we have looked at the relationship between social disadvantage and children's language competence. Differences have been observed in children from high- and low-SES backgrounds, and a range of explanations have been put forward: poverty, level of maternal education; the home environment; the relationship between mother and child including the nature of the interaction between mother and child; the quantity of speech to which the child is exposed; the nature of that speech and the language environment more generally. These explanations are highly intercorrelated, and recent research has attempted to disentangle them. We then considered the question of whether the language competence of children from low-SES backgrounds should be considered deficient, or merely different. Some researchers would argue that 'differences' are methodological artefacts arising from the way in which language competence is measured; others emphasise the roles of individual variation, language diversity and context-dependent differences. Given, however, the importance of oracy and literacy in education, I would argue that children who are already disadvantaged face the prospect of even greater disadvantage unless they are given the opportunity, through intervention, to make full use of the educational opportunities available to them.

REFERENCES

Adams, J. L. & Ramey, C.T. (1980). Structural aspects of maternal speech to infants reared in poverty. *Child Development*, **51**, 1280–1284.
Arriaga, R. I., Fenson, L., Cronan, T. & Pethick, S. J. (1998). Scores on the MacArthur Communicative Development Inventory of children from low- and middle income families. *Applied Psycholinguistics*, **19**(2), 209–223.
Baratz, J. C. (1970). Teaching reading in an urgan negro school system. In F. Williams (Ed.), *Language and poverty*. Chicago, IL: Markham Publishing Company.
Barnes, S., Gutfreund, M., Satterly, D. & Wells, G. (1983). Characteristics of adult speech which predict children's language development. *Journal of Child Language*, **10**, 65–84.
Bee, H. L., Van Egeren, L. F., Streissguth, A. P., Nyman, B. A. & Leckie, M. A. (1969). Social class differences in maternal teaching strategies and speech patterns. *Developmental Psychology*, **1**, 726–734.

Bee, H. L., Barnard, K. E., Eyres, S. J., Gray, C. A., Hammond, M. A., Spietz, A. L., Snyder, C. & Clark, B. (1982). Prediction of IQ and language skill from perinatal status, child performance, family characteristics and mother–infant interaction. *Child Development*, **53**, 1134–1156 .

Belsky, J. (1984). The determinants of parenting: A process model. *Child Development*, **55**, 83–96.

Bereiter, C. & Engelmann, S. (1966). *Teaching disadvantaged children in the pre-school*. Englewood Cliffs, NJ: Prentice-Hall.

Bernstein, B. (1958). Some sociological determinants of perception: An enquiry into sub-cultural differences. *British Journal of Sociology*, **9**(1), 159–174.

Bernstein, B. (1960). Language and social class: A research note. *British Journal of Sociology*, **11**(3), 271–276.

Bernstein, B. (1962a). Linguistic codes, hesitation phenomena and intelligence. *Language and Speech*, **5**(1), 31–46.

Bernstein, B. (1962b). Social class, linguistic codes and grammatical elements. *Language and Speech*, **5**(4), 221–240.

Bernstein, B. (1973). *Class, Codes and Control* (vol. 1). London: Routledge & Kegan Paul.

Bernstein, B. (1996). *Pedagogy, symbolic control and identity: theory, research, critique*. London: Taylor & Francis.

Bornstein, M. H., Haynes, M. O. & Painter, K. M. (1998). Sources of child vocabulary competence: A multivariate model. *Journal of Child Language*, **25**, 367–393.

Bradley, R. H. & Caldwell, B. M. (1984). The HOME Inventory and family demographics. *Developmental Psychology*, **20**, 315–320.

Bradley, R. H. & Corwyn, R. F. (2002). Socioeconomic status and child development. *Annual Review of Psychology*, **53**, 371–399.

Brooks-Gunn, J., Klebanov, P. K. & Duncan, G. J. (1996). Ethnic differences in children's intelligence test scores: Role of economic deprivation, home environment, and maternal characteristics. *Child Development*, **67**, 396–408.

Brophy, J. E. (1970). Mothers as teachers of their own preschool children: The influence of socioeconomic status and task structure on teaching specificity. *Child Development*, **41**, 79–94.

Bryant, P., MacLean, M. & Bradley, L. (1990). Rhyme, language and children's reading. *Applied Psycholinguistics*, **13**, 484–514.

Campbell, T. F., Dollaghan, C. A., Needleman, H. & Janosky, J. (1997). Reducing bias in language assessment: Processing-dependent measures. *Journal of Speech, Language, and Hearing Research*, **40**, 519–525.

Campbell, T. F., Dollaghan, C. A., Rockette, H. E., Paradise, J. L., Feldman, H. M., Shriberg, L. D., Sabo, D. L. & Kurs-Lasky, M. (2003). Risk factors for speech delay of unknown origin in 3-year-old children. *Child Development*, **74**(2), 346–357.

Chaney, C. (1992). Language development, metalinguistic skills, and print awareness in 3-year-old children. *Applied Psycholinguistics*, **13**, 485–514.

Chaney, C. (1994). Language development, metalinguistic awareness, and emergent literacy skills of three-year-old children in relation to social class. *Applied Psycholinguistics*, **15**, 371–394.

Chaney, C. (2000). Social class does not predict reading success, but language and metalin-guistic skills do. In M.R. Perkins & S. J. Howard (Eds.), *New directions in language development and disorders*. New York: Kluwer/Plenum.

Cooper, D. H., Roth, F. P., Speece, D. L. & Schatschneider, C. (2002). The contribution of oral language skills to the development of phonological awareness. *Applied Psycholinguistics*, **23**(3), 399–416.

Dickinson, D. K., McCabe, A., Anastasopoulos, L., Peisner-Feinberg, E. & Poe, E. (2003). The comprehensive language approach to early literacy: The interrelationships among vocabulary, phonological sensitivity, and print knowledge among preschool-aged children. *Journal of Educational Psychology*, **95**, 465–481.

Dollaghan, C. A., Campbell, T. F., Paradise, J. L., Feldman, H. M., Janosky, J. E., Pitcairn, D. N. & Kurs-Lasky, M. (1999). Maternal education and measures of early speech and language. *Journal of Speech, Language, and Hearing Research*, **42**, 1432–1443.

Duncan, G. J., Brooks-Gunn, J. & Klebanov, P. K. (1994). Economic deprivation and early childhood development. *Child Development*, **65**, 296–318.

Dunn, J., Wooding, C. & Herman, J. (1977). Mothers' speech to young children: variation in context. *Developmental Medicine and Child Neurology*, **19**, 629–638.

Entwisle, D. R. & Astone, N. M. (1994). Some practical guidelines for measuring youth's race/ethnicity and socioeconomic status. *Child Development*, **65**, 1521–1540.

Evans, G. (2004). The environment of childhood poverty. *American Psychologist*, **59**(2), 77–92.

Farran, D. C. & Haskins, R. (1980). Reciprocal influence in the social interactions of mothers and three-year-old children from different socioeconomic backgrounds. *Child Development*, **51**(3), 780–791.

Fish, M. & Pinkerman, B. (2003). Language skills in low-SES rural Appalachian children: Normative development and individual differences, infancy to preschool. *Applied Developmental Psychology*, **23**, 539–565.

Garcia Coll, C., Lamberty, G., Jenkins, R., Pipes McAdoo, H., Crnic, K., Hanna Wasik, B. & Vazquez Garcia, H. (1996). An integrative model for the study of developmental competencies in minority children. *Child Development*, **67**, 1891–1914.

Griffin, T. M., Hemphill, L. & Camp, L. (2004). Oral discourse in the preschool years and later literacy skills. *First Language*, **24**(2), 123–147.

Harris, M., Jones, D., Brookes, S. & Grant, J. (1986). Relations between the non-verbal context of maternal speech and rate of language development. *British Journal of Developmental Psychology*, **4**(3), 261–268.

Hart, B. & Risley, T. R. (1992). American parenting of language-learning children: Persisting differences in family–child interactions observed in natural home environments. *Developmental Psychology*, **28**, 1096–1105.

Hart, B. & Risley, T. R. (1995). *Meaningful differences in the everyday experience of young American children*. Baltimore, MD: Paul H. Brookes Publishing Co.

Hart, B. & Risley,T. R. (1999). *The social world of children learning to talk*. Baltimore, MD: Paul H. Brookes Publishing Co.

Hashima, P. Y. & Amato, P. R. (1994). Poverty, social support, and parental behavior. *Child Development*, **65**, 394–403.

Hernandez, D. J. (1997). Child development and the social demography of childhood. *Child Development*, **68**, 149–169.

Herrnstein, R. & Murray, C. (1996). *The bell curve: intelligence and class structure in American life*. New York: Simon and Schuster.

Hess, R. D. & Shipman, V. C. (1967). Cognitive elements in maternal behavior. In J. P. Hill (Ed.), *Minnesota symposia on child psychology*. Minneapolis, MN: University of Minnesota Press.

Hoff, E. (2003). Causes and consequences of SES-related differences in parent-to-child speech. In M. H. Bornstein & R. H. Bradley (Eds.), *Socioeconomic status, parenting, and child development* (pp. 147–160). Mahwah, NJ: Lawrence Erlbaum Associates.

Hoff, E. & Naigles, L. R. (2002). How children use input to acquire a lexicon. *Child Development*, **73**(2), 418–433.

Hoff-Ginsberg, E. (1991). Mother–child conversation in different social classes and communicative settings. *Child Development*, **62**, 782–796.

Hoff-Ginsberg, E. (1997). *Language development*. Pacific Grove, CA: Brooks/Cole.

Hoff-Ginsberg, E. (1998). The relation of birth order and socioeconomic status to children's language experience and language development. *Applied Psycholinguistics*, **19**, 603–629.

Huston, A. C., McLoyd, V. C. & Garcia Coll, C. (1994). Children and poverty: Issues in contemporary research. *Child Development*, **65**, 275–282.

Huttenlocher, J., Haight, W., Bryk, A., Seltzer, M. & Lyons, T. (1991). Early vocabulary growth: relation to language input and gender. *Developmental Psychology*, **27**, 236–248.

Huttenlocher, J., Vasilyeva, J., Cymerman, E. & Levine, S. (2002). Language input and child syntax. *Cognitive Psychology*, **45**, 337–374.

Jensen, A. (1969). How much can we boost IQ and scholastic achievement? *Harvard Educational Review*, **39**, 1–123.

Klebanov, P. K., Brooks-Gunn, J., McCarton, C. & McCormick, M. C. (1998). The contribution of neighborhood and family income to developmental test scores over the first three years of life. *Child Development*, **69**, 1420–1436.

Labov, W. (1969/1979). The logic of nonstandard English. In V. Lee (Ed.), *Language development*. London: Croom Helm and Open University, 1979.

Labov, W. & Harris, W. A. (1986). De facto segregation of black and white vernaculars. In D. Sankoff (Ed.), *Diversity and diachrony: Vol. 53. Current issues in linguistic theory*. Philadelphia, PA: John Benjamins.

Lawrence, V. W. & Shipley, E. F. (1996). Parental speech to middle- and working-class children from two racial groups in three settings. *Applied Psycholinguistics*, **17**, 233–255.

McLoyd, C. V. (1998). Socioeconomic disadvantage and child develoment. *American Psychologist*, **53**(2), 185–204.

Murray, A. D. & Hornbaker, A. V. (1997). Maternal directive and facilitative interaction styles: Associations with language and cognitive defvelopment of low risk and high risk toddlers. *Development & Psychopathology*, **9**(3), 507–516.

Naigles, L. R. & Hoff-Ginsberg, E. (1998). Why are some verbs learned before other verbs? Effects of input frequency and structure on children's early verb use. *Journal of Child Language*, **25**, 95–120.

Needleman, H. L., Schell, A., Bellinger, D., Leviton, A. & Allred, E. N. (1990). The long-term effects of exposure to low doses of lead in childhood: An 11-year follow-up report. *New England Journal of Medicine*, **322**, 83–88.

NICHD Early Child Care Research Network (2005). Pathways to reading: The role of oral language in the transition to reading. *Developmental Psychology*, **41**(2), 428–442.

Olson, S. L., Bates, J. E. & Kaskie, B. (1992). Caregiver–infant interaction antecedents of children's school-age cognitive ability. *Merrill-Palmer Quarterly*, **28**, 309–330.

Parks, P. L. & Smeriglio, V. L. (1986). Relationships among parenting knowledge, quality of stimulation in the home and infant development. *Family Relations*, **35**, 411–416.

Patterson, C. J., Kupersmidt, J. B. & Vaden, N. A. (1990). Income level, gender, ethnicity and household composition as predictors of children's school-based competence. *Child Development*, **68**, 807–819.

Peers, I. P., Lloyd, P. & Foster, C. (2000). *Clinical evaluation of language fundamentals-preschool, UK*. London: Psychological Corporation.

Raviv, T., Kessenich, M. & Morrison, F. J. (2004). A mediational model of the association between socioeconomic status and three-year-old language abilities: The role of parenting factors. *Early Childhood Research Quarterly*, **19**, 528–547.

Rice, M. L., Wexler, K. & Hershberger, S. (1998). Tense over time: The longitudinal course of tense acquisition in children with specific language impairment. *Journal of Speech, Language and Hearing Research*, **41**, 1412–1431.

Rosenthal, R. & Jacobson, L. (1968). *Pygmalion in the classroom*. London: Holt, Rinehart and Winston.

Roth, F. P., Speece, D. L. & Cooper, D. H. (2002). A longitudinal analysis of the connection between oral language and early reading. *The Journal of Educational Research*, **95**(5), 259–272.

Roth, F. P., Speece, D. L., Cooper, D. H. & De La Paz, S. (1996). Unresolved mysteries: How do metalinguistics and narrative skills connect with early reading? *Journal of Special Education*, **30**, 257–277.

Schwartz, R. G. & Terrell, B. Y. (1983). The role of input frequency in lexical acquisition. *Journal of Child Language*, **10**(1), 57–64.

Senechal, M. & LeFevre, J. (2002). Parental involvement in the development of children's reading skill: A five-year longitudinal study. *Child Development*, **73**, 445–460.

Shankweiler, D., Lundquist, E., Dreyer, L. G. & Dickinson, C. D. (1996). Reading and spelling difficulties in high school students: Causes and consequences. *Reading and Writing*, **8**(3), 267–294.

Siegel, L. (1982). Reproductive, perinatal and environmental factors as predictors of the cognitive and language development of preterm and full-term infants. *Child Development*, **53**, 963–973.

Smith, J. Brooks-Gunn, J. & Klebanov, P. (1997). Consequences in living in poverty for young children's cognitive and verbal ability and early school achievement. In G. Duncan & J. Brooks-Gunn (Eds.), *Consequences of growing up poor* (pp. 132–189). New York: Russell Sage Foundation.

Smith, L. (1999). Children's noun learning: How general learning processes make specialized learning mechanisms. In B. MacWhinney (Ed.), *The emergence of language* (pp. 277–304). Hillsdale, NJ: Erlbaum.

Snow, C. E. (2001). *The centrality of language: A longitudinal study of language and literacy development in low-income children*. London: University of London, Institute of Education.

Snow, C. E., Arlman-Rupp, A., Hassing, Y., Jobse, J. Joosten, J. & Vorster, J. (1976). Mothers' speech in three social classes. *Journal of Psycholinguistic Research*, **5**, 1–20.

Snow, C. E., Barnes, W. S., Chandler, J., Goodman, I. F. & Hemphill, L. (1991). *Unfulfilled expectations: home and school influences on literacy*. Cambridge, MA: Harvard University Press.

Snow, C. E., Burns, M. S. & Griffin, P. (Eds.) (1998). *Preventing reading difficulties in young children*. Washington, DC: The National Academies Press.

Snow, C. E., Dubber, D. & de Blauw, A. (1982). Routines in mother–child interaction. In L. Feagans and D. C. Farran (Eds.), *The language of children reared in poverty* (pp. 53–72). New York: Academic Press.

Stewart, W. A. (1970). Toward a history of American negro dialect. In F. Williams (Ed.), *Language and poverty*. Chicago, IL: Markham Publishing Company.

Tamis-LeMonda, C. S., Bornstein, M. H., Baumwell, L. & Damast, A. M. (1996). Responsive parenting in the second year: Specific influences on children's language and play. *Early Development and Parenting*, **5**(4), 173–183.

Tizard, B. & Hughes, M. (1984). *Young children learning: talking and thinking at home and at school*. London: Fontana.

Tomasello, M. & Todd, J. (1983). Joint attention and lexical acquisition style. *First Language*, **4**(12), 197–211.

Tough, J. (1977). *The Development of Meaning*. London: George Allen and Unwin Ltd.

Tough, J. (2000). Memorandum (EY 61). Appendix to the Minutes of Evidence presented to the Select Committee on Education and Employment, The United Kingdom Parliament. Retrieved 2 April, 2006, from http://www.publications.parliament.uk/pa/cm200001/cmselect/cmeduemp/33/33ap34.htm

Walker, D., Greenwood, C., Hart, B. & Carta, J. (1994). Prediction of school outcomes based on early language production and socioeconomic factors. *Child Development*, **65**, 606–621.

Wells, G. (1986). *The meaning makers: children learning language and using language to learn*. Portsmouth, NH: Heinemann Educational Books.

Wood, D. (1998). *How children think and learn* (2nd edn). Oxford: Blackwell.

Wooton, A. J. (1974). Talk in the homes of young children. *Sociology*, **8**, 277–295.

2 The Interplay between Language and Cognition in Typical and Atypical Development

NICOLA BOTTING

School of Psychological Sciences, University of Manchester, UK

INTRODUCTION

Language learning and cognitive development are complex processes. In this chapter, I will introduce and highlight some of the key issues surrounding research into language and the development of cognition in the early years. This chapter does not aim to provide an exhaustive review of the literature on these topics, which is vast. However, the ways in which we learn are relevant to the issue of language and social disadvantage that forms the focus of this volume. This chapter also aims to emphasise the interaction between these often theoretically separated areas of development and discusses this in the context of typical and atypical development.

EARLY COGNITIVE DEVELOPMENT

Unlike James's concept of the newborn's 'booming, buzzing confusion' (James, 1890), we now know that the development of cognition begins in utero and may continue well into early adulthood (Moshman, 1998). Differing theoretical approaches have changed the study of cognition over the decades. For example, the behaviourist trend throughout the 1950s minimised the study of cognition in development, preferring to focus only on aspects of behaviour that were directly observable (Watson, 1913) and arguing that much of language development occurs through systematic social reinforcement (Skinner, 1957) – a premise for which there is little empirical evidence. However, in more recent years this trend has reversed, and a cognitive approach to development has dominated much of the literature, leading to a number of advances in our knowledge of cognitive processes (Wood, 1991).

Importantly, the role of development per se has also begun to feature as an important topic of research where previously models derived from the study of adults were

Language and Social Disadvantage: Theory into Practice Edited by J. Clegg and J. Ginsborg
© 2006 John Wiley & Sons, Ltd

used to explain children's thinking and behaviour. This is particularly evident in the field of neuropsychology where, traditionally, findings relating to adult patients' acquired deficits have been used to inform research into childhood disorders. While these models may be used to complement a developmental approach, leaders in the field such as Karmiloff-Smith (1998) have urged us to question critically the implicit assumption of 'residual normality' that adult models sometimes bring, in which one skill can be entirely unaffected by impairment in another during development.

This developmental emphasis is not, of course, entirely new, and is evident in the highly influential work of Piaget who outlined various stages of cognitive development and highlighted the interrelatedness of different skills including language and cognition (Piaget, 1952). Although the ages at which Piaget suggested these stages develop have been questioned, along with some of the specifics of his theories, to date Piagetian theory remains crucial to current developmental research. Piaget's developmental stages begin with the sensori-motor stage in which the child explores the world almost entirely through touch and movement, relates only to the present and has little understanding of intention. Between the ages of about 2–6 years, according to Piaget, the child goes through a pre-operational or symbolic stage in which he or she develops the capacity to form the mental representations necessary for pretend play and language. The concrete operational stage is described as occurring at about 5–7 of age. This is where the child begins to develop strategies or rule bases for learning. Finally, the formal operational stage occurs at about 11 or 12 years of age in which the child develops more abstract mental abilities such as imagining themselves in different social scenarios and systematic problem solving.

For Piaget, these stages represented periods of qualitative change and 'leaps forward' in cognitive ability. Like James, however, Piaget underestimated the development of cognition in the young child. Furthermore, many researchers conceptualise the changes as more gradual. Recent trends in the study of cognitive development have emphasised the fact that 'stages' of development may not in fact be distinct time periods but are at least in part created by low-frequency time-sampling of behaviours. These behaviours may not even show linear patterns of change. Indeed the so called 'microgenetic' approach to cognitive development (Werner, 1948), in which change is intensively measured and analysed, has shown that skills sometimes decline, or at least show a period of unreliability and instability just preceding a breakthrough in learning (see Siegler, 2006, for a discussion). This research perspective takes a more quantitative approach to the examination of the development of cognitive processing, including skills such as decoding, storing, planning and analysing information.

COGNITIVE DEVELOPMENT

Two aspects of cognition implicated in language development and worth noting here are those of sociocognitive responsiveness and memory. Here, social responsiveness refers to a number of skills that underlie the communicative relationship between individuals such as joint attention and the understanding of intention, theory of mind and imitation. Sociocognitive skills, and their importance to language development, were also highlighted by earlier researchers such as Vygotsky (1962), who emphasised the social world of the child as a key factor in learning. In particular, Vygotsky postulated the Zone of Proximal Development (ZPD), which refers to the extended range of skills a child can develop in the context of full social interaction. For Vygotsky, optimum cognitive development can only be achieved in socially interactive environments. Vygotsky also suggests that sociocognitive actions, such as pointing, begin as meaningless gestures and become meaningful only through interaction (1978). Like Piaget, Vygotsky also believed that cognitive development is limited by the age of the child. These approaches may be of particular relevance in exploring the relationship between social disadvantage and language development since they emphasise the importance not only of the child's resources, but also features of the surrounding social environment.

Some sociocognitive responses appear to be available even to the newborn. Although Piaget believed that imitation cannot be said to be a true cognitive behaviour until the child is at least a year old, the imitation of facial expression, vowel sounds and other social behaviours has been observed in very young children (e.g. Anisfeld, 1991). Although most researchers would not consider all learning to be imitative, the ability to copy an action is clearly important in early language learning. Another form of social responsiveness is shown in basic forms of turn taking or 'proto-conversations' (Bateson, 1975) that have been recorded even in very young infants, who regulate their movements, sucking and vocalisations in rhythmic interactions with parental communication.

A number of studies have shown that 'joint attention' (the joint focus on or sharing of an item) primes the child to expect language related to that object or action. Children develop joint attention skills between 9 and 15 months of age, and progress from sharing attention, then following the direction of other people, to directing other people's attention themselves. These skills are related to early language and pre-verbal skills, and are also related to maternal social responsiveness (Carpenter, Nagell & Tomasello, 1998; Tomasello & Farrar, 1986). The understanding of intention is another key factor in sociocognitive skill. Some ingenious studies by Tomasello and colleagues (see Tomasello, 2001) have shown how important the understanding of speaker's intention is in early communicative learning and that sharing the same communicative goals is particular to human communication. In one set of studies, children were told that the researcher was looking for the 'Toma'. The researcher entered the room and found a novel item, but instead of looking pleased looked disappointed and moved to another location in which a second novel item was found. This time the researcher looked pleased and showed the child the item. Very young children of around 18 months were able to link the new word 'Toma' not just with the first item found but with the item the researcher 'intended' to find (Tomasello & Barton, 1994; Tomasello, Strosberg & Akhtar, 1995). The role of these types of interactive – as well as child-centred – factors has clear implications for the family with multiple incidences of language impairment, which may have more than one member experiencing impaired responsiveness.

As children near school age, other important sociocognitive skills appear. One of the main processes discussed in recent literature has been 'theory of mind', a term used to refer to the ability to take another's perspective. Like most abilities, this skill does not appear suddenly at the age of 3 or 4 years but is based on an increasingly sophisticated emotional knowledge, beginning with an increased understanding of intention, mental state terms, and with so called first order theory of mind ('I know what she's thinking') and mastery of false belief ('Teddy will think there are sweets in the Smarties tube even though I *know* there are stones in it'). Indeed, there appears to be an unstable or random pattern of passing and failing theory of mind tasks marking the transition between consistent failure and consistent success (Flynn, O'Malley & Wood, 2004; Wellman, Cross & Watson, 2001). As research progresses, we are developing a much deeper understanding of how this skill, which is based on the ability to meta-represent, relates to language development. Research into theories of mind has shown that although preschoolers are not as 'egocentric' as Piaget painted them, they have limitations in their understanding of individuals' unique perspectives on the world and have a tendency to believe that their own representations of the world are shared by everyone else. The gradual development of perspective-taking enables children to use increasingly subtle and sophisticated communicative devices including, for example, judging the optimum level of information relevant to the listener.

The second major post-Piagetian theme to be discussed is that of memory. Research into the *development* of memory is relatively recent. However, models of working memory such as that of Baddeley (1986) have helped us to conceptualise how memory and language might interrelate. In his original model, working memory has three parts: the visuo-spatial sketchpad, the central executive and the phonological loop. The last of these has, for obvious reasons, received much attention within the literature on language development and impairment and indeed the connection between language and verbal memory has now been established in a number of studies, such as that of Adams and Gathercole (2000) who showed that children with poor verbal memory skills were indeed also more likely to show poorer language skills. The use of verbal rehearsal, which is thought not to occur in younger children (Gathercole, Adams & Hitch, 1994), appears to be an important strategy in the development of more advanced cognition and learning. The effect of impaired language on this process, and on longer term memory is still relatively unknown, but may be important in explaining the cognitive difficulties now recognised in those with language impairment that are discussed below.

Until recently, however, little work existed that 'unpacked' the central executive portion of the model. This aspect has been described as including skills related to planning, fluency, inhibition, cognitive flexibility and working memory (Pennington & Ozonoff, 1996). The ability to inhibit, for example, may also affect how children learn the concepts necessary for developing language by helping them *not associate* certain atypical features of a concept and thus develop exemplar cases of that concept. Inhibitory control, however, is just one of the possible cognitive processes that could be examined in relation to language and which warrants further investigation.

The aspects of cognitive development highlighted here are only a part of the wider picture. They are intended to make salient a few aspects of early cognitive development and to illustrate that the development of cognition begins very early and is frequently intertwined with language learning. Although Piaget's ideas remain a strong influence in the field, a number of new themes such as those found in sociocognitive and information-processing models have enabled researchers to break some of his concepts down into more quantitative processes, to add cultural context to development and to challenge the ages at which children are able to master various skills.

EARLY LANGUAGE DEVELOPMENT

For many years the development of language was studied only in terms of expressive language partly because of the behaviourist trend to measure only observable behaviours, and partly due to limitations in experimental paradigms. However, more recently techniques relying on children's heart rate, head-turning, looking-time and sucking responses have meant that even very young infants can be participants in studies investigating the perception and understanding of language. We now know that, even in the mother's womb, babies in the last 6–3 months of gestation process speech sounds and begin to distinguish between these and other non-language sounds (Hepper, Scott & Shahidullah, 1993). The unborn child also seems to be sensitive to changes in style of music and can recognise his or her mother's voice over others at birth (De Casper & Fifer, 1980). Within the first few months, babies can identify differences in patterns of words (see below) and by 5 months prefer their own name to similar words (Mandel, Jusczyk & Pisoni, 1995). Between 8 and 10 months, children learn to understand simple phrases and, gradually, the meanings of individual words. At this age, children's receptive vocabulary ranges from about 10 to 150 words (Fenson, Dale, Reznick et al., 1994). By 18 months, a toddler can understand about 200–300 words and can infer meaning from the word order. For example, when given a sentence like 'Big Bird tickles Elmo', children of this age will attend longer to the correct picture of this action rather than an alternative depicting Elmo tickling Big Bird (Hirsch-Pasek & Golinkoff, 1996). Some researchers, such as Marcus, Vikayan, Bandi Rao and Vishton (1999), believe this 'knowledge' of grammar is evident much earlier, in the first few months of life. They have conducted rigorous experiments showing that infants as young as 2 months can detect changes and similarities in nonsense grammar: for example, FI-FI-FO is perceived by children as similar in kind to TA-TA-TO but different from FO-FI-FI.

Language production begins later than the understanding of words and becomes most evident with the emergence of single-word vocabulary. Infants usually start using real words, that is, referring to specific things rather than more generally used sounds, at about 10–15 months of age (Hoff, 2001). At this age, single words or set phrases are often used as 'holophrases', for example 'more' meaning 'I want more juice'. By the age of 2 years, typically developing children usually have at least 50 words in their spoken vocabulary. In more recent years, the documentation of vocabulary development has shown that as well as concrete nouns, more socially motivated words, such as 'more' and 'gone', and action words, such as 'up' and 'look', often make an early appearance in the child's language (Gopnik & Choi, 1995; Nelson, 1973). Between the acquisition of their first words, until they can produce about a hundred, children show a gradual pattern of lexical development – adding a few new words at a time. However, the majority of children appear to show a 'word spurt' at some point in lexical development in which vocabulary learning becomes much more rapid. This spurt tends to represent mainly object labels rather than other types of words, and the time it occurs seems to depend on a combination of age and sufficient vocabulary size. The precise cause of this spurt is not entirely known, although researchers have suggested that a critical mass of words enables the child to 'work out' how lexical items function (Smith, 1995) or that at this age language learning coincides with a conceptual leap that allows the child to group objects (Gopnik & Meltzoff, 1986).

Syntactic and lexical development occur in parallel. Thus, from about 18 months to 2 years of age, children appear to begin to use a 'cut and paste' strategy in which verbs are relatively 'fixed' to (i.e. used only in) the imitative context in which they are heard, while nouns are 'pasted' onto them in varying, more flexible slots (e.g. draw_). By about 3 years of age, children are able to use more verb-general constructions. However, not all verbs are treated the same at any given time; rather, some verbs are used more flexibly, earlier than others (Tomasello, 1999).

ISSUES IN LANGUAGE DEVELOPMENT

There are several different explanations for the way children learn language. The reader may be aware that much of the account given above, for example, reflects a mixture of theoretical approaches that influence my own non-nativist position on linguistic development. It is worth mentioning here the nature-nurture debate, which is still alive and well in the study of language development. All language researchers agree that there is some innate tendency for language to develop. At the same time, no one would argue that language input is irrelevant to the way we learn language. However, the degree to which these opposing sources are emphasised – innateness on the one hand, language input on the other – means that there is strong disagreement about children's language acquisition. It may seem surprising that, given the general shift towards general cognitive constructivism and sociocognitive research, many of those who study the development of language have been reluctant to move away from the nativist position as suggested by Chomsky (1957) and from an adult model of grammatical organisation (e.g. Pinker, 1994). This position suggests that the brain has specific knowledge about grammar from birth (a Universal Grammar), and that language input triggers this language-specific module into action. The theory also incorporates a finite set of different 'parameters' for language learning that can be adapted for each language (e.g. 'obligatory use of subject/non-obligatory use of subject'). These parameters make it simple for the innate system to adapt to whichever language community the child is born into. Findings such as those reported by Marcus et al. (1999), showing that even very young children are sensitive to grammar, support this Chomskian position that grammatical knowledge is inborn. However, part of the debate centres around the question of how non-specific 'grammar' can be before one calls it an ability to recognise 'same' and 'different' patterns (in any medium), which would then represent a more domain-general skill. Indeed, besides the nature-nurture debate, there is also a discussion about whether language development stems from highly specialised language systems, or if more global processing skills are sufficient to support language learning.

It seems unlikely that any one account can actually explain language development fully, and indeed many explanations fail to describe precisely how the process of language acquisition takes place with the ease that is seen in typical children. Alternative theories of language acquisition include socio-pragmatic and neuro-constructivist approaches. These suggest that children use a number of subtle social and pragmatic cues to guide their general cognitive predisposition for language learning. It may be helpful to take these different perspectives on language learning into account when we consider development.

The nature of the theories that inform our understanding of language learning is important when we consider potential environmental factors including social disadvantage. Some extreme cases of children who received virtually no language input and whose language development was severely impaired have been reported (e.g. by Curtiss, 1977: the case of 'Genie'), but far less is known about the more subtle effects of social disadvantage on language development (although much has been hypothesised: see Chapter 1, this volume) or, conversely, the nature of language difficulties that might result in social disadvantage.

HOW MIGHT LANGUAGE AND COGNITION INTERACT IN ATYPICAL POPULATIONS?

In typical populations, linguistic and cognitive skills often appear to develop along separate but parallel pathways. In those with generally delayed skills, this is also sometimes the case. However, other types of atypical development appear to reveal the more complex developmental process of language and cognition. At first glance, developmental disorders might seem to offer a further opportunity to 'separate' the two. Indeed, Specific Language Impairment (SLI) has sometimes been used to exemplify this disassociation of skills, along with Williams Syndrome – a disorder in which language skills appear at first to be relatively 'spared' compared with non-verbal skills, thus showing the opposite pattern of impairment. However, as research has progressed in this area, questions have been raised about whether these dissociations are in fact real in either disorder (Botting, 2005; Karmiloff-Smith, Grant, Berthoud et al., 1997).

Although development appears increasingly to be considered a focus of research in general, it is nevertheless a factor that has sometimes been overlooked in the study of SLI and other clinical groups. And yet the study of atypical populations may be even more in need of a developmental perspective and be able to inform us about developmental process to an even greater degree than the study of typically developing children. Thus, Hick, Botting and Conti-Ramsden (2005a, 2005b) showed that groups of children with Down syndrome, SLI, or who were developing typically, matched for non-verbal cognitive skills at baseline, developed these skills at a different *rate* over the following year. Surprisingly, it was the children with SLI who showed the least improvement on tests of non-verbal cognition. Furthermore, other recent work from Manchester (UK) and other centres has shown that individuals with SLI may have fluctuating or declining non-verbal IQ scores over time when compared with peers, showing a relative lag rather than any cognitive 'catch up' (Botting, 2005; Krassowski & Plante, 1997; Paul & Cohen, 1984). IQ is traditionally separated into verbal IQ and non-verbal IQ and these are intended to represent inherent cognitive ability for age compared with the general population. These constructs are usually assessed using a series of different psychometrically based subtests: those that involve language skills (verbal IQ) and those thought to involve other skills (non-verbal IQ). In some measurement tools, the scores from these two can then be combined to create separate verbal and non-verbal IQ scores respectively. Other tasks assess only non-verbal IQ. The IQ scores of people with SLI appear to decrease by between 10 and 20 points as they are reassessed from childhood through to adulthood (Botting, 2005; Krassowski & Plante, 1997; Paul & Cohen, 1984). Tomblin, Freese and Records (1992) report a mean decrease of about eight points in non-verbal IQ in a sub-sample of people with SLI between assessment in childhood and assessment 10 years later. Mawhood, Howlin and Rutter (2000) assessed 17 children with SLI when they were about 9 years old. When they were followed up, at the age of 19–21 years, their IQ scores had decreased by 14 points. However, Clegg, Hollis, Mawhood and Rutter (2005) report that the scores of this group had increased again when they were assessed at the age of 33–36 years. I have recently reported elsewhere a group of children with SLI who showed a mean drop of 23 points over a seven-year follow-up period (Botting, 2005). Importantly, the pattern of change in non-verbal IQ (NVIQ) was related to language outcome at 11 years of age even when initial NVIQ score was accounted for. The children with the more 'stable' IQ patterns showed the better language ability. Indeed, although in typical populations language and cognition may appear to be developing independently at around the same time, the more predictable nature of this change may mask a much closer interdependence. Furthermore, while IQ is usually the only measure taken of cognitive ability, other more specific tasks, paradigms that directly assess ability to learn (training tasks) or tools that measure level of functioning might also be aspects of cognitive ability that warrant more investigation.

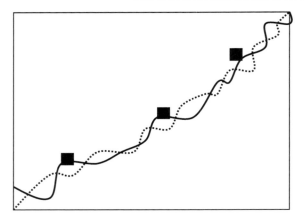

Figure 2.1. Speculative pattern of development in language and cognition

It is interesting to consider how cognition and language might develop in relation to one another and how we measure them. Figure 2.1 shows how a tightly knit interaction between language and cognition might theoretically occur in typical development. But if one imagines that only the square time-points were sampled, it is easy to see how development would appear as two linear and essentially independent skills, with one skill always more advanced than the other. The more detailed patterns in Figure 2.1, on the other hand, suggest that one skill may need to be at a certain level before the other can develop optimally.

If we extend this theoretical possibility to atypical populations, where both cognitive and language skills are slower to develop, we might expect to see much more of a recurring plateau effect in development, as shown in Figure 2.2, where one

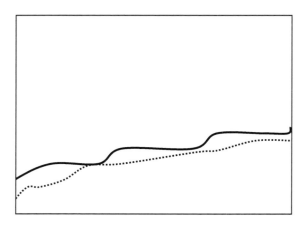

Figure 2.2. Potential pattern of *atypical* language and cognitive development

skill appears to 'struggle' without the other. This interactive pattern of development would also predict the initial 'specific' appearance of SLI with a later more general (but not entirely global) impairment, the pattern of 'illusory recovery' reported for children with SLI (Scarborough & Dobrich, 1990), and the slowed non-verbal development mentioned earlier (Hick, Botting & Conti-Ramsden, 2005b).

Of course these are merely speculations about possible patterns of development. However, the way we explain development informs the way we assess and treat children with SLI; these, in turn, influence outcomes. Thus our theoretical approach to language development is likely to affect how we study its role in social disadvantage too. If we take a strong developmental or constructivist approach, for example, this means we assume that there is the possibility for social skills to develop typically at first, but for atypical language development to interact with sociocognitive skills, leading back to less than optimal language development. If we take the modular position, however, we might predict that poor innate language skills need not impair the development of social skills. Ultimately, the theoretical beliefs we have (whether explicit or implicit) about the development of language and cognition affect the assumptions we make about language and social disadvantage.

SPECIFIC LANGUAGE IMPAIRMENT – HOW SPECIFIC IS IT?

Children with specific language impairment (SLI) are defined as having developmental language difficulties for which there is no obvious cause, such as hearing loss, neurological damage or generalised cognitive impairment. The language impairment may affect expressive (production of) language or receptive (understanding of) language, and often involves both (see Leonard, 1998). Difficulties may also be long-term (Clegg et al., 2005). SLI is thought to affect about 5% of the population (Law, Boyle, Harris, Harkness & Nye, 1998). However, despite the fact that language is the primary problem, individuals with SLI often experience difficulties with cognitive tasks at some point during development. These additional difficulties are seen in both verbal and non-verbal tasks.

In parallel with the theme of memory in studies of typical development, other lines of enquiry are emerging in research on verbal short-term memory, particularly relating to the ability of children with language difficulties to perform non-word repetition tasks. The relationship between this ability and language development in populations with language impairment is now established (Briscoe, Bishop & Norbury, 2001; Conti-Ramsden, Botting & Faragher, 2001; Gathercole & Baddeley, 1990). It is seen in the development of language over time (Botting & Conti-Ramsden, 2001) and appears to run in families (Bishop, North & Donlan, 1996). It is worth noting, however, that not all children with language impairment do poorly on non-word repetition tasks; nor do all children who do poorly on such tasks have language impairment. It must therefore be acknowledged that the overall positive predictive power of these tasks is unreliable. Other aspects of verbal memory, such as complex span have also been associated with SLI. For example, Ellis-Weismer and colleagues (1999) showed that working memory skill was clearly implicated in the language difficulties seen in their sample, and Montgomery (2003) showed that language comprehension skills were also linked with verbal short-term memory. Ongoing research by Chiat and Roy (Very Early Processing Skills Study) (2005) is investigating the role of both social responsiveness and phonological memory in predicting language outcome in children found to have very early language difficulties. Factors such as joint attention and imitation have already been highlighted recently as important additional predictors of the language learning in young children with autistic spectrum disorders (e.g. Charman, Baron-Cohen, Swettenham et al., 2003).

However, even the findings of research using memory tasks with children who have SLI clarify the nature of language impairments more generally: SLI appears to involve more than verbal deficits. Children with SLI have been shown to be poorer than their peers on tasks measuring visuo-spatial memory span (Hick et al., 2005b), symbolic play (Roth & Clark, 1987), spatial rotation (Johnston & Ellis-Weismer, 1983) and conservation tasks (Siegel, Lees, Allen & Bolton, 1981; see Leonard, 1998, for a full discussion).

Thus it appears that SLI cannot be used to argue convincingly for a dissociation between language and cognition. Indeed, recent findings almost imply the opposite – that a deficit in one area has an effect on the development of the other. As yet, the directional influence of these associations, however, and their potential outcome in terms of social development, is not fully understood. Furthermore, language profiles are also found to change over time within SLI (Conti-Ramsden & Botting, 1999). However, recent findings suggesting that the difficulties of children with SLI are more general may encourage theoreticians and professionals to reconsider the nature of cognition, and maybe even to conceptualise observed profiles as different 'dimensions' of skill and impairment.

LANGUAGE IMPAIRMENT AND COGNITION: A 'DOUBLE WHAMMY' FOR SOCIAL DISADVANTAGE

Considering the number and complexity of interactions between cognition and language development, the possibility arises that an impairment in language ability may quite often be coupled with cognitive difficulties of one sort or another. Furthermore, far from improving over time, this symbiosis of systems seems to lead to a worsening overall profile with age. For individuals with this pattern of difficulty, an outcome in which they are socially disadvantaged also seems plausible. Because of limitations on their language and cognition, not only are employment and housing opportunities less likely to be available to this group, but in addition, this population may be less enabled to protect their own rights in these matters or to put a case forward for improvements in quality of life. Even if support services are aware of a history of language impairment (and in our experience this is unlikely), the description of 'specific language impairment' may mask other difficulties that have developed over time and which may never have been fully addressed. However, SLI is very heterogeneous and appears to affect people from a wide range of social backgrounds, thus language difficulty is not exclusively associated with social disadvantage. Future research therefore needs to focus on identifying early factors that put particular individuals at most risk, so that this group can receive intensive and longer term support.

CIRCLE OF DISADVANTAGE: COGNITION AND LANGUAGE DIFFICULTIES IN THE FAMILY

Investigations into the family aggregation of language difficulty has shown repeatedly that a higher incidence of language impairment is evident in families of those with difficulties, with prevalence at about 30% compared with about 5–7% in the general population (Flax, Realpe-Bonilla, Hirsch et al., 2003; Tallal, Ross & Curtiss, 1989). The most recent of these studies have even begun to show promising links to particular chromosomal loci (16q and 19q) for expressive language ability (SLI Consortium, 2002). This tendency for impairments to be genetically inherited means that in a family with a child who has SLI, one or more parents are also more likely to be affected. Clearly, if a parent has language and – as is quite probable – cognitive difficulties, this in turn may limit their own ability to support and provide resources for the child, or to provide optimum models for cognitive and linguistic development. In some families, additional limitations may therefore include difficulties obtaining and remaining in employment, increased emotional difficulties, low income, smaller accommodation, lower educational achievement, and impoverished ability to provide educational and speech-language therapy assistance – factors often necessarily built into treatment. Thus, attempts to enhance the child's chances of developing better language skills and, ultimately, improved social outcomes, are at risk of being eroded by the same inherent language difficulties within the family itself. Chapter 1 of this volume focuses on the many ways in which social disadvantage may lead to and arise from impaired language and cognition.

IMPLICATIONS OF LANGUAGE AND COGNITIVE DEVELOPMENT FOR POLICY AND PRACTICE

This chapter began by outlining some key aspects of cognitive development, including the different stages of cognitive development proposed by Piaget, as well as more recent theories, which allow us to consider when and how cognitive changes take place. It sought to highlight the fact that even newborns have a number of cognitive skills and that by the time children reach school age a number of key cognitive skills, such as imitation, joint attention, understanding intention, working memory and theory of mind, as well as other factors, have contributed to their development of language. This then led on to a brief overview of language learning from early receptive skills to flexible and sophisticated syntactic ability. The nature of the interaction between language and cognition was then discussed in the context of atypically developing populations.

The chapter went on to argue that (1) developmental perspectives are crucial in understanding the development of language and that (2) in this developmental process, language and cognition are closely interdependent systems. These two points may seem obvious, but they are often ignored when decisions are made in both mainstream and clinical practice and policy. It may be that professionals working with atypical populations need particularly to focus on these important principles. Unless it is recognised, for example, that cognition in children with language difficulties develops at a different rate from that in typically developing children (Canivez & Watkins, 1998), assessment of cognitive skill will focus on single time points early on in the child's development. Later failure in academic tests may then be 'blamed' entirely on language difficulties when in fact substantial cognitive difficulties may also cause problems for the individual. Likewise, remediation and educational support are likely to focus solely on linguistic skill. However, our findings show that cognitive and sociocognitive difficulties may well exist alongside linguistic impairments and this issue needs to be addressed.

ACKNOWLEDGEMENTS

The author would like to thank the ESRC for fellowship grant: RES-000-27-0003 and Gina Conti-Ramsden for her continuous support.

REFERENCES

Adams, A. M. & Gathercole, S. E. (2000). Limitations in working memory: implications for language development. *International Journal of Language and Communication Disorders*, **35**, 95–116.
Anisfeld, M. (1991). Neonatal imitation. *Developmental Review*, **11**, 60–97.
Baddeley, A. D. (1986). *Working memory*. Oxford: Oxford University Press.
Bateson, M. C. (1975). Mother–infant exchanges: the epigenesis of conversational interaction. In D. Aaronson and R.W. Reiber (Eds.), *Developmental psycholinguistics and communication disorders; Annals of the New York Academy of Sciences*, **263**, 101–113. New York: New York Academy of Sciences.
Bishop, D. V. M., North, T. & Donlan, C. (1996). Non-word repetition as a behavioural marker for inherited language impairment: evidence from a twin study. *Journal of Child Psychology and Psychiatry*, **37**, 391–403.
Botting, N. (2005). Non-verbal cognitive development and language impairment. *Journal of Child Psychology and Psychiatry*, **46**, 317–326.

Botting, N. & Conti-Ramsden, G. (2001). Non-word repetition and language development in children with language impairments. *International Journal of Language and Communication Disorders*, **36**, 421–432.

Briscoe, J., Bishop, D.V.M. & Norbury, C. (2001). Phonological processing, language and literacy: a comparison of children with mild to moderate sensori-neural hearing loss and those with sepcific language impairment. *Journal of Child Psychology and Psychiatry*, **42**(3), 329–340.

Canivez, G. L. & Watkins, M. W. (1998). Long term stability of the Wechsler Intelligence Scale for Children Third Edition. *Psychological Assessment*, **10**, 285-291.

Carpenter, M. Nagell, K., & Tomasello, M. (1998). Social cognition, joint attention, and communicative competence from 9 to 15 months of age. *Monographs of the Society for Research in Child Development*, **63** (4, Serial No. 255).

Charman, T., Baron-Cohen, S., Swettenham, J., Baird, G., Drew, A. & Cox, A. (2003). Predicting language outcome in infants with autism and pervasive developmental disorder. *International Journal of Language and Communication Disorders*, **38**, 265–285.

Chiat, S. & Roy, P. (2005). Very Early Processing Skills as predictors of language disorders. Paper presented at NAPLIC conference, University of Warwick, March.

Chomsky, N. (1957). *Syntactic structures*. The Hague: Mouton.

Clegg, J., Hollis, C., Mawhood, L. & Rutter, M. (2005). Developmental Language Disorders – A follow-up in later adult life: cognitive, language and psychosocial outcomes.*Journal of Child Psychology and Psychiatry*, **46**, 128–149.

Conti-Ramsden, G. & Botting, N. (1999). Classification of children with specific language impairment. *Journal of Speech, Language and Hearing Research*, **42**, 1195-1204.

Conti-Ramsden, G., Botting, N. & Faragher, B. (2001). Psycholinguistic markers for SLI. *Journal of Child Psychology and Psychiatry*, **42**, 741–748.

Curtiss, S. (1977). *Genie: A psycholinguistic study of a modern day 'wild child'*. New York: Academic Press.

De Casper, A. J. & Fifer, W. P. (1980). Of human bonding: newborns prefer their mother's voices. *Science*, **208**, 1174–1176.

Ellis-Weismer, S., Evans, J. & Hesketh, L. J. (1999). An examination of verbal working memory capacity in children with specific language impairment. *Journal of Speech, Language and Hearing Research*, **42**, 1249–1260.

Fenson, L., Dale, P. S., Reznick, J. S., Bates, E., Thal, D. & Pethick, S. (1994). Variability in early communicative development. *Monographs of the Society for Research in Child Development*, **59**(5), Serial no. 242.

Flax, J., Realpe-Bonilla, T., Hirsch, L. S., Brzustowicz, L. M., Bartlett, C. W. & Tallal, P. (2003). Specific language impairment in families: Evidence for co-occurrence with reading impairments. *Journal of Speech, Language and Hearing Research*, **46**, 530–543.

Flynn, E., O'Malley, C., & Wood, D. (2004). A longitudinal, microgenetic study of the emergence of false belief understanding and inhibition skills. *Developmental Science*, **7**(1), 103-115.

Gathercole, S. E. & Baddeley, A. D.(1990). Phonological memory deficits in language disordered children: Is there a causal connection? *Journal of Memory and Language*, **29**, 336–360.

Gathercole, S. E., Adams, A. M. & Hitch, G. J. (1994). Do young children rehearse? An individual differences analysis. *Memory and Cognition*, **22**, 201–207.

Gopnik, A. & Choi, S. (1995). Names, relational words and cognitive development in English and Korean Speakers: Nouns are not always learned before verbs. In M. Tomasello &

W. Merriman (Eds.), *Beyond names for things: Young children's acquisition of verbs*. Mahwah, NJ: Erlbaum.

Gopnik, A. & Meltzoff, A. N. (1986). Relations between semantic and cognitive development in the one-word stage: the specificity hypothesis. *Child Development*, **57**, 1040–1053.

Hepper, P. G. Scott, D. & Shahidullah, S. (1993). Newborn and fetal response to maternal voice. *Journal of Reproductive & Infant Psychology*, **11**, 147–153.

Hick, R., Botting, N. & Conti-Ramsden, G. (2005a). Short-term memory and vocabulary development in children with Down syndrome and children with specific language impairment. *Developmental Medicine and Child Neurology*, **47**(8), 532–538.

Hick, R., Botting, N. & Conti-Ramsden, G. (2005b). Cognitive abilities in children with specific language impairment (SLI): Consideration of visuo-spatial skills. *International Journal of Language and Communication Disorders*, **40**(2), 137–149.

Hirsch-Pasek, K. & Golinkoff, R. M. (1996). *The origins of grammar: Evidence from early language comprehension*. Cambridge, MA: MIT Press.

Hoff, E. (2001). *Language development* (2nd edn). Belmont, CA: Wadsworth Press.

James, W. (1890). The principles of psychology (vols. 1 and 2). New York: Henry Holt.

Johnston, J. & Ellis-Weismer, S. (1983). Mental rotation abilities in language-disordered children. *Journal of Speech and Hearing Research*, **26**, 397–403.

Karmiloff-Smith, A. (1998). Development itself is the key to understanding developmental disorders. *Trends in Cognitive Science*, **2**, 389–399.

Karmiloff-Smith, A., Grant, J., Berthoud, I., Davies, M., Howlin, P. & Udwin, O. (1997). Language and Williams Syndrome: how intact is "intact"? *Child Development*, **68**(2), 246–262.

Krassowski, E., & Plante, E. (1997). IQ variability in children with SLI: Implications for use of cognitive referencing in determining SLI. *Journal of Communication Disorders*, **30**, 1–9.

Law, J., Boyle, J., Harris, F., Harkness, A. & Nye, C. (1998). Screening for speech and language delay: a systematic review of the literature. *Health Technology Assessment*, **2**(9), 184.

Leonard, L. B. (1998). *Children with Specific Language Impairment*. Boston, MA: MIT Press.

Mandel, D. R., Jusczyk, P. W. & Pisoni, D. B. (1995). Infants' recognition of the sound patterns of their own names. *Psychological Science*, **6**, 314–317.

Marcus, G. F., Vikayan, S. Bandi Rao, S. & Vishton, P.M. (1999). Rule learning by seven-month-old infants. *Science*, **283**, 77–80.

Mawhood, L., Howlin, P. & Rutter, M. (2000). Autism and Developmental Receptive Language Disorder – a comparative follow up in early adult life: I – cognitive and language outcomes. *Journal of Child Psychology and Psychiatry*, **41**, 547–559.

Montgomery, J. (2003). Working memory and comprehension in children with SLI: what we know so far. *Journal of Communication Disorders*, **36**, 221–231.

Moshman, D. (1998). Cognitive development beyond childhood. In W. Damon (Ed.), *Handbook of child psychology: Volume 2: Cognition, perception, and language* (pp. 947–978). New York, NY: John Wiley & Sons.

Nelson, K. (1973). Structure and strategy in learning to talk. *Monographs of the Society for Research in Child Development*. **38**, Serial no. 149.

Paul, R. & Cohen, D. (1984). Outcome of severe disorders of language acquisition. *Journal of Autism and Developmental Disorders*, **14**, 405–442.

Pennington, B. F. & Ozonoff, S. (1996). Executive functions and developmental psychopathology. *Journal of Child Psychology and Psychiatry*, **37**, 51–87.

Piaget, J. (1952). *The origins of intelligence in children.* New York: International Universities Press.

Pinker, S. (1994). *The language instinct: How the mind creates language.* New York: Morrow.

Roth, F. & Clark, D. (1987). Symbolic play and social participation abilities of language-impaired and normally-developing children. *Journal of Speech and Hearing Disorders,* **52**, 17–29.

Scarborough, H. S. & Dobrich, W. (1990). Development of children with early language delay. *Journal of Speech and Hearing Research,* **33**, 70–83.

Siegel, L., Lees, A., Allen, L. & Bolton, B. (1981). Nonverbal assessment of Piagetian concepts in preschool children with impaired language development. *Educational Psychology,* **1**, 153–158.

Siegler, R. S. (2006). Microgenetic analyses fo learning. In W. Damon & R. M. Lerner (Series Eds.) & D. Kuhn & R. S. Siegler (Vol. Eds.), Handbook of child psychology, Volume 2: Cognition, perception, and language (6th edn, pp. 464–510). Hoboken, NJ: Wiley.

Skinner, B. F. (1957). *Verbal behavior.* Englewood Cliffs, NJ: Prentice-Hall.

SLI consortium (2002). A genomewide scan identifies two novel loci involved in Specific Language Impairment. *American Journal of Human Genetics,* **70**, 384–398.

Smith, L. B. (1995). Self-organizing processes in learning to learn words: Development is not induction. In C.A. Nelson (Ed.), *New perspectives on learning and development: Minnesota Symposium for Child Development.* New York: Academic Press.

Tallal, P., Ross, R. & Curtiss, S. (1989). Familial aggregation in Specific Language Impairment. *Journal of Speech and Hearing Disorders,* **54**, 167–173.

Tomasello, M. (1999). *The cultural origins of human cognition.* Cambridge, MA: Harvard University Press.

Tomasello, M. (2001). Perceiving intentions and learning words in the second year of life. In M. Tomasello & E. Bates (Eds.), *Language Development: the essential readings* (pp. 111–128). Oxford: Blackwell.

Tomasello, M. & Barton, M. (1994). Learning words in non-ostensive contexts. *Developmental Psychology,* **30**, 639–650.

Tomasello, M. & Farrar, J. (1986). Joint attention and early language. *Child Development,* **57**, 1454–1463.

Tomasello, M., Strosberg, R. & Akhtar, N. (1995). Eighteen-month-old children learn words in non-ostensive contexts. *Journal of Child Language,* **22**, 1–20.

Tomblin, J. B., Freese, P. & Records, N. (1992). Diagnosing specific language impairment in adults for the purpose of pedigree analysis. *Journal of Speech, Language and Hearing Research,* **35**, 832–843.

Vygotsky, L. S. (1962). *Thought and language.* New York: Wiley.

Vygotsky, L. S. (1978). *Mind in society.* Cambridge, MA: Harvard University Press.

Watson, J. B. (1913). Psychology as the behaviorist views it. *Psychological Review,* **20**, 158–177.

Wellman, H. M., Cross, D. & Watson, J. (2001). A meta-analysis of false belief reasoning: The truth about false belief. *Child Development,* **72**, 655–684.

Werner, H. (1948). *Comparative psychology of mental development.* New York: International Universities Press.

Wood, D. (1991). *How children think and learn.* Cambridge, MA: Blackwell.

3 Literacy and Numeracy

IVY DOHERTY and JENNY LANDELLS

School of Allied Health Professions, Leeds Metropolitan University, UK

INTRODUCTION

There is an established and recognised relationship between the development of speech and language and the development of literacy and numeracy. Children with speech and language difficulties (SLD) often experience significant problems in the acquisition of literacy and numeracy. A developing body of research investigates this relationship and its underlying mechanisms. The chapter outlines the value of literacy and numeracy skills in today's society and describes the role of speech and language development in children's literacy and numeracy attainment. The literacy and numeracy profiles of children with SLD are then described. Finally, issues of socio-economic deprivation are addressed with respect to the association between language, literacy and numeracy.

THE VALUE OF LITERACY AND NUMERACY

Reading and writing are essential tools in today's society for both children and adults. Individuals who are not literate are severely disadvantaged in all aspects of daily life from education to employment, learning life skills and accessing social opportunities. It is estimated that some seven million adults in England lack basic literacy abilities (Moser, 1999). Although literacy attracts more attention, numeracy is equally essential to everyday life and many people are not proficient in basic numeracy skills (Basic Skills Agency, 1997).

SPEECH, LANGUAGE AND COGNITIVE SKILLS IN LITERACY DEVELOPMENT

Language has three components: phonology, syntax and semantics. Phonology is the understanding and organisation of sounds, including intonation and stress patterns

Language and Social Disadvantage: Theory into Practice Edited by J. Clegg and J. Ginsborg
© 2006 John Wiley & Sons, Ltd

specific to a language. Syntax is the level of language that is concerned with rules of word order and modifications of their forms, for example adding prefixes or suffixes to words to alter meaning. Semantics involves the understanding and use of meaning, of which vocabulary is a key part.

Working memory has a role in the development of language, literacy and numeracy. According to Baddeley and Hitch's (1974) model, information held in short-term memory decays and is lost unless it is rehearsed. This skill develops throughout childhood. Gathercole and Baddeley (1993) and Adams and Gathercole (1995, 2000) emphasise the importance of the phonological loop in developing language competence. In addition, cognitive abilities in areas such as attention and listening, sequencing and visual and auditory perception are essential prerequisites for literacy development. Furthermore, advanced literacy development requires metacognition, problem solving, reasoning, inference and the ability to generalise (Stothard, 1994).

Storch and Whitehurst (2002) identify the importance of both code-related skills and oral language ability in the development of literacy. Code-related skills include the knowledge that print goes from left to right, phoneme-grapheme correspondence, phonological awareness and basic writing skills. Oral language ability includes semantic, syntactic and conceptual knowledge. The extent of the contribution to literacy of these two skill sets is uncertain and there is much debate as to whether weaknesses in either skill set predicts problems in literacy development.

PHONOLOGICAL AWARENESS

A key aspect of both speech and language, and literacy development is phonological awareness. Children gradually learn to segment speech into its smaller units called phonemes in order to decode meaning and to develop vocabulary. The normal stages in the development of segmentation are awareness of words, syllables, onset-rime units and finally phonemes (Goswami & Bryant, 1990; Bishop, 1997). According to Carroll, Snowling, Hulme and Stevenson (2003), children first develop awareness of large units such as syllables and rime before small units such as phonemes. The resulting ability to perceive and manipulate individual speech sounds is generally referred to as phonological awareness, and is usually developed by children about the age of 3 years (Bryant & Bradley, 1983) with rime skills appearing before phoneme skills (Carroll et al., 2003). In literacy acquisition, phonological awareness precedes the skill of phoneme-grapheme matching. Hester and Hodson (2004) found that the ability to form and manipulate phonological representations – such as dividing words into their constituent parts and recombining them – is independent of IQ and receptive vocabulary. They argue that this ability underlies the decoding of letters, and should be taught to children in the early stages of literacy development.

Measures of phoneme awareness, such as deletion, oddity and detection – unlike onset-rime awareness – are strong predictors of reading (Hulme, Hatcher, Nation, et al., 2002). Phoneme deletion tasks demand well-specified phonemically structured phonological representations. Thus, the ability to learn to read effectively depends on forming associations between graphemes and orthographic representations and these phonological representations. If a child performs well on phonemic awareness tasks, this may be the best indicator available that his or her phonological representations are suitably organised to support the creation of mappings between orthography and phonology. Phonological awareness and knowledge of letter names are also powerful predictors of reading success (Muter, 1994). Those children who start school with the ability to recognise letters and who are able to segment spoken words into speech sounds are ready to start decoding print (Snowling, 2004).

DYSLEXIA

Children who experience difficulties in learning to read, associated with poor rime, phonological awareness, grapheme-phoneme recoding skills and a slow reading speed, are often diagnosed as dyslexic, particularly if they are of average or above-average intelligence (Critchley, 1970; Miles & Miles, 1999). Theorists and practitioners are currently much exercised as to the question of how dyslexia should be defined, although there is some evidence to suggest that both groups of children – poor readers and those with dyslexia – have deficits in the core skills of phonological processing, visual memory, syntactic ability and language ability regardless of any discrepancy between measured IQ and overall reading level (Siegel, 1999; Schneider, Roth & Ennemoser, 2000). A great deal of research has focused on the extent to which these skills are precursors of, or simply associated with, literacy. However, it should be noted that the inconsistency of the English orthographical system impacts on the literacy development of English language learners, since children cannot simply 'sound out' words to be read or written. Learners of other more orthographically consistent languages are better at identifying phoneme identification of words and non-words than children learning English, whether or not they are thought to be dyslexic (Bruck, 1992; Porpodas, 1999; Sprenger-Charolles, Cole, Lacert & Semiclaes, 2000). This finding supports the phoneme deficit account whereby children with dyslexia learning to read English are more likely to encounter disruptions in the development of stable phonological representations that are essential to phoneme-grapheme matching (Bowey, Cain & Ryan, 1992; Bruck, 1992; Goswami, 2002a, 2002b, 2002c; Swan & Goswami, 1997). The extent to which particular languages are orthographically consistent is also implicated in grapheme-phoneme recoding skills (Rack, Snowling & Olsen, 1990; Snowling, 1980; Van Ijzendoorn & Bus 1994) but deficits in reading speed seem to be cross-linguistic (Ziegler, Perry, Ma-Wyatt, Ladner & Schulte-Korne, 2003).

   Monaghan, Chater and Hulme (2005) argue that children develop awareness of language structure at different levels of granularity, progressing from larger units such as whole words, via onset-rime, to smaller units such as phonemes, and that this early, general, pattern of development provides the building blocks for later skilled reading. Thus, limited exposure to speech and language will result in poorer phoneme awareness skills, which may in turn affect literacy development. Ziegler and Goswami (2005) postulate that efficient processing skills at the smallest 'grain size' are disrupted in children with dyslexia. Children with phonological speech deficits are at risk of dyslexia in all languages, and children with milder phonological speech deficits who are given severely limited exposure to print will also be at risk of dyslexia in most languages. The critical factor would be the consistency of the orthography.

THE ROLE OF OTHER ASPECTS OF LANGUAGE IN DYSLEXIA

Snowling, Gallagher and Frith (2003) identified the precursors of dyslexia in 'high-risk' children aged 3 years and 9 months who were followed up when they were 8 years old and found to have developed reading difficulties. Their findings undermine the view that dyslexia is the consequence of a phonological deficit. Rather, they argue that early precursors of reading difficulty are to be found in language acquisition more generally, particularly the slow development of vocabulary, expressive and grammatical language skills. Snowling et al. (2003) postulate a model of literacy development that includes pathways for language, speech and letter knowledge. These can be of variable strength. Thus, if a child has better vocabulary than phonological skills at an early age, then the semantic pathway, rather than the phonological pathway, will be strengthened. This, in turn, will affect phonological awareness and thus word-level literacy. Snowling et al. found that children who were identified before the age of four as having weak phonological and spoken language pathways were likely to experience subsequent problems with reading, supporting the view that language impairments compromise the efficiency of the semantic route and its capacity to compensate (Nation & Snowling, 1998). The severity of such reading problems varies, of course, since it depends on the extent to which language skills other than phonology are affected. Snowling et al.'s study highlights the interactive nature of spoken language and literacy development. Although one can compensate for the other, this does not necessarily happen and a number of different routes to literacy may be taken. If a child learns to read relying on the semantic pathway, for example, their phoneme-grapheme mapping skills are likely to be weak and their spelling will suffer as a result.

INTERVENTION

Interventions can be very effective. For example, phonological awareness skills can be trained successfully; Elbro and Petersen (2004) report that the phonological awareness of poorest readers who took part in their study was more greatly improved than that of readers in the borderline range. Hatcher, Hulme, and Snowling (2004) advocate the teaching of phonic rather than rhyme skills in the early stages of learning to read. They do not believe, however, that typically-developing children need extra intervention; they found that a reading programme containing a highly structured phonic component was sufficient for most of the 4½-year-old children in their study to master the alphabetic principle and to learn to read effectively without any additional phonological training. Children with reading delays, on the other hand, did benefit from additional training in phonological awareness and linking letters to phonemes.

CHILDREN WITH SPEECH AND LANGUAGE DIFFICULTIES: LITERACY DEVELOPMENT

Children with SLD experience more difficulties acquiring literacy than children without SLD. In a longitudinal study, Bishop and Adams (1990) tracked a group of children with language difficulties from 4 years of age to determine the impact of the early language difficulty on literacy development. At 5½ years of age, the language difficulties of some of the children had resolved, whereas they persisted for the remainder. At the age of 8 years, the literacy abilities of the resolved group were good but those of the persisting group were much weaker. The strongest predictors of literacy difficulties were delayed receptive and expressive syntax. A 'critical age' hypothesis was formulated proposing that literacy development is dependent on adequate early speech and language and if speech and language development is still delayed at school entry age then literacy problems will follow. Further studies have confirmed the relationship between language and literacy development (Catts, 1993; Leitao, Hogben & Fletcher, 1997; Leitao & Fletcher, 2004; Magnusson & Naucler, 1990; Nathan, Stackhouse, Goulandris & Snowling, 2004a; Stothard, Snowling, Bishop, Chipchase & Kaplan, 1998). The analysis of different profiles of language and literacy skills indicates that early delays in phonological awareness and verbal naming lead to written word recognition difficulties, and early syntactic and semantic delays give rise to reading comprehension difficulties (Catts, 1993; Roth, Speece & Cooper, 2002).

Speech difficulties are also involved in literacy attainment (Nation & Snowling, 1998), although it has been suggested that children with pure speech difficulties are at less risk than those with language difficulties. Hesketh (2004) followed up children identified in a previous study (Hesketh, Adams, Nightingale & Hall, 2000) with moderate to severe speech disorders between the ages of 3½ and 5 years. When they were 6–7 years old, most of the children had developed typical speech, phonological awareness and literacy ability. However, literacy development was delayed in a small number of children. Poor early phonological awareness skills were the strongest predictor of literacy difficulties. Meanwhile Nathan et al. (2004a) argue, on the basis of similar findings, that persistent speech and language difficulties can affect literacy development. Nathan, Stackhouse, Goulandris and Snowling (2004b) also found persistent speech difficulties to have a significant impact on educational attainment. Children identified as having speech difficulties at the age of 4 years were followed up at the age of 7, when their performances in Key Stage 1 SATs were measured. There were differences in the levels achieved by children with resolved speech difficulties and children with persisting difficulties. The children in the resolved group scored at average or above average on reading, reading comprehension and mathematics, but not spelling. The scores of the children with persisting speech difficulties were much lower on all measures. The authors argue that even children with resolved speech difficulties may continue to experience problems with spelling.

There is support for the impact of phonological awareness intervention on the literacy development of children with specific SLD. Gillon (2000) investigated the benefits of phonological awareness; intervention for children with expressive phonological difficulties who also had delayed development of early reading. Three types of intervention were compared: specific phonological awareness; more generic intervention targeted at speech production and expressive language; and minimal input focusing on just speech production. The results showed the phonological awareness group made significant progress and reached levels similar to typically developing peers. Similar improvements in a smaller study were found by Major and Bernhardt (1998), but not by Denne, Langdown, Pring and Roy (2005), who cite the heterogeneity of children with speech impairments and the confusing terminology used to describe these children as the lack of comparability between studies.

SPEECH AND LANGUAGE DEVELOPMENT IN NUMERACY

In comparison to literacy, much less is known about numeracy acquisition. In typical development, infants only a few weeks old are able to recognise differences between small numbers of objects and even to show some reasoning ability with numbers, at least up to four (Tolchinsky, 2003; Wynn, 1998). Sophian (1998), on the other hand, argues that this merely demonstrates the ability to subitise, rather than to count. Subitising involves processing small numbers simultaneously rather than sequentially and is found in both children and adults.

Counting, however, forms the basis of arithmetic. First, children learn to recite numbers in the correct sequence by rote; this does not necessarily imply an understanding of the concepts underlying counting. This is demonstrated by the use of number words to represent non-specific quantities, for example 'I want three', meaning 'I want some' (Fazio, 1994). The concepts underlying counting have to be acquired (Sophian, 1998); they include one-to-one correspondence between words and objects, the stable-order principle whereby the sequence of numbers is invariant, and the cardinality principle whereby the final number represents the total number in the set (Gelman & Gallistel, 1978). Once children understand the cardinality principle, they can 'count on', adding a second set of numbers to one already counted. This is a precursor to understanding the place value rule, or recognising that the '1' in 10, 100, 1000 and so on represent cumulative powers of ten (Donlan, 1998).

Symbolic understanding, integrating the recognition of symbol representation and world knowledge is important for numeracy development (Munn, 1998). Children may be able to count three sweets and two cars and even to add them together, but to use the symbolic representation of $3 + 2 = 5$ requires abstract thinking. As understanding of number develops, increasing flexibility in thinking is required. Anghileri (2000) notes the importance of understanding relationships between numbers and number patterns. An example would be noticing that $2 + 2 + 2$ and 3×2 and 2×3

and $5+1$ are all equivalent to 6. Relationships are not always obvious. Some operations can be reversed, for example $(8+3 = 3+8$ and $8 \times 3 = 3 \times 8)$, but $8 \div 3$ is not equivalent to $3 \div 8$. Clearly understanding what is represented by the symbols '+', '×', '÷' and '=' is necessary, but it is also the case that many familiar words have specific uses, that have to be learned, in the context of arithmetic. For example, preschool children often use the word 'more' for a variety of purposes: to ask for extra chips at teatime, and to complain of unfairness: 'He's got more than me'. At school, however, the word 'more' can represent specific relationships between the values of numbers: 5 is three more than 2, 3 is one more than 2 and so on. According to Munn (1998), many children do not have this level of understanding when they start school.

CHILDREN WITH SPEECH AND LANGUAGE DIFFICULTIES: NUMERACY DEVELOPMENT

Some children with speech and language difficulties have problems acquiring numeracy skills. As we have seen, mathematical terms may have multiple meanings, causing confusion for many children. Zevenbergen (2001) cites the example of the child who looked puzzled when asked to calculate the volume of a box. When the teacher asked, 'Do you know what "volume" is?' the child replied, 'Yes, it is the button on the TV'. Homophones such as 'pie' and 'pi', and 'hole' and 'whole', can present similar challenges. Zevenbergen also highlights spatial terminology as being particularly difficult; for example, numbers are added 'up' but the answer is written at the bottom of the calculation. Problems can arise when teachers speak numbers aloud rather than writing them; for example, when the number spoken is '302' the listener must identify the 'hundred' as indicating the place. Numbers can only be written in one way; changing the order of the digits changes the number. Yet, 302 can be spoken as 'three oh two' or 'three hundred and two' (Tolchinsky, 2003). Grauberg (1998) notes that confusions can occur when children hear 'teen' and 'ty'; if they have poor auditory discrimination they may perceive 'sixteen' as 'sixty'. Further problems arise when such numbers are converted into place values; although both numbers, when spoken, start with six, the sequence is unhelpful, as the 'six' in sixteen refers to six units but the 'six' in sixty refers to six tens.

Fazio (1994) compared the performance of preschool children with SLI and two control groups of typically developing children (one younger, one older but matched for cognitive ability with the younger group) on a series of counting tasks using both oral and gestural output. The children with SLI made errors in sequencing numbers, on the oral tasks, which led to incorrect answers for the size of a set. On the other hand, they did show understanding of underlying rules such as the cardinality principle. They also performed better on the gestural tasks, where their verbal output did not interfere with their processing. The two control groups showed different patterns of results. Younger children performed as well on the oral tasks as on the gestural tasks. The older children however, performed better on the oral tasks than the gestural tasks. It may be that they were better at counting by rote because they had had more practice than the younger children, but they were having difficulty acquiring symbolic rules. Two years later, Fazio (1996) followed up the same groups of children. The children with SLI were not delayed in terms of their conceptual and procedural numeracy, but they still experienced difficulties with counting. They were therefore slow to learn new sequences of numbers, such as counting in tens. They also found it hard to retrieve mathematical 'facts' from memory, perhaps because they had found it hard to store phonological information relating to numbers.

There is continuing debate as to whether the children with specific SLD only experience difficulties processing linguistic information or if they have a more generalised cognitive processing deficit specific to numeracy. Stone and Connell (1993) suggest that children with specific language impairment (SLI) are poorer than typically-developing children at learning symbolic relationships, while Donlan, Bishop and Hitch (1998) argue that their understanding of symbolic relationships is merely restricted by linguistic impairment.

THE IMPACT OF SOCIO-ECONOMIC DEPRIVATION

There are fewer books available within the homes of children from low-SES backgrounds in comparison with those from higher-SES groups; perhaps as a result, they also tend to be read to less frequently (Whitehurst, 1997). When adults share books and read with young children, the style of language they use is particularly conducive to language development, but some children from low-SES backgrounds rarely have this experience. Purcell-Gates, L'Allier and Smith (1995) found that literacy practices varied widely among four families living in a large urban area in the USA. They were all literate – although they were divided into high- and low-literacy pairs – and from similar SES backgrounds. On average, the two high-literacy families engaged in eight times more literacy events per hour than the two low-literacy families. In addition, it is worth noting that the low literacy families did not engage in any 'storybook' activities. Whitehurst (1997) advocates a 'dialogic reading' approach whereby parents are taught to become facilitators, encouraging their children to take the lead when sharing storybooks and thus become the storytellers themselves. Torr (2004) also emphasises the importance of shared book reading and the role of the adult in helping the child to link knowledge and experiences to the text, which is a crucial part of literacy development. Torr compared interactions during shared reading between 4-year olds and their mothers and teachers. The mothers in the study had different educational backgrounds: half of them had left school at age 15–16, but the other half had educational qualifications up to degree standard. When the children were interacting with their mothers who had left school early they mostly listened and named objects pictured in the book. When they interacted with their teachers, however, they were more likely to make connections between the text and their own experiences. The other group of children, when reading with

their mothers who had been educated to degree level, interacted in similar ways
with their mothers and teachers. They too were more likely to make inferences and
generalise from the text and ask questions. Torr argues that the mothers with higher
levels of education used more grammatically complex language forms, which in
turn facilitated more sophisticated interactions.

Snow, Burns and Griffiths (1998) note that, in America, children from poor
families, those of African-American and Hispanic descent and children attending
urban schools are at much greater risk of poor reading outcomes than middle-class,
European-American and suburban children. Tikly, Haynes and Hill (2004) discuss
some of the barriers to achievement for children of mixed heritage in the UK.
Children from white/black Caribbean backgrounds form the largest group and are
also the group most at risk of low achievement. Many of these children come from
socially disadvantaged backgrounds, teachers' expectations of them are low and
they are more likely to be excluded from school than other cultural groups. In
contrast, pupils from white/Asian backgrounds achieve higher levels of educational
attainment regardless of SES. Parental levels of education have also been found
to be of significance in the educational achievement of their children. Davis-Kean
(2005), using data from a national cross-sectional study of African-Americans and
European-Americans, found that the total effect of parent educational achievement
was much stronger than the total effect of income in the European-American
group, but of lesser significance in the African-American sample. There is also
evidence that the level of parental involvement affects academic performance. Flouri
and Buchanan (2004) found that both fathers and mothers were important in the
academic development and success of boys and girls.

Given that there is a relationship between speech and language, and literacy, do
children from low socio-economic groups have similar difficulties with reading as
those children with speech and language difficulties, or are they different and need
to be treated differently? There is limited research focusing on the specific skills
needed to develop reading in children in the lower SES groups. Early studies by
Wallach, Wallach, Dozier and Kaplan (1977) reported SES-related differences in
preschool children's ability to segment, and Dickinson and Snow (1987) noted SES-
related differences in phonological sensitivity and other language and literacy skills.
Raz and Bryant (1990) found that low-SES children aged 4½ and 5½ from families
without employment had poorer letter knowledge and phonological processing skills
than children of the same age from families where at least one parent was in skilled
employment. There were strong SES-related differences in reading performance in
the older children. Lonigan, Burgess, Anthony and Barker (1998) carried out a large
study of children aged from 2 to 5 years from different SES backgrounds and found
social class differences in growth of phonological sensitivity. The differences were
small when the children were young but increased as the children grew older. Two
studies by Stuart (1999, 2004) demonstrate that the structured teaching of phonics
and phonological awareness skills for inner-city children (the majority of whom
were second language learners) can have a long-term impact on the development
of literacy skills. Whitehurst and Fischel (2000) believe that, in order to develop

adequate literacy skills, young children need a stimulating language environment but in addition they need, at the age of about 4–5 years, to be introduced specifically to the concepts of letters, sounds and print. As noted already, children who learn to read quickly are those who understand letters, grasp phoneme-grapheme correspondence and are able to print letters.

INTERVENTION FOR CHILDREN FROM LOW-SES BACKGROUNDS

The importance of early intervention to provide improved stimulation for young children in areas of social and economic deprivation is recognised through government-funded initiatives such as Head Start in America (Head Start Bureau, 2005) and Sure Start (2005) in Britain. Interventions such as the Hanen Parent Programme (Manolsen, 1992) have shown that changes to the style of parental interaction can have demonstrable effects on children's language development (Girolametto, Weitzman, Wiigs & Pearce, 1999; McDade & McCartan, 1998) but the time investment for carers and professionals is high. The necessity for appropriate training for early child educators has been highlighted in the National Service Framework for Children (Department of Health, 2004) and training packages to meet the needs of children with language impairments, provided by organisations such as I-CAN (2003), have been well received by staff in early education settings. A large-scale study of the provision of preschool education (Siraj-Blatchford, Sylva, Muttock, Gillon & Bell, 2002) found that education was effective, particularly for children from the most disadvantaged backgrounds. Specialised support in preschool, especially for language and prereading skills could be particularly beneficial. Outcomes for the children were related to the qualification levels of the staff – the higher the qualification, the more progress the children made. The importance of looking at the multifactorial components of both the home and child-care literacy environments when planning intervention is stressed by Weigel, Martin and Bennett (2005).

Despite the measures already put in place to improve early language and literacy skills, including the National Literacy Strategy (DfES, 1998) and National Numeracy Strategy (DfES, 1999), little overall change is apparent. Many children still leave school without basic literacy and numeracy skills and many of these are from low-SES groups. The long-term effects on employment prospects, personal and social development are significant and the percentage of individuals in the prison population with literacy difficulties (Bryan, 2004) provides another indication of the possible implications of poor academic achievement. However, not all children from low-SES backgrounds have poor academic achievement and some schools have good achievement from students who live in poverty (Adler & Fisher, 2001). While early language development must be recognised as an important factor in the acquisition of literacy and numeracy, the complexity of sociocultural factors must not be underestimated and must be taken into account when intervention is planned.

SUMMARY AND CONCLUSIONS

The majority of children develop literacy and numeracy skills without difficulty. Children with speech and language impairments are disadvantaged but not all children go on to have problems. Similarly many children from lower-SES backgrounds groups develop literacy and numeracy skills in the same way as their better-off peers, but some experience delays. The children particularly at risk are those from low-SES backgrounds who have persisting delays in their speech and language development.

Regardless of the *cause* of literacy delay, for example, access to appropriate language and literacy, or specific difficulties of language learning, all young at-risk groups can benefit from targeted intervention. Practitioners working with young children need to understand the complexities of literacy and numeracy development, to assess children carefully, to be trained to deliver intervention programmes and to involve parents and families from an early age in developing these skills which are crucial for access to education and skilled employment.

REFERENCES

Adams, A.-M. & Gathercole, S. E. (1995). *Phonological working memory and speech production in pre-school children.* Journal of Speech and Hearing Research, **38**, 403–414.

Adams, A.-M. & Gathercole, S. E. (2000). Limitations in working memory: implications for language development. *International Journal of Language and Communication Disorders*, **35**, 95–116.

Adler, M. A. & Fisher, C. W. (2001). Early reading programs in high-poverty schools: A case study of beating the odds. *Reading Teacher*, **54**, 616–619.

Anghileri, J. (2000). *Teaching number sense.* London: Continuum Books.

Baddeley, A. D. & Hitch, G. J. (1974). Working memory. In G. H. Bower (Ed.), *The psychology of learning and motivation: advances in research and theory, Vol. 8.* New York: Academic Press.

Basic Skills Agency (1997). *International numeracy survey. A comparison of the basic numeracy skills in adults 16–60 in seven countries.* London: Basic Skills Agency.

Bishop, D. V. M. (1997). *Uncommon understanding.* Hove: Psychology Press.

Bishop, D. V. M. & Adams, C. (1990). A prospective study of the relationship between specific language impairment and reading retardation. *Journal of Child Psychology & Psychiatry & Allied Disciplines*, **31**, 1027–1050.

Bowey, J. A., Cain, M. T. & Ryan, S. M. (1992). A reading-level design study of phonological skills underlying fourth grade children's word reading difficulties. *Child Development*, **63**, 999–1011.

Bruck, M. (1992). Persistence of dyslexics' phonological awareness. *Developmental Psychology*, **28**, 874–886.

Bryan, K. (2004). Preliminary study of the prevalence of speech and language difficulties in young offenders. *International Journal of Language & Communication Disorders*, **39**, 391–400.

Bryant, L. & Bradley, P. E. (1983). Categorising sounds and learning to read – a causal connection. *Nature*, **301**, 419–421.

Carroll, J. M., Snowling, M. J., Hulme, C. & Stevenson, J. (2003). The development of phonological awareness in pre-school children. *Developmental Psychology*, **39**(5), 913–923.

Catts, H. W. (1993). The relationship between speech-language impairments and reading disabilities. *Journal of Speech & Hearing Research*, **36**, 948–958.

Critchley, M. (1970). *The Dyslexic Child*. London: Heinemann.

Davis-Kean, P. E. (2005). The influence of parental education and family income on child achievement: the indirect role of parental expectations and the home environment. *Journal of Family Psychology*, **19**(2), 294–304.

Denne, M., Langdown, N., Pring, T. & Roy, P. (2005). Treating children with expressive phonological disorders: does phonological awareness therapy work in the clinic? *International Journal of Language & Communication Disorders*, **40**, 493–504.

Department of Health (2004). National Service Framework for children, young people and maternity services. Retrieved January, 2006, from www.dh.gov.uk/PolicyAndGuidance

DfES (1998). *The National Literacy Strategy*. Nottingham: DfES Publications Centre.

DfES (1999). *The National Numeracy Strategy*. London: Nottingham: DfES Publications Centre.

Dickinson, D. K. & Snow, C. E. (1987). Interrelationships among pre-reading and oral language skills in kindergartners from two social classes. *Early Childhood Research Quarterly*, **2**, 1–25.

Donlan, C. (1998). Number without language? Studies of children with specific language impairments. In C. Donlan (Ed.), *The development of mathematical skills*. Hove: Psychology Press.

Donlan, C., Bishop, D. V. M. & Hitch, J. (1998). Magnitude comparisons by children with specific language impairments: evidence of unimpaired symbolic processing. *International Journal of Language & Communication Disorders*, **33**, 149–160.

Elbro, C. & Petersen, D. K. (2004). Long term effects of phoneme awareness and letter sound training: an intervention study with children at risk for dyslexia. *Journal of Educational Psychology*, **96**(4), 660–670.

Fazio, B. (1994). Counting abilities of children with specific language impairment.: A comparison of oral and gestural tasks. *Journal of Speech & Hearing Research*, **37**, 358–368.

Fazio, B. (1996). Mathematical abilities of children with specific language impairment: a two year follow-up. *Journal of Speech & Hearing Research*, **39**, 839–849.

Flouri, E. & Buchanan, A. (2004). Early father's and mother's involvement and child's educational outcomes. *British Journal of Educational Psychology*, **74**, 141–153.

Gathercole, S. E. & Baddeley, A. J. (1993) Phonological working memory: a critical building block for reading development and vocabulary acquisition? *European Journal of Psychology of Education*, **8**, 259–272.

Gelman, R. & Gallistel, C. R. (1978). *The child's understanding of number*. Cambridge, MA: Harvard University Press.

Gillon, G. (2000). The efficacy of phonological awareness intervention for children with spoken language impairments. *Language Speech & Hearing Services in Schools*, **31**, 126–141.

Girolametto, L., Weitzman, E., Wiigs, M. & Pearce, P. S. (1999). The relationship between maternal language measures and language development in toddlers with expressive vocabulary delays. *American Journal of Speech-Language Pathology*, **8**, 364–374.

Goswami, U. (2002a). In the beginning was the rhyme? *Journal of Experimental Child Psychology*, **82**, 47–57.

Goswami, U. (2002b). Phonology, learning to read and dyslexia: a cross-linguistic analysis. In V. Csepe (Ed.), *Dyslexia: different brain, different behaviour* (pp. 1–40). Amsterdam: Kluwer Academic.

Goswami, U. (2002c). Phonology, reading development and dyslexia: a cross-linguistic perspective. *Annals of Dyslexia*, **52**, 1–23.

Goswami, U. & Bryant, P. E. (1990). *Phonological skills and learning to read*. Hove: Psychology Press.

Grauberg, E. (1998). *Elementary mathematics and language difficulties*. London: Whurr.

Hatcher, P. J., Hulme, C. & Snowling, M. J. (2004). Explicit phoneme training combined with phonic reading instruction helps young children at risk of reading failure. *Journal of Child Psychology & Psychiatry*, **45**(2), 338–358.

Head Start Bureau (2005). Retrieved January, 2006, from www2.acf.dhhs.gov/programs/hsb/

Hesketh, A. (2004). Early literacy achievement of children with a history of speech problems. *International Journal of Language and Communication Disorders*, **39**, 453–468.

Hesketh, A., Adams, C., Nightingale, C. & Hall, R. (2000). Phonological awareness therapy and articulatory training approaches for children with phonological disorders: a comparative outcome study. *International Journal of Language and Communication Disorders*, **35**, 337–354.

Hester, E. & Hodson, B. W. (2004). Role of phonological representation in decoding skills of young readers. *Child Language Teaching & Therapy*, **20**(2), 115–133.

Hulme, C., Hatcher, P. J., Nation, K., Brown, A., Adams, J. & Stuart, G. (2002). Phoneme awareness is a better predictor of early reading skill than onset-rime awareness. *Journal of Experimental Child Psychology*, **82**, 2–28.

I-CAN (2003). *Learning together, working together*. London: I-CAN.

Leitao, S. & Fletcher, J. (2004). Literacy outcomes for students with speech impairment: long-term follow-up. *International Journal of Language & Communication Disorders*, **39**, 245–256.

Leitao, S., Hogben, J. & Fletcher, J. (1997). Phonological processing skills in speech and language impaired children. *European Journal of Disorders of Communication*, **32**, 91–111.

Lonigan, C. J., Burgess, S. R., Anthony, J. L. & Barker, T. A. (1998). Development of phonological sensitivity in 2- to 5-year-old children. *Journal of Educational Psychology*, **90**(2), 294–311.

Magnusson, E. & Naucler, K. (1990). Reading and spelling in language-disordered children – linguistic and metalinguistic prerequisites: report on a longitudinal study. *Clinical Linguistics & Phonetics*, **4**(1), 49–61.

Major, E. & Bernhardt, B. (1998). Metaphonological skills of children with phonological disorders before and after phonological and metaphonological intervention. *International Journal of Language & Communication Disorders*, **33**, 413–444.

Manolsen, A. (1992). *It takes two to talk*. Toronto: The Hanen Centre.

McDade, A. & McCartan, P. (1998). 'Partnership with parents': a pilot project. *International Journal of Language and Communication Disorders*, **33** (Supplement).

Miles, T. R. & Miles, E. (1999). *Dyslexia: a hundred years on* (2nd edn). Buckingham: Open University Press.

Monaghan, P., Chater, N. & Hulme, C. (2005). *Levels of representation in language development*. York: University of York.

Moser, C. (1999). Improving literacy and numeracy. In 'The uses of literacy', *Economist*, 17 June, 355(8175).

Munn, P. (1998). Symbolic function in pre-schoolers. In C. Donlan (Ed.), *The development of mathematical skills*. Hove: Psychology Press.

Muter, V. (1994). Influence of phonological awareness and letter knowledge on beginning reading and spelling development. In C. Hulme & M. Snowling (Eds.), *Reading development & dyslexia*. London: Whurr.

Nathan, E., Stackhouse, J., Goulandris, N. & Snowling, M. J. (2004a). The development of early literacy skills among children with speech difficulties: A test of the critical age hypothesis. *Journal of Speech, Language &Hearing Research*, **47**, 377–391.

Nathan, E., Stackhouse, J., Goulandris, N. & Snowling, M. J. (2004b). Educational consequences of developmental speech disorder: Key Stage 1 National Curriculum assessment results in English and mathematics. *British Journal of Educational Psychology*, **74**, 173–186.

Nation, K. & Snowling, M. J. (1998). Semantic processing and the development of word recognition skills: Evidence from children with reading comprehension difficulties. *Journal of Memory and Language*, **39**, 85–101.

Porpodas, C. D. (1999). Patterns of phonological and memory processing in beginning readers and spellers of Greek. *Journal of Learning Disabilities*, **32**, 406–416.

Purcell-Gates, V., L'Allier, S. & Smith, D. (1995). Literacy at the Harts' and the Larsons': Diversity among poor, inner city families. *The Reading Teacher*, **48**(7), 572–578.

Rack, J. P., Snowling, M. J. & Olsen, R. (1990). The nonword reading deficit in developmental dyslexia: A review. *Reading Research Quarterly*, **27**, 29–53.

Raz, I. S. & Bryant, P. (1990). Social background, phonological awareness and children's reading. *British Journal of Developmental Psychology*, **8**, 209–225.

Roth, F. P., Speece, D. L. & Cooper, D. H. (2002). A longitudinal analysis of the connection between oral language and early reading. *Journal of Educational Research*, **95**, 259–272.

Schneider, W., Roth, E. & Ennemoser, M. (2000). Training phonological skills and letter knowledge in children at risk for dyslexia: a comparison of three kindergarten programs. *Journal of Educational Psychology*, **92**, 284–295.

Siegel, L. S. (1999). Learning disabilities: the roads we have travelled and the path to the future. In R. L. Sternberg & L. Spear-Swerling (Eds.), *Perspectives on learning disabilities. Biological, cognitive, contextual*. Boulder, CO: West View Press.

Siraj-Blatchford, I., Sylva, K., Muttock S., Gillon, R. & Bell, D. (2002). *Effective pedagogy in the early years*. Research report RR356. London: DfES.

Snow, C. E., Burns, M. S. & Griffiths, P. (1998). *Preventing reading difficulties in young children*. Washington: National Academy Press.

Snowling, M. J. (1980). The development of grapheme-phoneme correspondence in normal and dyslexic readers. *Journal of Experimental Child Psychology*, **29**, 294–305.

Snowling, M. J. (2004). Language skills and learning to read. *The Psychologist*, **17**(8), 438–441.

Snowling, M. J., Gallagher, A. & Frith, U. (2003). Family risk of dyslexia is continous: individual differences in the precursors of reading skill. *Child Development*, **74**(2), 358–373.

Sophian, C. (1998). A developmental perspective on children's counting. In C. Donlan (Ed.), *The development of mathematical skills*. Hove: Psychology Press.

Sprenger-Charolles, L., Cole, P., Lacert, P. & Semiclaes, W. (2000). On subtypes of developmental dyslexia: evidence from processing time and accuracy scores. *Canadian Journal of Experimental Psychology*, **54**, 87–103.

Stone, C. A. & Connell, P. J. (1993). Induction of a visual symbolic rule in children with specific language impairment. *Journal of Speech, Hearing and Research*, **36**, 599–608.

Storch, S. A. & Whitehurst, G. J. (2002). Oral and code-related precursors to reading: evidence from a longitudinal structural model. *Developmental Psychology*, **38**(6), 934–947.

Stothard, S. E. (1994). The nature and treatment of reading comprehension in children. In C. Hulme & M. Snowling (Eds.), *Reading development and dyslexia*. London: Whurr.

Stothard, S. E., Snowling, M. J., Bishop, D. V. M., Chipchase, B. B. & Kaplan, C. A. (1998). Language-impaired preschoolers: A follow-up into adolescence. *Journal of Speech, Language & Hearing Research*, **41**(2), 407–418.

Stuart, M. (1999). Getting ready for reading: Early phoneme awareness and phonics teaching improves reading and spelling in inner-city language learners. *British Journal of Educational Psychology*, **69**, 587–605.

Stuart, M. (2004). Getting ready for reading: A follow-up study of inner-city language learners at the end of Key Stage 1. *British Journal of Educational Psychology*, **74**, 15–36.

Sure Start (2005). Retrieved January, 2006, from www.surestart.gov.uk

Swan, D. & Goswami, U. (1997). Phonological awareness deficits in developmental dyslexia and the phonological representations hypothesis. *Journal of Experimental Child Psychology*, **66**, 18–41.

Tikly, L., Haynes, J. & Hill, J. (2004). *Understanding the educational needs of mixed heritage pupils*. Nottingham: DfES Publications.

Tolchinsky, L. (2003). *The cradle of culture and what children know about writing and numbers before being taught*. Mahwah, NJ: Lawrence Erlbaum Associates.

Torr, J. (2004). Talking about picture books: The influence of maternal education on four-year-old children's talk with mothers and pre-school teachers. *Journal of Early Childhood Literacy*, **4**(2), 181–207.

Van Ijzendoorn, M. H. & Bus, A. G. (1994). Meta-analytic confirmation of the nonword reading deficit in developmental dyslexia. *Reading Research Quarterly*, **29**, 266–275.

Wallach, L., Wallach, M. A., Dozier, M. G. & Kaplan, N. E. (1977). Poor children learning to read do not have trouble with auditory discrimination but do have trouble with phoneme recognition. *Journal of Educational Psychology*, **69**, 36–39.

Weigel, D. J., Martin, S. S. & Bennett, K. K. (2005). Ecological influences of the home and the child-care center on pre-school age children's literacy development. *Reading Research Quarterly*, **40**(2), 204–253.

Whitehurst, G. J. (1997). Language processes in context: language learning in children reared in poverty. In L. B. Adamson & M. A. Roinski (Eds.), *Communication and language acquisition – discoveries from atypical development*. London: Paul Brookes.

Whitehurst, G. J. & Fischel, J. E. (2000). A developmental model of reading and language impairments arising in conditions of economic poverty. In D. V. M Bishop & L. Leonard (Eds.), *Speech and language impairments in children: causes, characteristics, intervention and outcome*. Hove: Psychology Press.

Wynn, K. (1998). Numerical competence in infants. In C. Donlan (Ed.), *The development of mathematical skills*. Hove: Psychology Press.

Zevenbergen, R. (2001). Literacy demands of numeracy. *Primary Educator*, **7**, 16–20.

Ziegler, J. C. & Goswami, U. (2005). Reading acquisition, developmental dyslexia and skilled reading across languages: a psycholinguistic grain size theory. *Psychological Bulletin*, **131**, 3–29.

Ziegler, J. C., Perry, C., Ma-Wyatt, A., Ladner, D. & Schulte-Korne, G. (2003). Developmental dyslexia in different languages: language-specific or universal? *Journal of Experimental Child Psychology*, **86**, 169–193.

4 Childhood Speech and Language Difficulties and Later Life Chances

JUDY CLEGG

Human Communication Sciences, University of Sheffield

INTRODUCTION

This chapter describes long-term outcomes for children with speech and language difficulties and how speech and language difficulties (SLD) impact on later childhood and adult life chances. In the first section, the purpose and range of longitudinal studies in this area are described. This is followed by a synthesis of the research findings regarding outcomes for children with SLD across the domains of speech, language, cognition, educational attainment and psychosocial functioning. The second section deals with outcomes for children with delayed language from areas of social disadvantage and the extent to which delayed language impacts on later childhood and adult outcomes and ultimately life chances.

There are several reasons as to why there is an increasing interest in identifying outcomes for children with SLD. First, it used to be thought that SLD in children resolved over time leaving no lasting effects. However, preliminary research shows that for some children SLD can persist over time and have significant implications for other aspects of development. However, it is still not clear which children are at risk of persisting difficulties, and which are more resilient. The presentation of the initial speech and language difficulty often changes as children grow older; this has implications for understanding the aetiology of speech and language difficulties. Second, more and more children are being diagnosed with SLD. Research into the long-term outcomes for such children is essential for providing them, their parents, and often other professionals, with information about prognoses. Finally, increasing government emphasis on educational attainment has prompted health, educational and social services to consider how best to support pupils with SLD and meet their learning and other needs most effectively.

DEFINITIONS OF SPEECH AND LANGUAGE DIFFICULTIES

The term 'speech and language difficulty' refers to a range of problems in speech and/or language development. The physical articulation of speech sounds can be

Language and Social Disadvantage: Theory into Practice Edited by J. Clegg and J. Ginsborg

affected by physiological and structural abnormalities, such as cleft lip/palate, and neurological abnormalities leading to weakness of the speech musculature, known as dysarthria. However, the aetiology of other types of speech difficulty, such as phonological difficulties and verbal dyspraxia, is less clear. Language difficulties can involve problems in the development of both comprehension and production. Children's language is said to be 'delayed' when their language abilities are behind those expected for their chronological age, and 'impaired' when a language delay does not resolve and the child continues to experience difficulties. Speech and language difficulties often occur in children with physical disabilities, including hearing and neurological impairments, and/or developmental disorders such as Down syndrome and global learning delay. In these examples, SLD are usually attributed to and explained by an aetiological cause.

However, SLD do sometimes occur in the absence of an obvious identifiable cause. These difficulties – which used to be known as developmental receptive/expressive language disorder, childhood aphasia and developmental language disorder – are now usually referred to as Specific Language Impairment (SLI), because they are independent of cognitive ability; they are considered to affect 3–7% of all children (Fundudis, Kolvin & Garside, 1979; Richman, Stevenson & Graham, 1982; Tomblin, Records, Buckwalter et al., 1997). SLI is of particular interest to researchers, as well as clinicians, since its origins have yet to be determined. It can only be identified using standardised language and cognitive assessments, but there is some disagreement as to the criteria that should be used to establish a meaningful discrepancy between cognitive and language abilities. A liberal criterion stipulates a non-verbal IQ of 70 or above with performance on one standardised language measure one standard deviation below the mean (Johnson, Beitchman, Young et al., 1999). There is some evidence to suggest that this is consistent with speech and language therapists' judgement and referral practice (Records & Tomblin, 1994). A stringent criterion stipulates a non-verbal IQ of 85 or above with performance on at least two standardized language measures at least 1.5 SD below the mean (Leonard, 1997). Meanwhile, intermediate criteria are also used: for example, non-verbal IQ of 80 or above with language performance at least 1 SD below the mean on two out of four language measures (Norbury, Bishop & Briscoe, 2002). Advocates of liberal criteria claim that more stringent criteria may fail to identify children who are at risk of poor long-term outcomes (Johnson et al., 1999). However, Leonard (1997) argues that the liberal criterion identifies children who simply perform at the lower end of the normal distribution of language ability (according to Johnson et al.'s (1999) criterion, 16% of the general population would be classified with SLI) rather than presenting with significant language learning difficulties. There are two main reasons why it is hard to generalise from longitudinal studies of children with SLI. First, a variety of psychometric criteria are used. Second, children with SLI often have speech, as well as language, difficulties. Most research to date has focused on the latter. It is worth bearing in mind, therefore, that children with SLI are not a homogenous group; they present with a range of speech and language abilities.

LONGITUDINAL STUDIES OF CHILDREN WITH SLD

Longitudinal studies of children with speech and language difficulties date back to the late 1960s (Griffiths, 1969) and 1970s (Beagley & Wrenn, 1970; Garvey & Gordon, 1973; Hall & Tomblin, 1978). These were small studies ranging in design and age at which outcomes were measured, and often involved very heterogeneous groups of children with respect to the aetiology and severity of SLD. Furthermore, the majority were retrospective where researchers first saw participants at follow-up. Thus, information on their early language abilities and diagnosis had to be collated from clinical and, where available, educational records as often no detailed childhood cognitive and language assessments had been carried out. The 1990s saw an increase in prospective studies (Beitchman, Brownlie, Inglis et al., 1996a; Beitchman, Wilson, Brownlie, Walters & Larcee, 1996b; Clegg, Hollis, Mawhood & Rutter, 2005; Conti-Ramsden, Botting, Simkin & Knox, 2001b; Stothard, Snowling, Bishop, Chipchase & Kaplan, 1998) where participants are recruited in childhood and followed up subsequently. However, there is variation as to when final outcome assessments are made, ranging from middle childhood, adolescence, early adult to later adult life. Prospective studies assessing participants at several time points provide the most detailed developmental trajectories of children with speech and language difficulties. Some prospective studies also distinguish between children who meet the criteria for SLI and children whose language impairment is associated with low IQ and/or physical disabilities. Beitchman et al. (1996a, 1996b, 1996c) initiated a longitudinal study of a large Canadian community sample of 5-year-olds with a range of speech and language difficulties, identified using standardised measures. The outcomes for these children, across a range of domains, were identified when the children were 12 years (Beitchman et al., 1996a, 1996b), 14 years (Johnson et al., 1999) and 19 years old (Brownlie, Beitchman, Escobar et al., 2004; Young, Beitchman, Johnson et al., 2002). Given the size of the sample and the range of difficulties experienced by the children, the researchers were able to subgroup them into clusters based on their performance on a range of cognitive, speech and language measures. Outcomes for the children in each cluster could then be compared in order to identify the long-term effects of the difficulties experienced in childhood. Conti-Ramsden, Botting and Faragher (2001a) recruited children at 7 years of age from mainstream language units across the UK and identified outcomes at 11 years for three groups: children with persistent SLI, language impairment associated with low IQ and resolved SLI. A smaller UK cohort was recruited by Bishop and Edmundson and followed up at approximately 4–5 years (Bishop & Edmundson, 1987a, 1987b) and 15 years (Stothard et al., 1998). Again, outcomes for three groups were compared: adolescents with persistent SLI, resolved SLI and general delay. One of the longest follow-up studies compared two groups of boys, one with autism and the other with severe SLI, in childhood (when they were aged about 8 years old) (Bartak, Rutter & Cox, 1975), in middle childhood (Cantwell, Baker, Rutter & Mawhood, 1989) and in their early 20s (Mawhood, Howlin & Rutter, 2000; Howlin, Mawhood & Rutter, 2000). Over time, the boys with SLI developed more social and behavioural difficulties than originally anticipated and were the focus of the further follow-up in their mid-30s (Clegg et al., 2005). As we have seen, longitudinal studies can be problematic. For example, they should include comparison groups, in order to show the effects of SLD independent of those associated, for example, with low IQ and socio-economic status (SES) on later outcomes. However, with the exception of the Beitchman studies, most prospective longitudinal studies have neglected to do so. Conti-Ramsden and Botting (2004) included some normative data to assess the incidence of victimisation and bullying of children with SLI; Clegg et al. (2005) included comparison groups when they assessed outcomes in their participants' mid-30s to control for the effects of childhood intelligence and SES. Second, sample size varies hugely, from case studies to small groups (Aram, Ekelman & Nation, 1984; Paul & Cohen, 1984) and larger cohorts (Beitchman et al., 1996a, 1996b, 1996c; Conti-Ramsden et al., 2001b; Stern, Connell, Lee & Greenwood, 1995; Stothard et al., 1998). Third, the majority of studies to date have focused on outcomes in childhood and adolescence and only a few studies have reported adult outcomes (Clegg et al., 2005; Hall & Tomblin, 1978; Tomblin, Freese & Records, 1992). This will change as some of the more recent prospective studies continue to report later outcomes (Conti-Ramsden et al., 2001b; Stothard et al., 1998; Young et al., 2002).

We have already pointed out that the criteria for defining SLD are used inconsistently, and this is particularly the case in some of the older retrospective studies. Intelligence was not always assessed, and, even when it was, children with low IQs, extending into the learning disability range, were included (Aram & Nation, 1980; Aram et al., 1984; Paul & Cohen, 1984). Differing aetiologies also make it hard to interpret the findings of these earlier studies from which, for example children with physical impairments and autistic-type behaviours were not excluded (King, Jones & Lasky, 1982; Paul & Cohen, 1984). Some studies recruited participants with widely varying abilities. For example, Aram et al. (1984) and King et al. (1982) recruited all the children seen in particular clinics during a given period irrespective of their cognitive, motor or hearing impairments, thereby including children with concomitant disorders that may well have impacted significantly on outcomes. In many cases, detailed information about participants was lacking, and researchers were not able to investigate different patterns of development and outcomes attributable to different types of SLD. Despite these caveats, it is clear that many children who present with initial SLD continue to show persisting difficulties in later life. These include children who do and do not meet traditional psychometric criteria for SLI (Aram & Nation, 1980; King et al., 1982; Paul & Cohen, 1984). Longitudinal studies have focused on four broad domains in which outcome assessments are made: (1) speech, language and communication; (2) cognition, specifically verbal and non-verbal intelligence; (3) educational attainment; and (4) psychosocial functioning including aspects such as behaviour, in addition to broad measures of social functioning. Collectively, studies have attempted to track the changes in these areas over time.

SPEECH OUTCOMES

Interestingly, the developmental trajectories of children with pure speech difficulties such as dysfluency, verbal dyspraxia and cleft lip and palate have not been a specific focus of research and therefore much less is known about their trajectories and outcomes than for children with SLI. Although individuals with SLI often have additional speech difficulties, research to date has focused almost exclusively on the language involvement, and speech difficulties are often not described in detail. This may also be due to co-morbidity issues where, for example, cleft lip and palate are often part of a syndrome where general learning delay is a feature. However, there is an established literature concerning the relationship between the development of speech and literacy. Children with speech difficulties often have problems learning to read and write (Stackhouse, 2001) with subsequent implications for overall educational attainment. It seems to be the severity of the initial speech difficulty that predicts literacy outcome (Hesketh, 2004). Nathan, Stackhouse, Goulandris and Snowling (2004) tracked 4–5-year-old children with speech difficulties and typically developing controls until the age of 7 years, focusing on their attainment in Key Stage 1 Standard Assessment Tests (SATs). Children with persisting speech difficulties gained significantly lower SATs than controls on mathematics and English, with spelling a particular area of difficulty. Nash, Stengelhofen, Toombs, Brown and Kellow (2001) have found that adolescents with persisting speech difficulties as a result of cleft lip and palate experience similar psychosocial difficulties, such as bullying and poor academic attainment, to children with SLI. However, when compared to children with SLI and children with language impairment as a result of general delay, children with pure speech difficulties tend to have better outcomes (Beitchman et al., 1996a, 1996b, 1996c; Hall & Tomblin, 1978). Beitchman et al. (1996a, 1996b, 1996c) argue that children with pure speech difficulties have higher IQs and tend to be from areas of higher SES than children with more pervasive language difficulties. These demographic characteristics seem to act as protective factors, thus making these children more resilient over time.

LANGUAGE OUTCOMES

Over the lifespan, children with an initial profile of SLI continue to show impaired levels of receptive and expressive language development in later childhood (Aram & Nation, 1980; Stern et al., 1995), adolescence (Conti-Ramsden et al., 2001b) and even adult life (Clegg et al., 2005; Tomblin, Freese & Records, 1992). Later childhood and early adolescence appear to be a period where language abilities continue to develop albeit at a slower rate than typically developing controls (Beitchman et al., 1996b; Clegg et al., 2005; Conti-Ramsden et al., 2001a). However, fluctuations are evident in the developmental trajectory. In a large UK longitudinal study, Conti-Ramsden et al. (2001a) recruited 242 seven-year-olds with a range of speech and language difficulties (excluding hearing loss, major physical disability, autism and moderate learning disability) from mainstream language units. At 11 years of age, 200 children from the original sample were followed up, and several changes were observed. Non-verbal IQ had deteriorated for over a quarter of the sample. Children meeting traditional psychometric criteria for SLI fell from 84% to 40% (partly due to the fall in non-verbal IQ), and a complete resolution of SLI was identified in 16 of the children. When the boys with severe SLI recruited by Bartak et al. (1975) were followed up, verbal and non-verbal IQ remained within the normal range, albeit with significantly higher non-verbal than verbal IQ and some fluctuations throughout childhood and adult life. The severe receptive and expressive language impairment identified in childhood also persisted through adolescence and into adult life. Improvement in language ability occurred between childhood and early adolescence but then reached a plateau approximately equivalent to that expected in typically developing 9-year-olds. On the basis of the limited evidence available to us from longitudinal studies of children with SLI, language development would appear to reach a plateau well below the expected level around late adolescence with little subsequent improvement after this time (Beitchman et al, 1996b; Clegg et al., 2005; Johnson et al., 1999).

More recent prospective studies, as we have seen, subtyped large cohorts of children according to their initial SLD. As a result, different longitudinal trajectories and outcomes have been identified. Although, once again, the evidence is limited, language development in children with SLI over time does not seem to differ markedly from that in children with general cognitive delay (Beitchman et al., 1996a, 1996b, 1996c; Stothard et al., 1998). However, children with lower IQs and poor language comprehension make the least progress over time when compared with children with pure speech disorders and higher IQs (Beitchman et al., 1996a, 1996b, 1996c). The trajectories of children with resolved SLI are of particular interest. A substantial proportion of children who present with SLI in the preschool years develop age-appropriate language abilities by the time they are 5 years old (Bishop & Edmundson, 1987a, 1987b; Stothard et al., 1998) and their SLI is therefore considered to be resolved (Conti-Ramsden et al., 2001a; Stothard et al., 1998). However, these children can still have subtle difficulties with certain aspects of language, such as phonological processing, verbal working memory and reading (Conti-Ramsden et al., 2001a, 2001b; Stothard et al., 1998) later in life.

COGNITIVE OUTCOMES

There is much debate as to the relationship between language and cognition (e.g. Piaget, 1952; Vygotsky, 1962). SLI is of particular interest to researchers because it is considered to involve difficulties with language, but not cognition. Longitudinal studies have therefore aimed to recruit children who meet the criteria for SLI in order to measure the impact of language impairment independently of the effects of low intelligence. To reiterate: the criteria for SLI are represented by a discrepancy in performance on non-verbal IQ tests, since verbal IQ tests would be affected by language difficulties, and standardized language measures. However it is also important to measure intelligence over time, since this can offer insights into how it develops alongside selectively impaired language (as described by Botting in

Chapter 2, this volume). This was neglected, as we have seen, in some older studies (Aram & Nation, 1980; King et al., 1982). However, more recent research shows that children with low non-verbal IQ and language impairment have poorer outcomes in relation to language and educational attainment than children with language impairment but higher non-verbal IQ (Snowling, Adams, Bishop & Stothard, 2001). Generally, children with SLI have non-verbal IQ scores within the normal range although, unsurprisingly, their non-verbal IQ is usually higher than their verbal IQ. Both kinds of IQ score may fluctuate and indeed deteriorate over time, particularly in adolescence and later life (Botting, see Chapter 2, this volume; Clegg et al., 2005; Conti-Ramsden et al., 2001b; Tomblin et al., 1992). We have already noted that nearly half of the 5-year-old children with SLD in Conti-Ramsden et al.'s (2001b) study who initially met the criteria for SLI no longer did so at the age of 11, because their non-verbal IQ had fallen and there was no longer a discrepancy between their language and cognitive abilities. However, in the SLI cohort in Johnson et al.'s (1999) Canadian community sample, falls in non-verbal IQ were found not only for participants with SLI but also typically developing controls. This would seem to undermine the argument that IQ deteriorates over time as the result of SLI.

EDUCATIONAL ATTAINMENT

Research into SLD and educational attainment focuses on literacy and overall educational attainment as measured by examination performance. As mentioned previously, there is as strong an association between language and literacy development (Catts, Fey & Tomblin, 2002) as there is between speech and literacy development.

The development of literacy abilities in relation to language abilities in this population is unclear. However, preliminary evidence suggests that initial literacy abilities are poor and resolution is rarely reached, leaving individuals with low levels of literacy that have negative implications for education and academic achievement (Aram et al., 1984; Conti-Ramsden et al., 2001b; Stothard et al., 1998; Hall & Tomblin, 1978). Indeed, the participants initially recruited by Bishop and Edmundson (1987a) and studied at 15 years (Stothard et al., 1998) provide important information about educational achievement at 16/17 years. The GCSE grades of the young people in the four groups representing persisting SLI, resolved SLI, general delay and typically developing controls in Bishop and Edmundson's sample were obtained (Snowling et al., 2001). The resolved SLI group members were entered for more GCSEs and gained higher grades than those in the persisting SLI group and the general delay group. However, the resolved SLI group still underachieved compared with the typically developing controls. The persisting SLI and general delay groups performed at a similar level, averaging less than one GCSE pass at grade A-C, with the majority of their pass grades between D and G. More of the young people with resolved SLI went on to study A levels, whereas the majority of the persisting SLI group did not. Clegg et al. (2005) found that the persisting language impairment identified in SLI adults had a detrimental impact on academic outcome and subsequent employment opportunities. The SLI adults gained much lower academic qualifications compared with their siblings and a group matched on childhood IQ and socio-economic status. Of the 17 adults, only one adult had attained an academic qualification at age 16 years. The remainder had never passed an examination at this level or above.

PSYCHOSOCIAL OUTCOMES AND LIFE CHANCES

Interest in the social and behavioural development of children with speech and language difficulties stems from the work of Baker and Cantwell (1987a, 1987b) who studied the psychiatric outcomes for children with SLD in later childhood. A higher prevalence of psychiatric problems is found in children with speech and language difficulties when compared with controls. These earlier studies found that children with receptive language difficulties were more at risk of psychiatric problems than children with expressive difficulties. However, the heterogeneity of the children involved compromises the findings, thus making it difficult to identify the nature of the relationship between SLD and psychiatric problems. During the course of childhood, the risk of developing social and behavioural problems seems to increase (Bartak et al., 1975; Beitchman, Cohen, Konstantareas & Tannock, 1996d; Botting & Conti-Ramsden, 2000). Cantwell et al. (1989) compared the development of social and behavioural problems in boys with autism and boys with SLI. These were severe and persisting in boys with autism from the age of 8 years. In contrast, social and behavioural problems were not apparent in the boys with SLI when they were 8, but emerged in later childhood, worsening as they grew older (Howlin et al., 2000).

Both children and adults with persisting speech and language difficulties are more likely to experience emotional and behavioural problems than controls (Huaqing Qi & Kaiser, 2004). In addition, they are often bullied by peers and can even be targets for victimisation (Conti-Ramsden & Botting, 2004; Knox & Conti-Ramsden, 2003). As with other outcomes, children with lower IQs and receptive language impairments are at greater risk of developing social and behavioural difficulties in later childhood (Beitchman et al., 1996d; Botting & Conti-Ramsden, 2000). There is a possible association between SLD and the development of anti-social behaviour in early adult life. At the age of 19 years participants with SLD in the Canadian community sample did not show high levels of aggression but did have higher rates of arrests and convictions (Brownlie et al., 2004). The increase in social and behaviour problems may be the result of communication and interaction problems young people experience in conjunction with the increasing social and academic demands placed on them. However, it is hard to disentangle cause and effect when so many variables interact. SES, learning ability and type of educational placement no doubt also makes a contribution: for example, children with receptive language impairments and low IQs tend to be from areas of lower SES than children with higher IQs and expressive language difficulties (Beitchman et al., 1996a, 1996b, 1996c, 1996d). Therefore, SES and IQ are probably implicated in the development of social and behavioural difficulties as well as SLD.

The development of speech and language skills and the ability to communicate effectively are important prerequisites to psychosocial functioning in areas such as behaviour, employment, independent living, relationships and even quality of life. Records, Freese and Tomblin (1992) studied adults in their early 20s with histories of SLI and found similar levels of psychosocial adaptation to normal controls on a measure of quality of life. Although these young adults continued to show low scores on language measures, had left education earlier and had lower rates of pay than controls, they had the same generally positive attitude to life as the controls. However, they did express feelings of having less control, which was hypothesised to be related to lower language ability. In comparison, high levels of social maladaptation and poor psychosocial functioning were found in adults with SLI in comparison to normal controls (Clegg et al., 2005). In their mid-30s, only 10 of the men with SLI were in employment. Employment histories were unstable and the majority had experienced periods of unemployment lasting two years or more. Indeed, three men had never been in paid employment. Seven were living independently and the remainder lived either in the parental home or in supported accommodation nearby. Relationships were particularly difficult: more than half of the men had a limited range of friendships. As a cohort, they had experienced significantly fewer romantic relationships, with few in successful marriages or cohabiting relationships. Four men had developed serious mental health problems in adult life including schizophrenia, major clinical depression and personality disorder. The cause of their mental health problems is unclear but the high frequency of psychosocial difficulties experienced by the men with SLI, compared with controls, would suggest an association with SLI and consequent difficulties in social adaptation. However, this requires confirmation; there are few similar studies in this area, so it is not known how representative the findings of the Clegg et al. (2005) study are. Certainly, anecdotal accounts indicate that there is much variation and that not all children with SLI have such poor outcomes. Four pupils from a UK specialist school for children with SLD were followed up. Although as adults they had varying speech and language abilities, their psychosocial outcomes were similar. All the participants had been in employment since leaving full-time education, were either married or in a cohabiting relationship, living independently from their families and in satisfactory health. However, it can be hypothesised that these more positive outcomes were the result of their experiencing less severe speech and language difficulties and generally higher IQs in comparison with the adults with SLI in Clegg et al.'s study.

Although the findings outlined above need to be replicated, several explanations have been proposed for the association between SLI and social impairment. First, social impairment is a consequence of limited language and communication skills with implications for the development of relationships, the increased possibility of social rejection and the development of emotional and behavioural difficulties. Although this is a logical hypothesis, the nature of these associations is difficult to determine and further research is needed. Second, social impairment is an intrinsic part of SLI, where a higher risk of poor social functioning would be linked to the severity and persistence of the SLI. Studies of outcomes in adults identifying variations in social functioning would help to clarify this. Third, the observed deteriorations in the cognitive and language abilities of children and adolescents with SLI may be an important risk factor for psychosocial development. Finally, limitations in educational provision impact on the level of social functioning achieved. Historically, children with SLI received little support at secondary level and beyond (Clegg et al., 2005) and recent evidence suggests that there is still little SLT support available for secondary-school aged children with SLD (Lindsay, Soloff, Law et al., 2002). This lack of specialist support may hinder academic potential and therefore contribute to poor academic attainment. The consequences of this would be to limit further academic and occupational success, thus reducing opportunities for effective adult social functioning. Much more evidence is required to clarify the extent and nature of the association between SLI and adult social functioning and life chances.

Several issues arise when comparing the findings across studies. First, comparatively few longitudinal studies have been undertaken and therefore the conclusions drawn can only be limited. Sample sizes and outcome ages have differed markedly, as have the measures employed, ranging from standardised IQ and language assessments to parental and teacher ratings. Over time, the focus of longitudinal research has changed. Earlier studies have been discarded due to the heterogeneity of the samples with respect to intelligence and co-morbidity. In addition, the recent and increasing interest in SLI has led to the study of more specific abilities. Grammar development is thought to be specifically impaired in SLI (Rice & Wexler, 1996; van der Lely, 1996, 1998) as are aspects of information processing such as phonological working memory; more recent follow-up studies have concentrated on these aspects whereas the older studies did not. Variability is also a key factor to consider. Outcomes for adults in the cohort studied by Clegg et al. (2005) were much poorer than those found in three US longitudinal studies in which participants were followed up as adults (Hall & Tomblin, 1978; Records et al., 1992; Tomblin et al., 1992). Clegg et al.'s study may be unrepresentative; certainly, anecdotal accounts indicate that there is much variation and that not all children with SLI have such poor outcomes. While large-cohort studies also show variation, more detailed and perhaps smaller studies are needed to describe it and account for it.

LATER OUTCOMES: LOW SOCIO-ECONOMIC STATUS AND LANGUAGE DELAY

Low SES is implicated in speech and language development such that a large proportion of children from low SES backgrounds are reported to start school with speech and language abilities that are delayed in comparison with those expected for their chronological age (see Chapter 1, this volume, for a detailed review). Given that low SES is multifactorial, speech and language development may be one of the factors that influence general child development and subsequent outcomes in later childhood and adult life.

Why speech and language abilities often appear to be delayed in this population needs to be considered. The term 'delayed' is non-specific and does not adequately describe the range of speech and language difficulties experienced by children other than to say that the child's abilities are behind the level expected for the child's chronological age as measured by standardised assessments. This implies that delayed language would resolve with an adequate language-learning environment (see Chapter 1, p. 19, this volume). Some children described as having delayed language may have more specific language learning difficulties meeting criteria for SLI or even speech difficulties that are not directly linked to low SES but have a physiological basis. There may be reasons why these difficulties are not identified before children start school. For example, children from low-SES backgrounds tend to be 'hard to reach' and clinical services may not identify children due to missed appointments, parental expectations and attitudes.

It is known that SLI occurs in adequate language learning environments and therefore should not necessarily be attributed to low SES. Where SLI is not a factor, SLD associated with low SES is probably qualitatively different from SLI. As we have seen, the psychometric definition of SLI is problematic as studies have used different psychometric criteria to identify the presence and severity of SLI. Studies of low SES children seem to categorise children with delayed language with less stringent psychometric criteria than used to identify children with SLI. In a study of a large cohort of US children, for example, Whitehurst (1997) compared children from a Head Start programme with children from higher earning families, although both were considered as low SES. At 3, 4 and 5 years of age, a significant proportion of the children were one standard deviation below the mean on receptive and expressive language measures. Although impairments were identified in semantic measures, syntactic ability was within the normal range. Such a profile is not consistent with SLI, where traditionally syntactic ability is significantly impaired (Bishop, 1997). Thus speech and language ability in children with delayed language in areas of low SES may be qualitatively different to the SLI profile (although this requires confirmation). Alternatively, the theoretical definition and criteria of SLI may be an artificial construct to apply to the low SES population. In order to address these questions, much more needs to be known about the longitudinal speech and language profile of this population.

Social disadvantage has been linked to delayed language in the early years yet it is not known if the delayed language persists over time or resolves. If it persists, then on the basis of the longitudinal studies of children with SLD and SLI we can predict that this will have an impact on life chances independently of the initial effects of low SES in childhood, which have been shown to include poorer educational attainment, employment opportunities, general well-being and mental health, as well as an increased likelihood of involvement in antisocial behaviour. As we have seen, the findings of longitudinal studies of children with SLI suggest that there is a specific causal link between speech and language difficulty and negative outcomes in later childhood and adult life. However, these studies have yet to identify fully and therefore account for the impact of low SES on these outcomes. It will be interesting to see if follow-up studies of children from low-SES backgrounds with delayed language have outcomes similar to those found for children with SLI. Such studies will have to include rigorous research design in order to identify the specific effects of language delay where controlling for the effects of level of SES, IQ and possibly other social factors is imperative.

SUMMARY

In short, despite increasing interest in this area, research is as yet limited and the findings inconclusive: we still do not know enough about outcomes in later life for children with SLD. We do not know, in particular, the extent to which SLD are risk factors for negative outcomes and what the contribution of other factors might be. Nevertheless, we would argue that for some children, SLD is a risk factor for a wide range of problems later in childhood, adolescence and adulthood. If SLD are unresolved when children are 5 years old then it is likely to persist, and children with pervasive language impairments are more likely than children with speech impairments to experience educational and social difficulties later in life. Risk factors for poor outcomes are receptive language impairment, low IQ and low SES, whereas children who are more resilient to poor outcomes seem to have higher IQs, speech rather than language difficulties and to come from higher-SES backgrounds. Importantly, issues of social deprivation have not been fully addressed to date in longitudinal studies or included as explanations for the variation in adult outcomes.

REFERENCES

Aram, D. & Nation, J. (1980). Pre-school language disorders and subsequent language and academic difficulties. *Journal of Communication Disorders*, **13**, 159–198.

Aram, D. H., Ekelman, B. L. & Nation, J. E. (1984). Preschoolers with language disorders: 10 years later. *Journal of Speech and Hearing Research*, **27**, 232–244.

Baker, L. & Cantwell, D. P. (1987a). Factors associated with the development of psychiatric illness in children with early speech/language problems. *Journal of Autism & Developmental Disorders*, **17**, 499–510.

Baker, L. & Cantwell, D. P. (1987b). A prospective follow up of children with speech/language disorders. *Journal of the American Academy of Child & Adolescent Psychiatry*, **26**, 546–553.

Bartak, L., Rutter, M. & Cox, A. (1975). A comparative study of infantile autism and specific developmental receptive language disorders. I. The children. *British Journal of Psychiatry*, **126**, 127–145.

Beagley, H. A. & Wrenn, M. (1970). Clinical follow-up of 192 normally hearing children with delayed speech. *Journal of Laryngology and Otology*, **84**, 1001–1011.

Beitchman, J. H., Brownlie, E. B., Inglis, A., Wild, J., Ferguson, B., Schachter, D., Lancee, W., Wilson, B. & Mathews, R. (1996a). Seven-year follow up of speech/language impaired and control children: psychiatric outcome. *Journal of Child Psychology & Psychiatry*, **37**, 961–970.

Beitchman, J. H., Wilson, B., Brownlie, E. B., Walters, H. & Lancee, W. (1996b). Long-term consistency in speech/language profiles: I. Developmental and academic outcomes. *Journal of the American Academy of Child & Adolescent Psychiatry*, **35**(6), 804–814.

Beitchman, J. H., Wilson, B., Brownlie, E. B., Walters, H., Inglis, A. & Lancee, W. (1996c). Long term consistency in speech/language profiles: II. Behavioural, emotional and social outcomes. *Journal of the American Academy of Child & Adolescent Psychiatry*, **35**(6), 815–824.

Beitchman, J., Cohen, N. J., Konstantareas, M. M. & Tannock, R. (Eds) (1996d). *Language, learning and behavior disorders: Developmental, biological and clinical perspectives.* New York: Cambridge University Press.

Bishop, D. V. M. (1997). *Uncommon Understanding: Development and disorders of language comprehension in children.* Hove: Psychology Press.

Bishop, D. V. M. & Edmundson, A. (1987a). Language impaired four-year-olds: Distinguishing transient from persistent impairment. *Journal of Speech and Hearing Disorders*, **52**, 156–173.

Bishop, D. V. M. & Edmundson, A. (1987b). Specific language impairment as a maturational lag: Evidence from longitudinal data on language and motor development. *Developmental Medicine and Child Neurology*, **29**, 442–459.

Botting, N. & Conti-Ramsden, G. (2000). Social and behavioural difficulties in children with language impairment. *Child Language Teaching and Therapy*, **16**, 10–21.

Brownlie, E. B., Beitchman, J. H., Escobar, M., Young, A., Atkinson, L., Johnson, C., Wilson, B. & Douglas, L. (2004). Early language impairment and young adult delinquent and aggressive behaviour. *Journal of Abnormal Child Psychology*, **32**(4), 453–467.

Cantwell, D., Baker, L., Rutter, M. & Mawhood, L. (1989). Infantile autism and developmental receptive dysphasia: a comparative follow-up into middle childhood. *Journal of Autism and Developmental Disorders*, **19**, 19–32.

Catts, H. W., Fey, M. E. & Tomblin, J. B. (2002). A longitudinal investigation of reading outcomes in children with language impairments. *Journal of Speech, Language & Hearing Research*, **45**(6), 1142–1157.

Clegg, J., Hollis, C., Mawhood, L. & Rutter, M. (2005). Developmental language disorders – a follow-up in later adult life. Cognitive, language and psychosocial outcomes, *Journal of Child Psychology & Psychiatry*, **46**(2), 128–149.

Conti-Ramsden, G. & Botting, N. (2004). Social difficulties and victimization in children with SLI at 11 years of age. *Journal of Speech, Language and Hearing Research*, **47**(1), 145–161.

Conti-Ramsden, G., Botting, N. & Faragher, B. (2001a). Psycholinguistic markers for specific language impairment (SLI). *Journal of Child Psychology and Psychiatry*, **42**, 741–748.

Conti-Ramsden, G., Botting, N., Simkin, Z. & Knox, E. (2001b). Follow-up of children attending infant language units: outcomes at 11 years of age. *International Journal of Language & Communication Disorders*, **36**, 207–220.

Fundudis, T., Kolvin, I. & Garside, R. (Eds). (1979). *Speech retarded and deaf children: their psychological development.* London: Academic Press.

Garvey, M. & Gordon, N. (1973). A follow-up study of children with disorders of speech development. *British Journal of Disorders of Communication*, **4**, 46–56.

Griffiths, C. P. S. (1969). A follow-up study of children with articulation and language disorders. *Journal of Speech and Hearing Disorders*, **43**, 227–241.

Hall, P. & Tomblin, J. (1978). A follow-up study of children with articulation and language disorders. *Journal of Speech and Hearing Disorders*, **43**, 227–241.

Hesketh, A. (2004). Early literacy achievement of children with a history of speech problems. *International Journal of Language & Communication Disorders*, **39**(4), 453–468.

Howlin, P., Mawhood, L. & Rutter, M. (2000). Autism and developmental receptive language disorder – a follow up comparison in early adult life, II: social, behavioural, and psychiatric outcomes. *Journal of Child Psychology and Psychiatry*, **41**, 561–578.

Huaqing Qi, C. & Kaiser, A. P. (2004). Problem behaviour of low income children with language delays: an observation study. *Journal of Speech, Language & Hearing Research*, **47**(3), 595–609.

Johnson, C. J., Beitchman, J. H., Young, A., Escobar, M., Atkinson, L., Wilson, B., Brownlie, E. B., Douglas, L., Taback, N., Lam, I. & Wang, M. (1999). Fourteen-year follow up of children with and without speech/language impairments: Speech/language stability and outcomes. *Journal of Speech, Language and Hearing Research*, **42**, 744–760.

King, R. R., Jones, C. & Lasky, E. (1982). In retrospect: a fifteen-year follow-up report of speech-language-disordered children. *Language, Speech and Hearing Services in Schools*, **13**, 24–32.

Knox, E. & Conti-Ramsden, G. (2003). Bullying risks of 11-year-old children with specific language impairment (SLI): does school placement matter? *International Journal of Language & Communication Disorders*, **38**(1), 1–12.

Leonard, L. N. (1997). *Children with specific language impairment*. Cambridge, MA: MIT Press.

Lindsay, G., Soloff, N., Law, J., Band, S., Peacey, N., Gascoigne, M. & Radford, J. (2002). Speech and language therapy services to education in England and Wales. *International Journal of Language & Communication Disorders*, **37**(3), 273–288.

Mawhood, L., Howlin, P. & Rutter, M. (2000). Autism and developmental receptive language disorder – a comparative follow up in early adult life. I: cognitive and language outcomes. *Journal of Child Psychology and Psychiatry*, **41**, 547–559.

Nash, P., Stengelhofen, J., Toombs, L., Brown, J. & Kellow, B. (2001). An alternative management of older children with persisting communication problems. *International Journal of Language and Communication Disorders; Proceedings of the Colleges 2001 Conference* (supplement), **36**, 179–184.

Nathan, L., Stackhouse, J., Goulandris, N. & Snowling, M. (2004). Educational consequences of developmental speech disorder: Key stage I National Curriculum assessment results in English and mathematics. *British Journal of Educational Psychology*, **74**, 173–186.

Norbury, C. F., Bishop, D. V. M. & Briscoe, J. (2002). Does impaired grammatical comprehension provide evidence for an innate grammar module? *Applied Psycholinguistics*, **23**, 247–268.

Paul, R. & Cohen, D. (1984). Outcomes of severe disorders of language acquisition. *Journal of Autism and Developmental Disorders*, **14**, 405–422.

Piaget, J. (1952). *The origins of intelligence in children*. New York: International Universities Press.

Records, N. & Tomblin, J. B. (1994). Clinical decision making: describing the decision rules of practicing speech language pathologists. *Journal of Speech and Hearing Research*, **37**, 144–156.

Records, N., Freese, P. & Tomblin, J. B. (1992). The quality of life of young adults with histories of specific language impairment. *American Journal of Speech & Language Pathology*, **1**, 44–53.

Rice, M. L. & Wexler, K. (1996). Toward tense as a clinical marker of specific language impairment in English-speaking children. *Journal of Speech and Hearing Research*, **39**, 1239–1257.

Richman, N., Stevenson, J. E. & Graham, P. J. (1982). *Behavioural development.* London: Academic Press.

Snowling, M. J., Adams, J. W., Bishop, D. V. M. & Stothard, S.E. (2001). Educational attainments of school leavers with a preschool history of speech-language impairments. *International Journal of Language and Communication Disorders*, **36**, 173–183.

Stackhouse, J. (2001). Identifying children at risk for literacy problems. In J. Stackhouse & B. Wells (Eds.), *Children's speech and literacy difficulties: Identification and intervention, Bk. 2* (pp. 1–40). London: Whurr.

Stern, L. M., Connell, T. M., Lee, M. & Greenwood, G. (1995). The Adelaide preschool language unit: results of a follow up. *Journal of Paediatrics and Child Health*, **31**, 207–212.

Stothard, S. E., Snowling, M. J., Bishop, D. V. M., Chipchase, B. B. & Kaplan, C. A. (1998). Language-impaired preschoolers: a follow-up into adolescence. *Journal of Speech and Language Hearing Research*, **41**, 407–418.

Tomblin, J. B., Freese, P. R. & Records, N. L. (1992). Diagnosing specific language impairment in adults for the purpose of pedigree analysis. *Journal of Speech and Hearing Research*, **35**, 832–843.

Tomblin, J. B., Records, N., Buckwalter, P., Zhang, X., Smith, E. & O'Brien, M. (1997). Prevalence of specific language impairment in kindergarten children. *Journal of Speech, Language and Hearing Research*, **40**, 1245–1260.

van der Lely, H. K. J. (1996). Specifically language impaired and normally developing children: Verbal passive vs. adjectival passive sentence interpretation. *Lingua*, **98**, 243–272.

van der Lely, H. K. J. (1998). SLI in children: movement, economy, and deficits in the computational-syntactic system. *Language Acquisition*, **7**, 161–192.

Vygotsky, L. S. (1962). *Thought and language.* New York: Wiley.

Whitehurst, G. J. (1997). Language processes in context: Language learning in children reared in poverty. In L. B. Adamson & M. A. Romski (Eds.), *Communication and language acquisition.* Baltimore, MD: Brookes.

Young, A. R., Beitchman, J. H., Johnson, C., Douglas, L., Atkinson, L., Escobar, M. & Wilson, B. (2002). Young adult academic outcomes in a longitudinal sample of early identified language impaired and control children. *Journal of Child Psychology & Psychiatry*, **43**(5), 635–645.

5 Language and the Development of Social and Emotional Understanding

MARION FARMER
Division of Psychology, School of Psychology and Sports Sciences, University of Northumbria

INTRODUCTION

Many studies have found adjustment and socio-emotional difficulties in children with language impairments (Beitchman,Wilson, Brownlie et al., 1996b; Conti-Ramsden & Botting, 2004; Lindsay & Dockrell, 2000; Redmond & Rice, 1998). It is also noted that anxiety and mental health problems are major hazards to be faced by children with communication disorders (Beitchman, Wilson, Johnson et al., 2001; Beitchman et al., 1996b; Beitchman, Brownlie, Inglis et al., 1996c; Gillott, Furniss & Walter, 2001; Howlin & Rutter, 1987). Even in the very early years (21–31 months), children who lag behind others in their expressive language are more likely to experience depression and withdrawal, and show less social relatedness and interest in play than their typically developing (TD) peers (Irwin, Carter & Briggs-Gowan, 2002).

   This chapter outlines our current understanding of the role of language in the development of social and emotional understanding. It also attempts to indicate how delays or difficulties in the development of language may affect this development. Four areas of socio-emotional development are addressed: the development of self–other awareness and social cognition; the development of emotional understanding and self-regulation; the development of self-concept and self-esteem; and the development of peer relationships. The main argument put forward here is that language is at the heart of self–other awareness, emotional understanding and social cognition, and that these are, in turn, the bases for socio-emotional adjustment. It will also be argued that the two main sources of the child's development in this area are the child's individual cognitive endowment relating to the processing and output of linguistic information and the communicative environment in which he or she finds herself. The interaction between these two initially independent factors will mediate the children's levels of understanding and expression of the relevant concepts. This in turn will regulate the input they receive, their understanding of self and other, their interaction with others and, finally, their social competence and

Language and Social Disadvantage: Theory into Practice Edited by J. Clegg and J. Ginsborg
© 2006 John Wiley & Sons, Ltd

experience. In particular, the importance of early conversational experience will be a recurrent theme. Here it must be noted that much of the research has been concerned with the development of children with specific language impairment (SLI) and a question lies over the applicability of the findings from this research to the development of children where environmental factors may be primary in causing language delay. It may be necessary to distinguish between children who have lower levels of vocabulary development and literacy-related language skills, due to environmental input, from children with language impairments. Meanwhile, the question as to whether language delay is really language difference is not addressed here (see Chapter 1, this volume).

In the course of this chapter, some attempt will be made, rather, to consider possible differences in the relationships between social development and language, depending on the origin of the developmental difficulty. However, the precise balance of the roles played by environmental and genetic factors in the manifestation of language delay and impairment is still unclear. It may be that given the natural distribution of language abilities in any population there are some children who, if given an average or better early language environment, will develop language competencies in the normal range, albeit below average. However, these children, if brought up in a less than stimulating language environment, may later present as language-delayed or impaired.

LANGUAGE AND THE DEVELOPMENT OF SELF–OTHER UNDERSTANDING AND SOCIAL COGNITION

The development of self-other understanding depends on the development of self-awareness or knowledge of the self as an entity separate from other selves. It is an essential aspect of social cognition. This can be defined as our cognitions about the social world – our perceptions and understanding relating to ourselves as part of the social world, our interactions with others and the interactions between others. Table 5.1 outlines key aspects of the rapid development of self-understanding and social cognition in young children up to the age of 4 years. Developments in this area do not suddenly stop at this age, of course. Understanding of the self and others and cognitions about the social world continue to develop and change throughout the individual's lifetime. The focus here is on early developments since these are seen as the foundations for entrance into the social world. Research has shown that children with higher levels of sociocognitive development have higher levels of social competence (Cassidy, Werner, Rourke, Zubernis & Balaraman, 2003; Lalonde & Chandler, 1995; Watson, Nixon, Wilson & Capage, 1999). Research has also shown that there is a strong relationship between language development and sociocognitive development (e.g. Cutting & Dunn, 1999; Jenkins & Astington, 1996). The origins and nature of this relationship will be explored here.

The awareness of the self as opposed to the other is fundamental to social cognition; indeed the emergence of self-awareness is 'one of the most fundamental developmental tasks faced by the young child' (Ruble, Alvarez, Bachman et al.,

Table 5.1. Some milestones in the development of self–other understanding and social cognition

Age found	Behaviour	Implications for self–other awareness and reasoning about self and other
Neonate	Imitation of facial gestures and expressions	Theory: this matching of behaviours establishes communication between infant and other and enables the infant to identify persons
1–3 months	Matching of the *affective* states/behaviours of caregivers	Infants engage in *dialogues* and expect others to engage in mutual *turn-taking* with them. Implies that infants perceive the effects of their own actions during interaction and are capable of understanding their partners' internal states and adapting to their subjective control
4 months +	Interactional games such as peek-a-boo	Development of understanding of conventionalisation (rules) of dialogue and conversational turn-taking with the other
From 9 months	Comprehension of pointing	
From 12 months	Use of pointing	*Pointing* is an act of social cognition which directs the attention of another. Joint attention is the ability to coordinate attention toward a social partner and an object of mutual interest. Individual differences in engagement in joint attention predict later language development
From 12 months	Social referencing	The use of the emotional signals of others to appraise events and guide action
From 15 months	Self-recognition in mirrors	Key evidence for the development of a concept of the identity of the individual self
21 months +	Use of 1st person pronouns	Labelling of self and use of pronouns 'I', 'me', 'mine' denote understanding of individuality
2 years +	Questions about others' emotions and intentions	Indicates concern about origins and meaning of the behaviours of others
	Emotions of embarrassment and shame	Indicate concern with the ways in which others view the self
	Categorisation of self as boy/girl, child/adult	Indicates development of understanding of own identity
	Role-taking in pretence	Reflects understanding of others' psychological functioning and develops that understanding
	Connection of desires to action	Shows understanding that other people act in accordance with their own desires which may be different from the child's
3 years +	Connection of beliefs to action	Shows understanding that beliefs influence behaviour (e.g. the child may say that someone is looking for their dog because 'He thinks the dog ran away')
4 years +	Understanding of false beliefs in others: 'Theory of mind'	The child knows that mental representations are different in kind from physical realities (e.g. the child has hidden her mother's hat behind a chair and knows that her mother will look for it in the cupboard where it is normally kept. The child understands her mother has a false belief)

2004, p. 30). The 'self' concept has been defined as consisting of a personal self – a sense of self as different from the other – and a social self – a sense of self as connected to the other (Ruble et al., 2004). Clearly here self and other awareness are inextricably linked. Research into the development of self–other understanding throws some interesting light on the role of language in this process.

In general, we consider that children's language reflects the concepts that they are developing or have already acquired (Barrett, 1995; Gopnik, 1981) and that the words they use are salient to them perceptually. We find that references to the self appear in children's vocabulary almost as soon as they start to talk. Very young children label their body parts and talk about physical sensations, action plans and ongoing actions, showing that they are aware of themselves as agents. Typically developing children refer to a range of feeling states by the age of 2 years. At about the age of 3 years, they start to talk about the causes and consequences of feelings and to discuss a wide variety of feeling states. Through these conversations they are able to gain insight into the behaviours of others. At this age, children also begin to use words such as 'think' and 'know' referring to the thoughts and beliefs of themselves and others (van der Meulen, 2001).

Research also shows that conversational interactions with caregivers are of great importance here in giving the child the vocabulary to identify concepts and feelings. Beeghly, Bretherton, and Mervis (1986) found that that the total amount of internal state utterances and the number of different internal state utterances of caregivers were positively correlated with children's frequency of use of different internal state words, and number of different internal state words referring to self and other. Furrow, Moore, Davidge and Chiasson (1992) showed that at 3 years of age children's use of cognitive state terms is similar to their mothers' use. Children respond to their parents' input but also parents appear to be sensitive to the changes in their children's awareness. Booth, Hall, Robison and Kim (1997) found that parents comment more often on their children's internal states as the children grow older and they 'become more cognitively capable' (p. 597). They suggest that it seems likely that this change in parents' language matches the now differentiated self–other awareness of the children.

Children not only identify and discuss feelings, beliefs and intentions of the self and other in conversation with caregivers, they also develop understanding of their own social identities. Forrester (2001) puts language to the fore in the development of the self. He analyses in detail the conversations between a young child, from the age of 19–28 months, and her father, showing how the child's understanding of her 'membership categorisation' as a small member of human society is shaped in dialogue. In such dialogues, an early understanding of category membership and identity can be developed, together with expectations of that identity and the identity of the others who engage in dialogue, and the ways in which mutual understanding and cooperation can be achieved.

Rudimentary as the child's expressive language skills may be in these dialogues, we can see their importance in enabling the child to engage her parent in this type of exchange. By contrast, we can imagine the child whose expressive language has not yet emerged, or the child whose receptive skills prevent understanding, as being highly disadvantaged, even unable to participate in such an exchange and therefore lagging behind in the development of basic social understanding. There is, however, little research into the development of talk about the self in children with language development difficulties. In one of the few relevant studies published to date, Lee and Rescorla (2002) found that young children with delayed expressive language (late talkers) made fewer references to cognitive states and more references to physiological states than typically developing (TD) age-matched children. Similarly, their mothers made fewer references to cognitive states than did the mothers of the TD children. Mothers of the late talkers appeared to be matching the conceptual level of their talk to the expressive language levels of their children and treating their children as if they were cognitively delayed. In sum, this research makes a convincing case for the role of early conversation in the development of self-awareness. It also indicates that from an early age, the development of self-understanding in children unable to participate in these conversational opportunities is likely to be compromised.

A further key to the development of an understanding of self and one's identity is through personal narrative. According to social constructionist accounts (theories which suggest that our knowledge and concepts about our world are socially constructed), we develop our personal narratives about ourselves in social interaction with others (Fivush, 1994). Young children engage in conversations about their past experiences as early as 18 months of age (Eisenberg, 1985; Miller & Sperry, 1988), with adults structuring their recall by conversational means. The child's active role in remembering develops from dependence on the adult's input to total independence in narrative recall in the preschool years. Eder (1994) highlights three important functions of personal story telling: self-construction, self-regulation and self-presentation. Stories convey information about the significance of a child's experiences and help the child to organise those experiences. They provide the child with links between actions and intentions. They provide many opportunities for social comparison (Miller, 1994). Children also hear stories told about themselves and participate in the joint construction of stories with others.

Here again we can see that children with language development delays or difficulties will be disadvantaged at many levels. Their ability to follow and join in with narrative is likely to be impaired. Although most of the studies of parental conversations with children with SLI have concentrated on aspects of parental input that would relate to grammatical development, one study by Rescorla, Bascome, Lampard and Feeny (2001) found that in these conversations late talkers provided fewer answers to maternal questions, made fewer declarative statements, and were less likely to elaborate on their own topic than comparison children. Mothers of late talkers produced significantly more utterances and asked many more questions. Yont, Hewitt and Miccio (2002) found that even when children with language difficulties are intelligible, mothers have more difficulty understanding them because of ambiguous utterances and underspecified pronouns, or because of semantically inappropriate or inaccurate information. This would suggest that communicative flow between mothers and children with language difficulties is impaired, impeding the production of joint narratives. Interestingly, the level of narrative skills displayed by young children has been found to be an excellent predictor of later persistent language impairment (Bishop & Edmundson, 1987). The greater the difficulty the child has in producing a narrative the greater the likelihood of persistent language impairment.

Turning our attention to the child's understanding of 'the other', many links have been found between communicative and sociocognitive developmental competencies. First, studies of TD children seem to demonstrate the strong link between the early sociocognitive abilities shown by normal infants in joint attention episodes with others and the development of reference and vocabulary (Harris, Barlow-Brown & Chasin, 1995; Tomasello & Farrar, 1986). Further developmental research on peer interaction shows that children's ability to understand the intentions of others and coordinate interactive play with their peers between 19 months and 39 months is correlated with specific linguistic developments (Smiley, 2001). We also find a wealth of research relating to the influence of language development and conversational interactions on the child's 'theory of mind' – the understanding that others have intentions, beliefs and emotions that are different from their own and that these guide behaviour. Studies of TD children show that there is a strong predictive relationship between measures of language development and successful performance on experimental tasks that assess a child's theory of mind, although there are controversies relating to the roles of syntax and semantics in this relationship (Cheung, Hsuan-Chih, Creed et al., 2004; de Rosnay, Pons, Harris & Morrell, 2004; de Villiers & Pyers, 2002; Shatz, Diesendruck, Martinez-Beck & Akar, 2003; Slade & Ruffman, 2005). Recent investigations of children with language impairment have shown that some children, at least, in this heterogeneous grouping have deficits in social cognition (Bishop, 1997; Farmer, 2000; Marton, Abramoff & Rosenzweig, 2005). The role of language experience as opposed to language difficulty is difficult to disentangle here. Certainly, compared with chronological age-matched peers, there is a developmental delay in this area.

As with self-understanding, research into the understanding of others' minds has shown fairly consistently that conversational processes in the family are associated with the process of the development of these particular sociocognitive abilities (Dunn, 1996; Lewis, 1994; Lewis, Freeman, Kyriakidou, Maridaki-Kassotaki & Berridge, 1996; Ruffman, Perner, Natio, Parkin & Clements, 1998). It has also been shown that children from more disadvantaged backgrounds are delayed in their development of theory of mind in comparison with children from middle-class homes (Cutting & Dunn, 1999; Hughes, Jaffee, Happe et al., 2005; Shatz et al., 2003). One possible explanation is that 'mind-mindness' (talk about internal states and intentions) is more prevalent in conversations between middle-class caregivers and their children. Hughes et al. (2005) make a clear case for this position, although it has yet to be substantiated by research. Another possible explanation is that, as Shatz et al. argue, language influences understanding of mind in a variety of ways and that 'the reported relations between various language skills and false belief reasoning mostly reflect not specific direct linguistic influences . . . but rather more general, indirect influences of language use on the speeded cognitive development one finds in children from advantaged backgrounds' (Shatz et al., 2003, p. 726). Whatever the exact nature of this relationship it is clear that language and discourse are of key importance in this development. Carpendale and Lewis (2004) contend that 'the extent and nature of the social interaction children experience will influence the development of their social understanding. Increased opportunity to engage in cooperative social interaction and exposure to talk about mental states should facilitate the development of social understanding' (p. 79).

LANGUAGE AND THE DEVELOPMENT OF EMOTIONAL UNDERSTANDING AND REGULATION

Research into the socio-emotional adjustment of children has shown the importance of the development of emotional understanding and emotional self-regulation. Table 5.1 shows some aspects of this development. Children's knowledge and understanding of emotion and emotional self-regulation in the preschool years have been shown to be strong predictors of later social competence (Calkins, Gill, Johnson & Smith, 1999; Izard, Fine, Schultz et al., 2001; Schultz, Izard, Ackerman & Youngstrom, 2001).

Children develop their understanding of emotions through interactions with others; they learn to recognise emotions, to name them and to identify causes and effects of emotional states (see discussion of the development of self–other understanding, above). Learning to represent emotion internally is of key importance in interpreting and handling one's emotions (Saarni, 1997). Language plays a critical role in internal presentation. Language allows one to reflect on one's feelings and experience, mediate one's responses and direct one's behaviour. The acquisition of internal state language in the toddler years is therefore an important aspect of development in the preschool years (Repacholi & Gopnik, 1997). Level of language comprehension has been shown to be an independent predictor of emotional understanding in TD children aged 4–11 years (Pons, Lawson, Harris & de Rosnay, 2003). Cutting and Dunn (1999) found that language ability was independently related to both false belief (sociocognitive) understanding and emotional perspective-taking. Little attention has been given to this topic with children with SLI, but one study carried out by Ford and Milosky (2003) found that children aged 5–6 years old with language impairments were similar to chronological age-matched TD children in their ability to label emotions but had more difficulty than TD children in making inferences about a character's feelings in a story. Such inferences are essential to anticipating and responding to emotional reactions in others.

As with sociocognitive understanding so emotional understanding and empathic responding have also been shown to be influenced by the conversations and language to which a child is exposed in the early years (Garner, 2003; Garner, Jones, Gaddy & Rennie, 1997; Harris, 1994). Some research has shown that parents' education and occupation are good predictors of their children's emotional understanding (Dunn & Brown, 1994; Dunn, Brown, Slomkowski, Tesla & Youngblade, 1991).

It seems, therefore, that, as with the development of sociocognitive understanding, the development of emotional understanding is likely to be impeded for young children with delays and difficulties in language development. Indeed, as noted at the beginning of this chapter, it has frequently been shown that children with language difficulties are likely to have difficulties of socio-emotional adjustment. Conversely it has also consistently been shown that children with emotional and behavioural difficulties are likely to have language development deficits (Benner, Nelson & Epstein, 2002).

One aspect of emotional development with an important role to play is emotional self-regulation. This has been defined by Eisenberg, Cumberland, Spinrad et al. (2001, p. 1114) as 'the process of initiating, maintaining, modulating, or changing the occurrence, intensity, or duration of internal feeling states, emotion-related physiological processes, and the behavioural concomitants of emotion (e.g. facial expressions) in the service of accomplishing goals'. Well-adjusted children are expected to be 'relatively high in the ability to voluntarily control their attention and behaviour as needed to respond in an adaptive manner' (Eisenberg et al., 2001, p. 1114). The authors distinguish between passive, reactive control and active, effortful control. Effortful control is thought to be related to social competence, empathy and sympathy, low levels of aggression, negative emotionality and the development of conscience.

Although the research cited above suggests that language has an important role to play in the development of emotional self-regulation, there is again a paucity of research relating to the effects of a child's delayed or impaired language on this development. One study by Stansbury and Zimmermann (1999), however, found that mothers of preschool children with poorer language comprehension skills used less sophisticated strategies to help their children regulate their emotion than did mothers of children with more typical language abilities. These parents, in regulating the child's behaviour, relied on demands for compliance without also offering an explanation for the need for compliance. They did not apparently support the child's attempts to self-regulate. These parent–child dyads were also likely to have longer negative emotional episodes. Dyads in which children had both poor expressive language skills and poor verbal comprehension were the most dysfunctional. Stansbury and Zimmermann suggest that an 'autocratic' style, involving the use of shorter utterances, is adopted by parents in response to a child's lack of comprehension; they do not believe that the child's lower level of verbal comprehension is the result of the style of parental input. Interestingly, they found that language skill was not directly related to children's behaviour problems, but the use of a dysfunctional emotion regulation strategy was associated with both internalising and externalising behaviour problems.

The children in Stansbury and Zimmerman's study represented a range of TD children and children with behaviour problems. They were not selected as having difficulties in language development. A study by Fujiki, Brinton and Clarke (2002) looked at the development of emotional regulation abilities in older children with SLI. They found that children with SLI aged between 6 and 13 years of age had significantly lower scores on an Emotion Regulation Checklist than typically developing children matched for chronological age. Indeed the scores of the children with SLI decreased with age, indicating a deteriorating picture of adjustment and coping. Emotion regulation abilities were not, however, directly correlated with levels of receptive or expressive language in the SLI group. Fujiki et al. suggest that not only does language help one to regulate one's emotions but emotional regulation abilities may also influence the opportunities for social interaction and language development. They suggest that it may be difficult for children with poor emotional regulation to take part in sustained verbal interactions with caregivers and with others. Children with language difficulties may rely on non-linguistic means to regulate their feelings and to communicate them to others. It seems possible that children who are disadvantaged by their lack of earlier exposure to conversations and explanations about self-regulation and emotion, for whatever reason may, as a result, be increasingly deviant in their socio-emotional adjustment.

LANGUAGE AND THE DEVELOPMENT OF SELF-ESTEEM AND SELF-WORTH

An important aspect of the development of the self, related to socio-emotional adjustment, is the development of self-esteem or self-worth. Self-esteem represents an aspect of self-cognition that reflects one's perceptions about oneself. Self-esteem derives from one's evaluation of the self-concept, which is defined as a conceptual system made up of one's thoughts and attitudes about oneself, including thoughts about one's physical being, social characteristics and psychological functioning (inner thoughts and emotional states). It is the result of one's experiences of life and is in turn considered to affect one's ability to adapt to environmental demands, one's general state of well-being and academic achievements (Battle, 1992).

Much research has been devoted to considering the development of self-esteem as the child progresses from preschool to adulthood and the factors which may be associated with individual differences in this development. In general, it is considered that initially children have an undifferentiated self-concept relating to self-esteem, but that as they go beyond the preschool years the self-concept is differentiated into separate sub-components: general, social, academic and parent related (e.g. Harter, 1983, 1985). General self-esteem is an overall perception of the person's self-worth, social self-esteem is the perception of relationship quality with others, academic self-esteem is the perceptions of abilities to achieve academically and parent-related self-esteem is the perception of status at home and caregivers' views of the self. Evaluations of one's worth are affected by comparing one's own competencies and attributes with those of others and internalising evaluations of others. It is thought that children with positive views about themselves feel more efficacious and able to tackle difficulties and problems. This will enable them to persevere in problem-solving and in the face of challenge.

Little attention has been paid to the relationship between children's language development and their self-esteem. Two reported studies of self-esteem in children with SLI (Jerome, Fujiki, Brinton & James, 2002; Lindsay & Dockrell, 2000) show that the levels of self-esteem of younger children aged 6–9 years do not differ from those of TD children. However, one study with a slightly older group of children aged 7–10 years (Marton, Abramoff & Rosenzweig, 2005) shows lower social self-esteem in these children. The age difference between the groups may account for this difference. Jerome et al. found that older children aged 10–13 years had lower self-esteem relating to scholastic competence, social acceptance and behavioural conduct. Longitudinal studies have shown that the socio-emotional adjustment of children with SLI tends to deteriorate rather than improve (Conti-Ramsden & Botting, 2004; Fujiki et al., 2002). The findings related to self-esteem would seem to accord with this research. Two possibilities may account for the difference between the findings in two of the studies above for older and younger children. Chafel (2003) reports that social comparisons are not frequent in the talk of young children and Mintz (1995) suggests that social comparison behaviour increases with age. It is therefore quite possible that younger children's difficulties are not often commented on by their peers. The other possibility is that the increasing emphasis on language competence in handling the academic and social demands of school may lead children to have increasing awareness of their difficulties and increasingly negative self evaluations. It is clear that at school many comparisons will be made relating to the generally lower levels of literacy and academic achievement that are common in children with SLI (Beitchman, Wilson, Brownlie et al., 1996a). Most recent research seems to suggest that pupils with learning difficulties have lower levels of academic self-esteem than their TD peers, but similar levels of global self-worth (Bear, Minke & Manning, 2002; Frederickson & Jacobs, 2001; Gans, Kenny & Ghany, 2003). Competence in language and literacy skills are the main keys to school achievement. Children with lower levels of language development inevitably have lower levels of achievement in literacy and therefore are at risk for the development of low self-esteem in this area.

Differentiating between children with congenital SLI and children with delayed language development due to environmental causes (under-stimulation, exposure to limited language, etc.) may be important. Children with SLI are often found to have difficulties in peer acceptance and difficulties in academic achievement. It could be expected that these children will have lowered feelings of self-worth in these areas. Children with lower competencies in language skills due to environmental causes will almost certainly have lower levels of academic success, but may not have similar difficulties in peer acceptance. Here the models of the relationship between language skills and social competence differ. One model suggests that lower levels of language skill lead to lower ability to participate in social interaction, which in turn leads to fewer engagements in social interaction and fewer opportunities to develop social skills. Another model suggests that language is the basis for the development of social cognition, which leads to social comprehension and social understanding, and that children with lower levels of language development will have lower abilities to understand the intentions and social interactions of others. Clearly children whose language disadvantage derives from environmental factors may differ from children with specific language impairment depending on the importance of language in facilitating and developing social understanding and social interaction. The evidence given above in the sections on social cognition and emotional development suggests that conversational interaction is essential to these developments; however this remains to be proven. It is also important to clarify what level of conversational deprivation would constitute an impediment to these developments.

LANGUAGE AND THE DEVELOPMENT OF PEER RELATIONSHIPS

Children's peer relations have been extensively studied and findings from psychological studies indicate that peer acceptance during the school years is strongly predictive of later socio-emotional adjustment in adult life (Bagwell, Newcomb & Bukowski, 1998; Parker & Asher, 1987). Anthropological studies of peer groups and peer culture show the high importance of talk for the construction of social meanings and social norms within the peer group. Talk is used to elaborate games and codes of behaviour, to organise and elaborate play, to resolve conflicts, construct identities, to resist adult norms and thus establish a sense of peer group (Kyratzis, 2004). Communicative competence in this arena entails not only the use and understanding of appropriate vocabulary and sentence structures but also the use of specific linguistic devices such as the imitation of other characters' voices and speaking styles, the presentation of position by means of narrative and argument, the ability to use different voices and codes for different occasions. Generally, studies of everyday behaviour in normally developing children show connections between measures of communicative competence and ratings of social understanding and competence (Black & Hazen, 1990; Black & Logan, 1995; Brown, Donelan-McCall & Dunn, 1996; Slomkowski & Dunn, 1996).

Findings from research studies and from clinical and educational observation indicate that many children with deficits in communication skills have difficulties in peer interaction. Studies of preschool children with communication difficulties in integrated settings (Redmond and Rice, 1998; Rice, 1993) show that, compared to chronological age-mates in group settings, preschool children with communication disorders interact more with adults than peers, tend to be ignored more often by peers and are less likely to respond to the initiations of others. Gertner, Rice and Hadley (1994) found that preschool children with impaired language were less likely than TD children to be wanted as playmates in dramatic play. Horwitz et al. (2003) found that among preschool children, expressive language delays were strongly linked to lower rates of social competence in interacting with peers. In a number of studies, Brinton, Fujiki and colleagues have found lower levels of social acceptance and social competence in pre-adolescent children with SLI in mainstream educational settings (Brinton & Fujiki, 1999; Brinton, Fujiki & Higbee, 1998a; Brinton, Fujiki & McKee, 1998b; Fujiki, Brinton & Todd, 1996; Fujiki, Brinton, Hart & Fitzgerald, 1999a). Fujiki et al. (1996) also found that children with SLI experienced higher levels of loneliness than age-matched controls. Research tends to show that children with language development difficulties tend to be withdrawn and to show internalising problems rather than to externalise their problems in acting out behaviours such as aggression to others (Fujiki, Brinton, Morgan & Hart, 1999b; Redmond and Rice, 1998). Fujiki, Brinton, Isaacson and Summers (2001) found that children with impaired language spent significantly less time interacting with their peers in the playground than TD children and showed significantly more withdrawn behaviours. Brinton et al. (1998a) found that 8–12-year-old children with impaired language were also less active in cooperative work groups that their TD peers.

Withdrawal, rejection and neglect by peers do not tell the whole story. Conti-Ramsden and Botting (2004), in a longitudinal study of a large cohort of children attending language units in the UK, found that about 40% of children with SLI aged 11 years were rated by their teachers as having difficulties in social behaviour and peer relationships. Over and above this, they also found that 36% of these children reported being victimised and the target of bullying, compared with 12% of TD children. They found that social difficulties appear to increase over the years; at 11 years of age, more than half the children were showing clinical-level social difficulties. The authors suggest that there is 'an increased risk of being victimized and of social withdrawal; research needs to address the role of low self-esteem, depression and social avoidance in children who have long-term persistent language difficulties' (p. 159).

On the other hand, however, some studies (Fujiki et al., 1999a; Guralnick, Connor, Hammond, Gottman & Kinnish, 1996; Howlin & Rutter, 1987; McCabe & Meller, 2004) show that some children with SLI are accepted by their peers and demonstrate considerable social competence. Fujiki et al. (1999a) found that in one classroom a child with SLI was amongst the most rejected in the class, but another child with SLI was the most popular in the classroom. There appears to be variability within the SLI population in terms of social acceptance. Language ability alone does not decide social status. Redmond and Rice (1998) provide evidence that suggests that young children with SLI develop their socially maladaptive behaviours as the results of their deviant social experience. It is certainly possible that experience may be an important deciding factor in this variability. As we have seen, conversational input influences the development of children's self-awareness, emotional understanding and social cognition. It is possible that children with better socio-emotional adjustment and peer relations are those whose input has been more facilitative in this respect.

INTERVENTION TO IMPROVE SOCIO-EMOTIONAL ADJUSTMENT

It has been argued here that one key to the development of socio-emotional understanding is the development of appropriate language and concepts and that conversational interaction with caregivers has a key role to play. However, it seems that not all families may provide this. Additionally, studies of interaction in preschool settings suggest that interactions between adults and children may also be less than ideal (Girolametto, Hoaken, Weitzman & van Lieshout, 2000; Massey, 2004). However, the within-child factors that the child brings to interactions have been shown, at least in some studies, to moderate the type of input he or she receives (Stansbury & Zimmermann, 1999).

What seems to be required is responsive, child-centred interaction, which is adjusted to the level of the child's understanding and communicative ability, and which deals with issues relating to emotions, intentions, beliefs and knowledge through narration and discussion. An awareness of issues relating to within-child factors is clearly essential here. The social interactionist approaches advocated by a number of language intervention programmes suggest that child-centred adults' social responsiveness and modified language input assist the children in the language learning process and also in social adjustment (Farmer, 2002; Farmer & Griffiths in Chapter 9.3, this volume; Robertson & Weismer, 1999). If we consider work such as that of Stansbury and Zimmermann (1999), discussed above, then early interventions in the family setting that target language and communication skills alone may be the key. Ward (1999) shows the advantageous effects on communication skills of identification and intervention with children at risk during the first year of life. Hughes et al. (2005) also suggest that programmes boosting child-centred family talk may be the most effective provision here. If, on the other hand, very early intervention within families is not possible, as may well be the case, then intervention within the preschool or school classroom may be the way forward. There are many books and other publications relating to the development of emotional literacy but little evaluation of such approaches is available. A paper by Webster-Stratton and Reid (2004) reviews different types of intervention and reports a promising programme for the development of socio-emotional competence in early years settings. Clearly there are many issues not yet addressed by research but, considering the evidence here, very early intervention for children at risk would seem to be of utmost importance in the prevention of later socio-emotional difficulties.

REFERENCES

Bagwell, C. L., Newcomb, A. F. & Bukowski, W. M. (1998). Preadolescent friendship and peer rejection as predictors of adult adjustment. *Child Development*, **69**(1), 140–153.
Barrett, M. (1995). Early lexical development. In P. Fletcher & B. MacWhinney (Eds.), *The handbook of child language*. Cambridge: Blackwell.

Battle, J. (1992). *Culture Free Self Esteem Inventories (2nd edn)*. Austin, TX: Pro-Ed.

Bear, G. G., Minke, K. M. & Manning, M. A. (2002). Self-concept of students with learning disabilities: A meta-analysis. *School Psychology Review*, **31**(3), 405–427.

Beeghly, M., Bretherton, I. & Mervis, C. B. (1986). Mothers' internal state language to toddlers. *British Journal of Developmental Psychology*, **4**(3), 247–260.

Beitchman, J. H., Wilson, B., Brownlie, E. B., Walters, H., Inglis, A. & Lancee, W. (1996a). Long-term consistency in speech/language profiles: Developmental and academic outcomes. *Journal of the American Academy of Child and Adolescent Psychiatry*, **35**(6), 804–814.

Beitchman, J. H., Wilson, B., Brownlie, E. B., Walters, H., Inglis, A. & Lancee, W. (1996b). Long-term consistency in speech/language profiles, 2: behavioural, emotional and social outcomes. *Journal of the American Academy of Child and Adolescent Psychiatry*, **35**(6), 815–825.

Beitchman, J. H., Brownlie, E. B., Inglis, A., Wild, J., Ferguson, B., Schachter, D., Lancee, W., Wilson, B. & Matthews, R. (1996c). Seven-year follow-up of speech/language impaired and control children: Psychiatric outcome. *Journal of Child Psychology and Psychiatry and Allied Disciplines*, **37**(8), 961–970.

Beitchman J. H., Wilson, B., Johnson, C. J., Atkinson, L., Young, A., Adlaf, E., Escobar, M. & Douglas, L. (2001). Fourteen-year follow-up of speech/language-impaired and control children: Psychiatric outcome. *Journal of the American Academy of Child and Adolescent Psychiatry*, **40**(1), 75–82.

Benner, G. J., Nelson, J. R. & Epstein, M. H. (2002). Language skills of children with EBD: A literature review. *Journal of Emotional and Behavioral Disorders*, **10**(1), 43–59.

Bishop, D. V. M. (1997). *Uncommon understanding*. Hove: Psychology Press.

Bishop, D. V. M. & Edmundson, A. (1987). Language-impaired 4-year-olds – distinguishing transient from persistent impairment. *Journal of Speech and Hearing Disorders*, **52**(2), 156–173.

Black, B. & Hazen, N. L. (1990). Social status and patterns of communication in unacquainted and acquainted preschool children. *Developmental Psychology*, **26**, 379–387.

Black, B. & Logan, A. (1995). Links between communication patterns in mother–child, father–child and child–peer interactions and children's social status. *Child Development*, **66**, 255–271.

Booth, J. R., Hall, W. S., Robison, G. C. & Kim, S. Y. (1997). Acquisition of the mental state verb know by 2 to 5-year-old children. *Journal of Psycholinguistic Research*, **26**(6), 581–603.

Brinton, B. & Fujiki, M. (1999). Social interactional behaviors of children with specific language impairment. *Topics in Language Disorders*, **19**(2), 49–69.

Brinton, B., Fujiki, M. & Higbee, L. M. (1998a). Participation in cooperative learning activities by children with specific language impairment. *Journal of Speech, Language and Hearing Research*, **41**(5), 1193–1206.

Brinton, B., Fujiki, M. & McKee, L. (1998b). Negotiation skills of children with specific language impairment. *Journal of Speech, Language and Hearing Research*, **41**(4), 927–940.

Brown, J. R., Donelan-McCall, N. & Dunn, J. (1996). Why talk about mental states? The significance of children's conversations with friends, siblings and mothers. *Child Development*, **67**(3), 836–849.

Calkins, S. D., Gill, K. L., Johnson, M. C. & Smith, C. L. (1999). Emotional reactivity and emotional regulation strategies as predictors of social behavior with peers during toddlerhood. *Social Development*, **8**(3), 310–334.

Carpendale, J. I. M. & Lewis, C. (2004). Constructing an understanding of mind: The development of children's social understanding within social interaction. *Behavioral and Brain Sciences*, **27**(1), 79+.

Cassidy, K. W., Werner, R. S., Rourke, M., Zubernis, L. S. & Balaraman, G. (2003). The relationship between psychological understanding and positive social behaviours. *Social Development*, **12**(2), 198–221.

Chafel, J. A. (2003). Socially constructing concepts of self and other through play. *International Journal of Early Years Education*, **11**(3), 213–222.

Cheung, H., Hsuan-Chih, C., Creed, N., Ng, L., Wang, S. P. & Mo, L. (2004). Relative roles of general and complementation language in theory-of-mind development: Evidence from Cantonese and English. *Child Development*, **75**(4), 1155–1170.

Conti-Ramsden, G. & Botting, N. (2004). Social difficulties and victimization in children with SLI at 11 years of age. *Journal of Speech Language and Hearing Research*, **47**(1), 145–161.

Cutting, A. L. & Dunn, J. (1999). Theory of mind, emotion understanding, language, and family background: Individual differences and interrelations. *Child Development*, **70**(4), 853–865.

de Rosnay, M., Pons, F., Harris, P. L. & Morrell, J. M. B. (2004). A lag between understanding false belief and emotion attribution in young children: Relationships with linguistic ability and mothers' mental-state language. *British Journal of Developmental Psychology*, **22**(2), 197–218.

de Villiers, J. G. & Pyers, J. E. (2002). Complements to cognition: a longitudinal study of the relationship between complex syntax and false-belief-understanding. *Cognitive Development*, **17**(1), 1037–1060.

Dunn, J. (1996). The Emanuel Miller Memorial lecture 1995. Children's relationships: bridging the divide between cognitive and social development. *Journal of Child Psychology and Psychiatry and Allied Disciplines*, **37**(5), 507–518.

Dunn, J. & Brown, J. (1994). Affect expression in the family, children's understanding of emotions, and their interactions with others. *Merrill-Palmer Quarterly Journal of Developmental Psychology*, **40**(1), 120–137.

Dunn, J., Brown, J., Slomkowski, C., Tesla, C. & Youngblade, L. (1991). Young children's understanding of other people's feelings and beliefs: Individual differences and their antecedents. *Child Development*, **62**, 1352–1366.

Eder, R. A. (1994). Comments on children's narratives. In U. Neisser & R. Fivush (Eds.), *The remembered self*. Cambridge: Cambridge University Press

Eisenberg, A. R. (1985). Learning to describe past experience in conversation. *Discourse Processes*, **8**, 177–204.

Eisenberg, N., Cumberland, A., Spinrad, T. L., Fabes, R. A., Shepard, S. A., Reiser, M., Murphy, B. C., Losoya, S. H. & Guthrie, I. K. (2001). The relations of regulation and emotionality to children's externalizing and internalizing problem behaviour. *Child Development*, **72**(4), 1112–1134.

Farmer, M. (2000). Language and social cognition in children with SLI. *Journal of Child Psychology and Psychiatry*, **41**(5), 627–636.

Farmer, M. (2002). Social interactionism in practice: a review. In F. Griffiths (Ed.), *Communication counts: speech and language difficulties in the early years*. London: David Fulton Publishers.

Fivush, R. (1994). Constructing narrative, emotion and self in parent–child conversations about the past. In U. Neisser & R. V. Fivush (Eds.), *The remembered self*. Cambridge: Cambridge University Press.

Ford, J. A. & Milosky, L. M. (2003). Inferring emotional reactions in social situations: Differences in children with language impairment. *Journal of Speech Language and Hearing Research*, **46**(1), 21–30.

Forrester, M. A. (2001). The embedding of the self in early interaction. *Infant and Child Development*, **10**(4), 189–202.

Frederickson N. & Jacobs S. (2001). Controllability attributions for academic performance and the perceived scholastic competence, global self-worth and achievement of children with dyslexia. *School Psychology International*, **22**(4), 401–416.

Fujiki, M., Brinton, B. & Todd, C. M. (1996). Social skills of children with specific language impairment. *Language Speech and Hearing Services in Schools*, **27**(3), 195–202.

Fujiki, M., Brinton, B., Hart, C. H. & Fitzgerald, A. H. (1999a). Peer acceptance and friendship in children with specific language impairment. *Topics in Language Disorders*, **19**(2), 34–48.

Fujiki, M., Brinton, B., Morgan, M. & Hart, C. H. (1999b). Withdrawn and sociable behavior of children with language impairment. *Language Speech and Hearing Services in Schools*, **30**(2), 183–195.

Fujiki, M., Brinton, B., Isaacson, T. & Summers, C. (2001). Social behaviors of children with language impairment on the playground: A pilot study. *Language Speech and Hearing Services in Schools*, **32**(2), 101–113.

Fujiki, M., Brinton, B. & Clarke, D. (2002). Emotion regulation in children with specific language impairment. *Language Speech and Hearing Services in Schools*, **33**(2), 102–111.

Furrow, D., Moore, C., Davidge, J. & Chiasson, L. (1992). Mental terms in mothers' and children's' speech – similarities and relationships. *Journal of Child Language*, **19**(3), 617–631.

Gans, A. M., Kenny, M. C. & Ghany, D. (2003). Comparing the self-concept of students with and without learning disabilities. *Journal of Learning Disabilities*, **36**(3), 285–293.

Garner, P. W. (2003). Child and family correlates of toddlers' emotional and behavioral responses to a mishap. *Infant Mental Health Journal*, **24**(6), 580–596.

Garner, P. W., Jones, D. C., Gaddy, G. & Rennie, K. M. (1997). Low-income mothers' conversations about emotions and their children's emotional competence. *Social Development*, **6**(1), 37–52.

Gertner, B. L., Rice, M. L. & Hadley, P. A. (1994). Influence of communicative competence on peer preferences in a preschool classroom. *Journal of Speech and Hearing Research*, **37**(4), 913–923.

Gillott, A., Furniss, F. & Walter, A. (2001). Anxiety in high-functioning children with autism. *Autism*, **5**(3), 277–286.

Girolametto, L., Hoaken, L., Weitzman, E. & van Lieshout, R. (2000). Patterns of adult-child linguistic interaction in integrated day care groups. *Language Speech and Hearing Services in Schools*, **31**(2), 155–168.

Gopnik, A. (1981). The development of non-nominal expressions in 1–2-year-olds: Why the first words aren't about things. In P. Dale & D. Ingram (Eds.), *Child Language: An International Perspective*. Baltimore, MD: University Park Press.

Guralnick, M. J., Connor, R. T., Hammond, M. A., Gottman, J. M. & Kinnish, K. (1996). The peer relations of preschool children with communication disorders. *Child Development*, **67**(2), 471–489.

Harris, P. L. (1994). The child's understanding of emotion – developmental change and the family environment. *Journal of Child Psychology and Psychiatry and Allied Disciplines*, **35**(1), 3–28.

Harris. M., Barlow-Brown, F. & Chasin, J. (1995). The emergence of referential understanding: Pointing and the comprehension of object names. *First Language*, **15**, 19-34.

Harter, S. (1983). Developmental perspectives on the self-system. In E. Hetherington (Ed.),
Handbook of child psychology: vol 4. Socialisation, personality and social development.
New York: Wiley.

Harter, S. (1985). Competence as a dimension of self-evaluation: Towards a comprehensive
model of self-worth. In R. L. Leahy (Ed.), *The development of self.* Orlando, FL: Academic
Press.

Horwitz, S. M., Irwin, J. R., Briggs-Gowan, M. J., Heenan, J. M. B., Mendoza, J. &
Carter, A. S. (2003). Language delay in a community cohort of young children. *Journal
of The American Academy of Child And Adolescent Psychiatry*, **42**(8), 932–940.

Howlin. P. & Rutter, M. (1987). The consequences of language delay for other aspects
of development. In M. Yule & M. Rutter (Eds.), *Language development and disorders.
Clinics in developmental medicine No.101/102.* Oxford: Blackwell.

Hughes, C., Jaffee, S. R., Happe, F., Taylor, A., Caspi, A. & Moffitt, T. E. (2005). Origins
of individual differences in theory of mind: From nature to nurture? *Child Development*,
76(2), 356–370.

Irwin, J. R., Carter, A. S. & Briggs-Gowan, M. J. (2002). The social-emotional development
of 'late-talking' toddlers. *Journal of the American Academy of Child and Adolescent
Psychiatry*, **41**(11), 1324–1332.

Izard, C., Fine, S., Schultz, D., Mostow, A., Ackerman, B. & Youngstrom, E. (2001). Emotion
knowledge as a predictor of social behavior and academic competence in children at risk.
Psychological Science, **12**(1), 18–23.

Jenkins, J. M. & Astington, J. W. (1996). Cognitive factors and family structure associated
with theory of mind development in young children. *Developmental Psychology*, **32**(1),
70–78.

Jerome, A. C., Fujiki, M., Brinton, B. & James, S.L. (2002). Self-esteem in children with
specific language impairment. *Journal of Speech Language and Hearing Research*, **45**(4),
700–714.

Kyratzis, A. (2004). Talk and interaction among children and the co-construction of peer
groups and peer culture. *Annual Review of Anthropology*, **33**, 625–649.

Lalonde, C. E. & Chandler, M. J. (1995). False belief understanding goes to school: on the
social-emotional consequences of coming early or late to a first theory of mind. *Cognition
and Emotion*, **9**(2/3), 167–185.

Lee, E. C. & Rescorla, L. (2002). The use of psychological state terms by late talkers at age
3. *Applied Psycholinguistics*, **23**(4), 623–641.

Lewis, C. (1994). Episodes, events and narratives in the child's understanding of mind.
In C. Lewis & P. Mitchell (Eds.), *Children's early understanding of mind: origins and
development.* Hove: Lawrence Erlbaum Associates.

Lewis, C., Freeman, N. H., Kyriakidou, C., Maridaki-Kassotaki, K. & Berridge, D. M.
(1996). Social influences on false belief access: specific sibling influences or general
apprenticeship? *Child Development*, **67**, 2930–2947.

Lindsay, G. & Dockrell, J. (2000). The behaviour and self-esteem of children with specific
speech and language difficulties. *British Journal of Educational Psychology*, **70**, 583–601.

Marton, M., Abramoff, B. & Rosenzweig, S. (2005). Social cognition and language in
children with specific language impairment (SLI). *Journal Of Communication Disorders*,
38(2), 143–162.

Massey, S. L. (2004). Teacher–child conversation in the preschool classroom. *Early Childhood Education Journal*, **31**(4), 227–231.

McCabe, P. C. & Meller, P. J. (2004). The relationship between language and social competence: How language impairment affects social growth. *Psychology in the Schools*, **41**(3), 313–321.

Miller, P. J. (1994). Narrative practices: their role in socialisation and self-construction. In U. Neisser & R. Fivush (Eds.), *The remembered self*. Cambridge: Cambridge University Press.

Miller, P. J. & Sperry, L. L. (1988). Early talk about the past – the origins of conversational stories of personal experience. *Journal of Child Language*, **15**(2), 293–315.

Mintz, J. (1995). Self in relation to other: preschoolers verbal social comparisons within narrative discourse. In L. Sperry & P. Smiley (Eds.), *Exploring young children's concepts of self and other through conversation* (pp. 61–73). San Francisco, CA: Jossey Bass.

Parker, J. G. & Asher, S. R. (1987). Peer relations and later personal adjustment – are low-accepted children at risk? *Psychological Bulletin*, **102**(3), 357–389.

Pons, F., Lawson, J., Harris, P. L. & de Rosnay, M. (2003). Individual differences in children's emotion understanding: Effects of age and language. *Scandinavian Journal of Psychology*, **44**(4), 347–353.

Redmond, S. M. & Rice, M. L. (1998). The socioemotional behaviors of children with SLI: Social adaptation or social deviance? *Journal of Speech Language and Hearing Research*, **41**(3), 688–700.

Repacholi, B. M. & Gopnik, A. (1997). Early reasoning about desires: Evidence from 14- and 18-month-olds. *Developmental Psychology*, **33**(1), 12–21.

Rescorla, L., Bascome, A., Lampard, J. & Feeny, N. (2001). Conversational patterns in late talkers at age 3. *Applied Psycholinguistics*, **22**(2), 235–251.

Rice, M. L. (1993). Don't talk to him he's weird: A social consequences account of language and social interactions. In A. P. Kaiser & D. B. Gray (Eds.), *Enhancing children's communication: Research foundations for intervention*. Baltimore, MD: Brookes Publishing Company.

Robertson, S. B. & Weismer, S. E. (1999). Effects of treatment on linguistic and social skills in toddlers with delayed language development. *Journal of Speech Language and Hearing Research*, **42**(5), 1234–1248.

Ruble, D. N., Alvarez, J., Bachman, M., Cameron, J., Fuligni, A., Garcia Coll, C. & Rhee, E. (2004). The development of a sense of 'we': The emergence and implications of children's collective identity. In M. Bennett & F. Sani (Eds.), *The development of the social self*. Hove and New York: Psychology Press.

Ruffman, T., Perner, J., Natio, M., Parkin, L. & Clements, W. A. (1998). Older (but not younger) siblings facilitate false belief understanding. *Developmental Psychology*, **34**(1), 161–174.

Saarni, C. (1997). Coping with aversive feelings. *Motivation and Emotion*, **21**(1), 45–63.

Schultz, D., Izard, C. E., Ackerman, B. P. & Youngstrom, E. A. (2001). Emotion knowledge in economically disadvantaged children: Self-regulatory antecedents and relations to social difficulties and withdrawal. *Development and Psychopathology*, **13**(1), 53–67.

Shatz, M., Diesendruck, G., Martinez-Beck, I. & Akar, D. (2003). The influence of language and socioeconomic status on children's understanding of false belief. *Developmental Psychology*, **39**(4), 717–729.

Slade, L. & Ruffman, T. (2005). How language does (and does not) relate to theory of mind: A longitudinal study of syntax, semantics, working memory and false belief. *British Journal of Developmental Psychology*, **23**(1), 117–141.

Slomkowski, C. & Dunn, J. (1996). Young children's understanding of other people's beliefs and feelings and their connected communication with friends. *Developmental Psychology*, **32**, 442–447.

Smiley, P. A. (2001). Intention understanding and partner-sensitive behaviors in young children's peer interactions. *Social Development*, **10**(3), 330–354.

Stansbury, K. & Zimmermann, L. K. (1999). Relations among child language skills, maternal socialization of emotion regulation, and child behaviour problems. *Child Psychiatry and Human Development*, **30**(2), 121–142.

Tomasello, M. & Farrar, M. J. (1986). Joint attention and early language. *Child Development*, **57**, 1454–1463.

van der Meulen, M. (2001). Self-references among children's first fifty words: Indications for an emerging sense of self in Dutch-speaking children. *Infant and Child Development*, **10**(4), 161–171.

Ward, S. (1999). An investigation into the effectiveness of an early intervention method for delayed language development in young children. *International Journal of Language and Communication Disorders*, **34**(3), 243–264.

Watson, A., Nixon, C., Wilson, A. & Capage, L. (1999). Social interaction skills and theory of mind in young children. *Developmental Psychology*, **35**(2), 386–391.

Webster-Stratton, C. & Reid, M. J. (2004). Strengthening social and emotional competence in young children – the foundation for early school readiness and success. *Infants and Young Children*, **17**(2), 96–113.

Yont, K. M., Hewitt, L. E. & Miccio, A. W. (2002). 'What did you say?': understanding conversational breakdowns in children with speech and language impairments. *Clinical Linguistics and Phonetics*, **16**(4), 265–285.

6 Language, Behaviour and Social Disadvantage

HELEN STRINGER[1] **and JUDY CLEGG**[2]

[1]*School of Education, Communication and Language Sciences, University of Newcastle upon Tyne; Newcastle upon Tyne Hospitals NHS Trust*
[2]*Department of Human Communication Sciences, University of Sheffield*

INTRODUCTION

In the UK, the behaviour of some young people is currently an issue of concern, addressed by several government initiatives (Home Office, 2003). Another focus of government policy is young children's early speech and language development (DfES, 2003a) and indeed links have been proposed between early speech and language difficulties and the development of behaviour difficulties (Botting & Conti-Ramsden, 2000; Cohen, Vallance, Barwick et al., 2000; Cross, 2004). An association between language and behaviour was first documented in the middle of the last century (Beckey, 1942). However, it is only recently that researchers and practitioners in many disciplines, including education, psychology, child and adolescent mental health, and speech and language therapy, have begun to explore the complexities of this association. Typically, research has focused on children and young people who present with difficulties in both their speech and language development, and in their emotional and behavioural development. We begin this chapter by describing two perspectives on children experiencing speech, language and communication difficulties (SLCD) and emotional and behavioural disorders (EBD). We go on to consider the emotional and behavioural development of children with SLCD, and the speech, language and communication abilities – and difficulties – of children with EBD, arguing that these are frequently under-identified. This has implications for educational outcomes, particularly in relation to literacy development. We discuss possible explanations for the association between SLCD and EBD, and end by considering issues relating to intervention.

CHILDREN AND YOUNG PEOPLE WITH SLCD AND EBD

Historically, research has addressed the association between SLCD and EBD from two perspectives. The first approach examines the trajectories of children with primary

---

Language and Social Disadvantage: Theory into Practice Edited by J. Clegg and J. Ginsborg
© 2006 John Wiley & Sons, Ltd

speech and language difficulties who develop secondary EBD as they grow older. The second, more recent, approach is based on assessments of groups of children and young people with primary EBD revealing previously-undetected SLCD that are thought to contribute to the EBD. Implicit in these two approaches is the distinction between primary and secondary difficulties. 'Primary' difficulties are those identified first, as the child is growing up, and therefore other difficulties identified subsequently are usually considered the consequence of, or 'secondary' to, the primary difficulty. Whichever approach is taken, children and young people present with a wide variation in the type and severity of the SLCD and EBD they experience. It is therefore very hard to specify the nature and causes of the association between them.

EBD can be divided into externalising and internalising disorders. Generally, externalising disorders include anti-social and aggressive behaviour, whereas internalising disorders involve mood and anxiety. The Diagnostic and Statistical Manual of Mental Disorders (DSM-IV) (American Psychiatric Association, 1994) sets out three categories of EBD. These are: (1) pervasive developmental disorders such as autism; (2) behavioural disorders such as Attention Deficit Hyperactivity Disorder (ADHD), oppositional, defiant and conduct disorders; and (3) emotional disorders, for example mood and anxiety disorders.

The two perspectives described above are reflected in current UK referral practices whereby children and young people tend to be categorised as having primary SLCD or primary EBD. Those with SLCD are referred to speech and language therapy (SLT) services and those with EBD to Child and Mental Health Services (CAMHS). In some areas of the UK, SLT services and CAMHS work in collaboration (Clegg & Hartshorne, 2004; Cross, 1999; Cross, 2004; Cross, Blake, Tunbridge & Gill, 2001). However, some children who are identified by educational professionals as having EBD are not referred to CAMHS (Crawford & Simonoff, 2003; Gilmour, Hill, Place & Skuse, 2004). Rather, they receive statements of Special Educational Need (SEN) and as a result are placed in settings such as pupil referral units and exclusion units for children with EBD with little access to external agencies; Place, Wilson, Martin and Hulsmeier (2000) found that over 50% of pupils in a primary school for excluded children with EBD had psychiatric disorders, but few had received psychiatric diagnoses. It is not clear why this was the case, but it may have been due to lack of access to CAMHS or other professionals specialising in children's EBD. Without diagnosis, however, appropriate treatment and management cannot be offered – and the consequences of EBD for these children are comparable to those with clinically diagnosed disorders (Rutter, 2003). For the purposes of this chapter, then, we will use the term EBD to refer to all children identified with EBD, with or without a formal psychiatric diagnosis.

THE EMOTIONAL AND BEHAVIOURAL DEVELOPMENT OF CHILDREN WITH PRIMARY SLCD

A higher prevalence of EBD has been identified in children with SLCD compared to those without (Baker & Cantwell, 1987a, 1987b; Beitchman, Hood, Rochon &

Peterson, 1989; Beitchman, Brownlie, Inglis et al., 1996a; Beitchman, Wilson, Brownlie et al., 1996b; Botting & Conti-Ramsden, 2000; Cantwell & Baker, 1977). This has led researchers to propose a direct pathway from early SLCD to the development of EBD. Research examining the prevalence of EBD in cohorts of children with primary SLCD suggests that a wide range of EBD is associated with SLCD over time, including anxiety-related symptoms, social and behavioural difficulties, attention-deficit problems and even antisocial or criminal behaviour (Baker & Cantwell, 1987a, 1987b; Beitchman et al., 1996a, 1996b; Botting & Conti-Ramsden, 2000; Brownlie, Beitchman, Escobar et al., 2004; Fundudis, Kolvin & Garside, 1979; King, Jones & Lasky, 1982; Silva, Justin, McGee & Williams, 1984). Longitudinal studies show that EBD persist and the reported incidence of EBD increases when children reach adolescence (Baker & Cantwell 1987a, 1987b; Beitchman et al., 1996a, 1996b) and early adulthood (Clegg, Hollis, Mawhood & Rutter, 2005).

On the basis of these studies, we estimate that about 40–60% of children with SLCD, not including those diagnosed with autistic spectrum disorders (Burden, Scott, Forge & Goodyer, 1996), also experience secondary EBD. However, this estimate should be treated with caution. The findings of the majority of studies are based on research with heterogeneous groups of children experiencing a range of SCLD, varying in both type and severity. They identify and quantify EBD using measures ranging from teacher reports to formal psychiatric diagnoses. Moreover, all of the studies cited above have identified a proportion of children with SCLD – again, about 40–60% – who do not develop EBD over time. The notion of a direct developmental pathway between early SLCD and later EBD is therefore questionable.

THE SPEECH, LANGUAGE AND COMMUNICATION ABILITIES OF CHILDREN WITH PRIMARY EBD

Researchers have recently begun to examine the prevalence of SLCD in children and young people with formal psychiatric diagnoses of primary EBD (Clegg & Hartshorne, 2004; Cross et al., 2001; Giddan, Milling & Campbell, 1996; Prizant, Audet, Burke et al., 1990; Stringer, 2004; Stringer, Lozano & Dodd, 2004). As many as one third of children referred for psychiatric intervention have unidentified SLCD (Cohen, 1996; Cohen, Davine, Horodezky, Lipsett & Isaacson, 1993; Warr-Leeper, Wright & Mack, 1994). Furthermore, Warr-Leeper et al. estimate that the prevalence of SLCD in children and adolescents with psychiatric disorders is 10 times greater than in the general school population. Higher rates of previously unidentified SLCD are found in children with externalising rather than internalising disorders (Cohen et al., 1993; Cohen, Barwick, Horodezky, Vallance & Im, 1998). Cohen et al. (1998) conducted a large-scale study of 4–8-year-old children receiving psychiatric treatment in the USA. Formal assessments showed that 40% experienced SLCD that had not previously been identified. Similarly, 60% of 5–13-year-olds in a child and adolescent psychiatric unit in the USA experienced a range of SLCD, from fluency and vocal resonance difficulties to severe receptive language difficulties (Giddan et al., 1996). Bilingual children are currently the focus of attention in the USA. It is often argued that exposure to, and learning to speak more than one language places children at greater risk of developing EBD. Toppelberg, Medrano, Morgens and Nieto-Castanon (2002) examined the cognitive and language abilities of 50 children, speaking both English and Spanish, who were referred to an outpatient psychiatry clinic over a 30-month period. Forty-one per cent of the children were found to have a range of SLCD and EBD. Although this is an interesting study, which highlights the importance of language, its findings must be interpreted with caution, as it is unlikely that bilingualism is a specific cause of EBD.

Although the majority of the studies cited above were carried out in the USA, some research is being undertaken in the UK (Clegg & Hartshorne, 2004; Cross, Blake, Tunbridge & Gill, 2001; Stringer et al., 2004). Cross et al. (2001) report a case study of an adolescent with EBD who, despite average levels of intelligence, had significant language and literacy impairments. Speech and language intervention resulted in improvement in his communication abilities and a reduction in his inappropriate behaviour. Clegg and Hartshorne (2004) highlight the language and communication difficulties of children with Attention Deficit Hyperactivity Disorder (ADHD). Burgess and Bransby (1990) studied 17 children with EBD aged between 6 and 13 years in a psychiatric unit to find that 16 of the children presented with SLCD. Interestingly, the staff only rated five of these children as having communication difficulties. Observation of the language used by the staff showed that it was equivalent in complexity to that used in mainstream classes for children of similar ages, suggesting that staff were over-estimating the children's ability to communicate. Fourteen years later, in a similar study in the UK, Stringer et al. (2004) assessed the speech, language and communication (SLC) abilities of 19 pupils aged between 8 and 14 years who attended a special school for children with EBD. Fourteen of the pupils were found to have SLCD, but only eight of these had been identified by their teachers as having a speech or language difficulty. Teachers' descriptions of their pupils' difficulties ranged from 'poor vocabulary' to 'difficulty understanding instructions'. One teacher accurately identified all of the children with SLCD in her class, whereas other teachers did not identify any. Two of the boys with SLCD were currently known to the local SLT service and a further boy was receiving SLT for a speech difficulty.

As we have seen, children identified as having EBD are often excluded from mainstream school, even when they do not have a formal psychiatric diagnosis. In the UK, exclusions can be temporary or permanent. When exclusion is permanent, the child is removed from the school register and the Local Education Authority is required to find alternative and appropriate educational provision. Children who are excluded on the grounds of EBD and in special educational provision usually have a Statement of SEN (special educational needs). More boys than girls, and a high proportion of children in local authority care, as well as those in areas of recognised socio-economic deprivation, are permanently excluded (DfES, 2002, 2003b).

A handful of researchers in the UK have started to explore the speech, language and communication profiles of children and young people who have been excluded from school or who are at risk of permanent exclusion. The primary aim of such research is to determine whether SLCD contributed to the behaviour resulting in the exclusion. Preliminary findings indicate that some of these children and young people do have SLCD. In a small exploratory study, six out of eight primary school-aged children in an exclusion unit had speech and language profiles meeting the criteria for Specific Language Impairment (SLI) when assessed on a range of standardised cognitive and language measures (Clegg, 2004). Law and Sivyer (2003) conducted one of the first speech and language intervention studies with primary school-aged children at risk of exclusion from school. The children recruited to both the treatment and the control groups were at risk of exclusion and all presented with language and communication difficulties. Compared with the control group, the treatment group made gains in their language, communication and self-esteem, but interestingly these improvements did not result in a significant reduction in the children's challenging behaviour. Finally, Gilmour et al. (2004) compared the pragmatic communication abilities of children between the ages of 5 and 10 years excluded from school or at risk of exclusion from school with those of children with conduct disorders and autistic spectrum disorders. They found that the excluded or at-risk children had similar pragmatic abilities to both the comparison groups, indicating that they too have significant communication difficulties that impact on their behaviour.

SPEECH, LANGUAGE AND COMMUNICATION DIFFICULTIES IN CHILDREN WITH EBD

Longitudinal studies of children with primary SLCD suggest that early receptive language difficulties are more likely to lead to EBD than expressive language difficulties (Beitchman et al., 1989; Beitchman et al., 1996a, 1996b; Botting & Conti-Ramsden, 2000; Hooper, Roberts, Zeisel & Poe, 2003). Interestingly, children with speech difficulties are less at risk (Baker & Cantwell, 1987a, 1987b; Beitchman et al., 1996a, 1996b; Haynes & Naidoo, 1991), although Nash, Stengel-hofen, Toombs, Brown and Kellow (2001) argue that older children with persisting speech difficulties due to cleft lip and palate are also vulnerable. As with other later outcomes (see Chapter 4 this volume), it is the involvement of language, particularly receptive language difficulty, as opposed to pure speech disorder, that seems to carry a greater risk of EBD. Meanwhile Baker and Cantwell (1987a, 1987b) suggest that internalising disorders are more common when children experience speech difficulties, while externalising disorders are more common with language difficulties. However, we would argue that such categorisation is arbitrary, as children rarely present with isolated difficulties in either speech or language, and the co-morbidity of psychiatric disorders is usually high.

Pragmatic language ability involves the appropriate use and interpretation of language in relation to the context in which it occurs (Bishop, 1997) and requires skill in turn-taking, topic maintenance, attention control, interpreting subtle non-literal aspects of meaning, conversation repair and listener empathy (McTear & Conti-Ramsden, 1992; Ripley, Barrett & Fleming, 2001). The development of pragmatic language ability is thought to be dependent on interactions between linguistic, social, cognitive and emotional aspects of development. Pragmatic language difficulties can be a secondary consequence of SLCD. They can also represent a more specific language difficulty, such as that identified using the profile of Pragmatic Language Impairment described by Bishop and Frazier Norbury (2003). Pragmatic language difficulties are often associated with EBD (Gilmour et al., 2004), particularly ADHD (Cohen et al., 2000; Tannock, Purvis & Schachar, 1993). Vallance, Im and Cohen (1999) compared the elicited narratives of a group of children aged between 7 and 12 years with EBD and SLCD. They concluded that the children with co-morbid SLCD and EBD showed more discourse deficits than controls. Deficits included difficulties with pronominal reference and with internal state relationships involving cause, result or purpose (involving 'because' or 'so' structures). The unclear and ambiguous way in which the children referred to themselves and other people disrupted their overall communicative competence and led to listener confusion.

ADHD is one of the most commonly reported psychiatric disorders associated with SLCD (Cantwell & Baker, 1991; Love & Thompson, 1988; Tirosh & Cohen, 1998). In ADHD, specific language difficulties seem to consist of both receptive and expressive problems (Kim & Kaiser, 2000; Oram, Fine, Okamoto & Tannock, 1999) and pragmatic language difficulties (Kim & Kaiser, 2000; Tannock et al., 1993; Westby, 1999), such as excessive talking and poor topic maintenance. To date, these studies have compared ADHD children with normal language controls rather than with children with primary SLCD or other types of behaviour difficulties. Such comparisons would help to determine the specificity of the SLC profile found in ADHD compared to other EBD and children with primary SLCD. For example, Stringer (2004) recruited 50 children and adolescents with co-occurring language impairment and EBD (including ADHD) to study their performance on a series of language tasks. In this group, performance at word-level was superior for expressive vocabulary than for receptive vocabulary. However, at sentence-level, performance was superior for receptive rather than expressive language. Comparisons between the children with ADHD and the children with other types of EBD did not find any significant differences between their performance on these measures, indicating that the profile of SLCD was similar for children with ADHD and other subcategories of EBD. A distinct SLC profile for children with ADHD was therefore not identified.

LITERACY DEVELOPMENT IN CHILDREN WITH SLCD AND EBD

We have already seen in Chapter 2 that children with SLCD are at more risk of developing literacy difficulties. This is the case, too, for children with EBD, who have high rates of literacy difficulties (Carroll, Maughan, Goodman & Heltzer,

2005). However, there is little agreement as to why EBD affects the development of language and literacy. Tomblin, Zhang, Buckwalter and Catts (2000) argue that literacy difficulties are the result of SLCD. Snowling, Bishop and Stothard (2000) propose that early phonological difficulties place children at risk of failure in the early stages of reading, but later impairments of other language skills compromise the development of reading to adult levels of fluency. Thus, if EBD are also present they must be independent of language and literacy development. In contrast, Adams and Snowling (2001) suggest that the core cognitive deficits in executive function associated with ADHD are independent of the phonological deficits associated with reading difficulties. This would support the view of Williams and McGee (1996) who argue that disruptive behaviour in preschool children is already associated with their poor language skills, and that reading disorders stem from language difficulties from school entry onwards.

Sanson, Prior and Smart (1996) conducted a longitudinal study of four groups of children. The first had literacy difficulties, the second had EBD, the third had co-morbid literacy and EBD difficulties, and the fourth group had neither. The authors found that the developmental trajectories of the children with co-morbid literacy difficulties and EBD differed from those with 'pure' literacy difficulties. Surprisingly, only 10% of the co-morbid literacy-EBD group also presented with SLCD. This may, however be an underestimate of the true incidence as the data was collected via report rather than direct assessment. Beitchman et al. (1996a) showed that 57% of children with SLCD who developed EBD also had literacy difficulties. Of the children with SLCD who did not develop EBD there was a much smaller proportion who presented with literacy difficulties. Carroll et al. (2005) found in a large-scale study that low levels of in-attention and socio-economic deprivation were mediating factors in the relationship between ADHD, conduct disorders and literacy attainment. Thus, the direction of risk for some children is from the EBD to literacy difficulties with or without the involvement of language. However, the authors acknowledge that there is insufficient evidence fully to support either view of the association between SLCD, EBD and literacy difficulties. It should be clear that many children and adolescents have co-occurring SLCD, EBD and literacy difficulties; however, due to the heterogeneity of the populations studied, the complexities of these associations are poorly understood, and therefore only limited conclusions can be drawn.

PATHWAYS

Developmental and biological mechanisms have been proposed to explain the association between primary SLCD and the later development of EBD. According to the developmental account, children with SLCD may be rejected by their peers, affecting their self-confidence and self-esteem, and therefore their subsequent emotional and behavioural development (see Chapter 5, this volume, for a detailed discussion of the issues). Rejection may be a direct result of the child's communication difficulties, eliciting negative perceptions and impeding the formation of friendship networks, or the indirect result of academic failure arising from SLCD, such as literacy problems or poor performance on SATs (Nathan, Stackhouse, Goulandris & Snowling, 2004). According to the biological account, some children may have genetically-inherited cerebral abnormalities as indicated by fMRI studies (Plante, Swisher, Vance & Rapsack, 1991). Such abnormalities could be responsible for a 'neurodevelopmental delay', that is, delays in general cognition, visuo-spatial abilities and motor coordination (Beitchman, 1985). These in turn affect both speech, language and communication development, and emotional and behavioural development. The proposed mechanisms are difficult to isolate, however, as they are likely to operate in conjunction with one another. They involve both genetic and environmental factors, which interact in such a way that it is impossible to determine how individuals will develop. Some children with SLCD do not subsequently develop EBD; it may be that they are particularly resilient, protected by their higher levels of intelligence, less severe SLCD (e.g. speech rather than language difficulties), higher socio-economic status or other aspects of their environment.

It is unlikely that children with primary EBD, such as those identified as having ADHD, go on to develop secondary SCLD. Rather, we would argue, the EBD and SLCD are co-morbid. For example, children with ADHD may fail to develop adequate SLC abilities because of their difficulties attending to and engaging with the environment; impulsivity and distractibility may distort their social interactions reducing their opportunities to develop and practise appropriate pragmatic skills. However, as we have seen, mild SLCD are unlikely to be identified – and therefore treated – in children with EBD (Burgess & Bransby, 1990; Clegg & Hartshorne, 2004; Stringer et al., 2004); behaviour management is more often thought to be the priority. Thus 'secondary' SLCD diagnoses in children with EBD should most properly be considered the late identification of pre-existing difficulties. Yet – aside from those children with EBD who have unidentified SLCD – not all children with EBD go on to develop SLCD. In other words, adequate SLC abilities do not necessarily protect children from developing EBD. Nevertheless, we would argue that certain factors affecting children's development such as low intelligence, large family size, neglect, pre- and peri-natal problems and parental mental illness can all explain both SLCD and EBD. These factors are more common in areas of socio-economic deprivation, where there are also high proportions of children and young people with SLCD and EBD.

INTERVENTION

There are several reasons why the SLCD of children with EBD are not routinely identified, even when children are referred appropriately. Receptive language difficulties are not as obvious as expressive language difficulties, and they are thus more likely to be overlooked. Also, many children develop compensatory strategies in order to hide their receptive language difficulties. Pragmatic language difficulties – such as not knowing how to take turns in a conversation, and therefore interrupting, and talking over other people – may be interpreted as negative behaviour. Children's SLCD would be more likely to be identified if more SLT and CAMH professionals worked together.

In a recent review of the role of speech and language therapy in CAMHS, however, Law and Garrett (2004) comment that 'the relationship between behaviour and language development appears to be more widely recognised in the literature than it is in practice' (p. 50). SLT services do not routinely cater for children labelled with 'primary' EBD and referrals by psychiatric services to SLT services are not common, even though they are advocated by the research literature (Cohen et al., 1993). When SLCD are suspected, an appropriate assessment should be conducted and the results used to inform treatment and management. Where co-morbid SLCD and EBD are diagnosed, the SLCD need to be considered when intervention is planned. For example, when professionals talk to children, they must take the child's level of understanding into account.

Speech and language therapy can be successful in improving socialisation and therefore behaviour in young children with SLCD and secondary EBD (Sparrow, Balla & Cichetti, 1984). Here the effects of SLT on EBD are termed 'second order' (Law & Garrett, 2004) as treatment is primarily targeted at the SLCD. Currently, however, there is only limited evidence to show that improving the SLC abilities of children with EBD can result in a reduction of EBD. Despite improving the language and communication abilities of children at risk of exclusion from school, Law and Sivyer (2003) were not able to show a significant reduction in negative and anti-social behaviours, although some improvement was reported. The results of an intervention study with secondary school-age pupils (Chapter 9.6, this volume) showed that their language abilities improved, and – according to teachers' and parents' reports – their behaviour improved, too, but this was not confirmed using objective measures. Future research needs to be based on reliable, un-biased, assessments of behaviour.

CONCLUSIONS

In this chapter, we have shown that SLCD can give rise to secondary EBD, and that SLCD can exist alongside EBD, although it is often undetected when EBD is diagnosed. However, many children with SLCD do not develop EBD, and many children with EBD do not have SLCD; it is thus unlikely that SLCD are a specific cause of EBD independent of other genetic and environmental factors. The causes of the association between SLCD and EBD remain unclear; we would argue that there are several possible developmental and biological pathways, and children from socio-economically deprived backgrounds are particularly at risk. Meanwhile, collaboration between SLT and CAMH services would enable early, accurate identification of both types of difficulty to be made, and interventions to be put in place in order to improve children's SLC abilities and behaviour.

REFERENCES

Adams, J. W. & Snowling, M. (2001). Executive function and reading impairments in children reported by their teachers as 'hyperactive'. *British Journal of Developmental Psychology*, **19**, 293–307.

American Psychiatric Association (APA) (1994). *Diagnostic and statistical manual of mental disorders* (4th edn). Washington DC: APA.

Baker, L. & Cantwell, D. P. (1987a). Factors associated with the development of psychiatric illness in children with early speech/language problems. *Journal of Autism and Developmental Disorders*, **17**, 499–510.

Baker, L. & Cantwell, D. P. (1987b). A prospective follow up of children with speech/language disorders. *Journal of the American Academy of Child and Adolescent Psychiatry*, **26**, 546–553.

Beckey, R. (1942). A study of certain factors related to retardation of speech. *Journal of Speech Disorders*, **7**, 223–249.

Beitchman, J. H. (1985). Speech and language impairment and psychiatric risk: toward a model of neurodevelopmental immaturity. *Symposium on Child Psychiatry*, **8**, 721–735.

Beitchman, J. H., Hood, J., Rochon, J. & Peterson, M. (1989). Empirical classification of speech/language impairment in children II. Behavioural characteristics. *Journal of the American Academy of Child and Adolescent Psychiatry*, **28**, 118–123.

Beitchman, J. H., Brownlie, E. B., Inglis, A., Wild, J., Ferguson, B., Schachter, D., Lancee, W., Wilson, B. & Mathews, R. (1996a). Seven–year follow up of speech/language impaired and control children: psychiatric outcome. *Journal of Child Psychology & Psychiatry*, **37**, 961–970.

Beitchman , J. H., Wilson, B., Brownlie, E. B., Walters, H., Inglis, A. & Lancee, W. (1996b). Long term consistency in speech/language profiles: II. Behavioural, emotional and social outcomes. *Journal of the American Academy of Child & Adolescent Psychiatry*, **35**(6), 815–824.

Bishop, D. V. M. (1997). *Uncommon understanding: development and disorders of language comprehension in children*. Hove: Psychology Press.

Bishop, D. V. M. & Frazier Norbury, C. (2003). Exploring the borderlands of autistic disorder and specific language impairment: a study using standardised diagnostic instruments. *Journal of Child Psychology and Psychiatry*, **43**, 917–929.

Botting, N. & Conti-Ramsden, G. (2000). Social and behavioural difficulties in children with language impairment. *Child Language Teaching & Therapy*, **16**, 105–120.

Brownlie, E. B., Beitchman, J. H., Escobar, M., Young, A., Atkinson, L., Johnson, C., Wilson, B. & Douglas, L. (2004). Early language impairment and young adult delinquent and aggressive behavior. *Journal of Abnormal Child Psychology*, **32**, 453–467.

Burden, V., Scott, C. M., Forge, J. & Goodyer, I. (1996). The Cambridge Language and Speech Project (CLASP). I. Detection of language difficulties at 36–39 months. *Developmental Medicine and Child Neurology*, **38**, 613–631.

Burgess, J. & Bransby, G. (1990). An evaluation of the speech and language skills of children with emotional and behavioural problems. *College of Speech and Language Therapists Bulletin*, January, 2–3.

Cantwell, D. P. & Baker, L. (1977). Psychiatric disorder in children with speech and language retardation. *Archives of General Psychiatry*, **34**, 583–591.

Cantwell, D. P. & Baker, L. (1991). *Psychiatric and developmental disorders in children with communication disorder*. Washington DC: American Psychiatric Press.

Carroll, J. H., Maughan, B., Goodman, R. & Heltzer, H. (2005). Literacy difficulties and psychiatric disorders: evidence for comorbidity. *Journal of Child Psychology & Psychiatry*, **46**, 524–532.

Clegg, J. (2004). Language and behaviour: an exploratory study of pupils in an exclusion unit. Proceedings of the British Psychological Society Developmental Section Annual Conference, Leeds September.

Clegg, J. & Hartshorne, M. (2004). Speech and language therapy in hyperactivity: a United Kingdom perspective in complex cases. *Seminars in Speech and Language*, **25**, 263–271.

Clegg, J., Hollis, C., Mawhood, L. & Rutter, M. (2005). Developmental language disorders – a follow-up in later adult life. Cognitive, language and psychosocial outcomes, *Journal of Child Psychology & Psychiatry*, **46**(2), 128–149.

Cohen, N. J. (1996). Unsuspected language impairments in psychiatrically disturbed children: developmental issues and associated conditions. In J. H. Beitchman, N. J. Cohen, M. M. Konstantareas & R. Tannock (Eds.), *Language, learning and behaviour disorders: developmental, biological and clinical perspectives* (pp. 105–127). New York: Cambridge University Press.

Cohen, N. J., Davine, M., Horodezky, N., Lipsett, L. & Isaacson, L. (1993). Unsuspected language impairment in psychiatrically disturbed children: Prevalence and language and behavioural characteristics. *Journal of the American Academy of Child and Adolescent Psychiatry*, **32**, 595–603.

Cohen, N. J., Barwick, M. A., Horodezky, N. B., Vallance, D. D. & Im, N. (1998). Language, achievement and cognitive processing in psychiatrically disturbed children with previously identified and unsuspected language impairments. *Journal of Child Psychology & Psychiatry*, **39**, 865–877.

Cohen, N. J., Vallance, D. D., Barwick, M., Im, N., Menna, R., Horodezky, N. B. & Isaacson, L. (2000). The interface between ADHD and language impairment: an examination of language, achievement, and cognitive processing. *Journal of Child Psychology & Psychiatry*, **41**, 353–362.

Crawford, T. & Simonoff, E. (2003). Parental views about services for children attending schools for the emotionally and behaviourally disturbed (EBD): a qualitative analysis. *Child: Care, Health & Development*, **29**, 481–491.

Cross, M. (2004). *Children with emotional and behavioural difficulties and communication problems*. London: Jessica Kingsley Publishers.

Cross, M. (1999). Lost for words. *Child and Family Social Work*, **4**, 249–257.

Cross, M., Blake, P., Tunbridge, N. & Gill, T. (2001). Collaborative working to promote the communication skills of a 14-year-old student with emotional, behavioural, learning and language difficulties. *Child Language Teaching and Therapy*, **17**, 227–246.

DfES (2002). *Permanent exclusions from maintained schools in England*. Statistical Release 10/2002. London: Department for Education and Skills. Available at www.dfes.gov.uk/statistics.

DFES (2003a). *Every child matters*. London: Department for Education and Skills (DfES).

DfES (2003b). *Permanent exclusions from maintained schools in England.* Statistical Release 16/2003. London: Department for Education and Skills. Available at www.dfes.gov.uk/statistics.

Fundudis, T., Kolvin, I. & Garside, R. (Eds). (1979). *Speech retarded and deaf children: their psychological development.* London: Academic Press.

Giddan, J. J., Milling, L. & Campbell, M. D. (1996). Unrecognised language and speech deficits in preadolescent psychiatric inpatients. *American Journal of Orthopsychiatry,* **66**, 85–92.

Gilmour, J., Hill, B., Place, M. & Skuse, D. H. (2004). Social communication deficits in conduct disorder: a clinical and community survey. *Journal of Child Psychology & Psychiatry,* **45**, 967–978.

Haynes, C. & Naidoo, S. (1991). *Children with specific speech and language impairment* (Vol. 119). Oxford: Blackwell Scientific Publications.

Home Office (2003). *Respect and responsibility: taking a stand against anti-social behaviour.* London: The Home Office, Government Publication.

Hooper, S. J., Roberts, J. E., Zeisel, S. A. & Poe, M. (2003). Core language predictors of behavioural functioning in early elementary school children: concurrent and longitudinal findings. *Behavioural Disorders,* **29**, 1–21.

Kim, O. H. & Kaiser, A. P. (2000). Language characteristics of children with ADHD. *Communication Disorders Quarterly,* **21**, 154–165.

King, R. R., Jones, C. & Lasky, E. (1982). In retrospect: a fifteen year follow-up report of speech-language-disordered children. *Language, Speech and Hearing Services in Schools,* **13**, 24–32.

Law, J. & Garrett, Z. (2004). Speech and language therapy: Its potential role in CAMHS. *Child and Adolescent Mental Health,* **9**, 50–55.

Law, J. & Sivyer, S. (2003). Promoting the communication skills of primary school children excluded from school or at risk of exclusion: an intervention study. *Child Language Teaching and Therapy,* **19**, 1–27.

Love, A. J. & Thompson, M. G. (1988). Language disorders and attention deficit disorders in young children referred for psychiatric services: analysis of prevalence and a conceptual synthesis. *American Journal of Orthopsychiatry,* **58**, 52–64.

McTear, M. & Conti-Ramsden, G. (1992). *Pragmatic disability in children.* London: Whurr.

Nash, P., Stengelhofen, J., Toombs, L., Brown, J. & Kellow, B. (2001). An alternative management of older children with persisting communication problems. *International Journal of Language & Communication Disorders; Proceedings of the Colleges 2001 Conference* (supplement), **36**, 179–184.

Nathan, L., Stackhouse, J., Goulandris, N. & Snowling, M. (2004). Educational consequences of developmental speech disorder: Key stage I National Curriculum assessment results in English and mathematics. *British Journal of Educational Psychology,* **74**, 173–186.

Oram, J., Fine, J., Okamoto, C. & Tannock, R. (1999). Assessing the language of children with Attention Deficit Hyperactivity Disorder. *American Journal of Speech-Language Pathology,* **8**, 72–80.

Place, M., Wilson, J., Martin, E. & Hulsmeier, J. (2000). The frequency of emotional and behavioural disturbance in an EBD school. *Child Psychology & Psychiatry Review,* **5**, 76–80.

Plante, E., Swisher, L., Vance, R. & Rapsack, S. (1991). MRI findings in boys with specific language impairment. *Brain and Language,* **41**, 52–66.

Prizant, B., Audet, L., Burke, G., Hummel, L., Maher, S. & Theadore, G. (1990). Communication disorders and emotional/behavioural disorders in children and adolescents. *Journal of Speech and Hearing Research*, **55**, 179–192.

Ripley, K., Barrett, J. & Fleming, P. (2001). *Inclusion for children with speech and language impairments*. London: David Fulton.

Rutter, M. (2003). Commentary: Nature-nuture interplay in emotional disorders. *Journal of Child Psychology & Psychiatry*, **44**, 934–944.

Sanson, A., Prior, M. & Smart, D. (1996). Reading disabilities with and without behaviour problems at 7–8 years: prediction from longitudinal data from infancy to 6 years. *Journal of Child Psychology & Psychiatry*, **37**, 529–541.

Silva, P., Justin, C., McGee, R. & Williams, S. (1984). Some development and behavioural characteristics of seven-year old children with delayed speech development. *British Journal of Disorders of Communication*, **19**, 107–154.

Snowling, M., Bishop, D. V. M. & Stothard, S. E. (2000). Is pre-school language impairment a risk factor for dyslexia in adolescence? *Journal of Child Psychology & Psychiatry*, **4**, 587–600.

Sparrow, S. S., Balla, D. A. & Cichetti, D. V. (1984). *Vineland Adaptive Behaviour Scales*. Circle Pines, MN: American Guidance Service.

Stringer, H. (2004). *Children and adolescents with emotional and behavioural disorders and speech and language impairment: incidence, nature and intervention*. Newcastle upon Tyne: University of Newcastle upon Tyne.

Stringer, H., Lozano, S. & Dodd, B. (2004). The link between language disorders and behavioural difficulties in adolescents. *Afasic News*, Winter, 12–13.

Tannock, R., Purvis, K. L. & Schachar, R. (1993). Narrative abilities in children with attention deficit hyperactivity disorder. *Journal of Abnormal Child Psychology*, **21**, 103–117.

Tirosh, E. & Cohen, A. (1998). Language deficits in ADD: a prevalent comorbidity. *Journal of Child Neurology*, **13**, 493–497.

Tomblin, J. B., Zhang, X., Buckwalter, P. & Catts, H. (2000). The association of reading disability, behavioural disorders and language impairment among second-grade children. *Journal of Child Psychology & Psychiatry*, **41**, 473–482.

Toppelberg, C. O., Medrano, L., Morgens, L. P. & Nieto-Castanon, A. (2002). Bilingual children referred for psychiatric services: associations of language disorders, language skills and psychopathology. *Journal of the American Academy of Child and Adolescent Psychiatry*, **41**, 712–722.

Vallance, D. D., Im, N. & Cohen, N. J. (1999). Discourse deficits associated with psychiatric disorders and with language impairments in children. *Journal of Child Psychology & Psychiatry*, **40**, 693–704.

Warr-Leeper, G., Wright, N. A. & Mack, A. (1994). Language disabilities of antisocial boys in residential treatment. *Behavioural Disorders*, **19**, 159–169.

Westby, C. (1999). Assessment of pragmatic competence in children with psychiatric disorders. In D. Rodgers-Adkinson & P. Griffith (Eds.), *Communication disorders and children with psychiatric and behavioural disorders* (pp. 177–258). San Diego: Singular Publishing Group.

Williams, S. & McGee, R. (1996). Reading in childhood and mental health in early adulthood. In J. H. Beitchman, N. J. Cohen, M.M. Konstantareas & R. Tannock (Eds.), *Language, learning and behaviour disorders. Developmental, biological and clinical perspectives* (pp. 530–554). Cambridge: Cambridge University Press.

7 Language and Communication in Young People with Learning Difficulties

MONICA BRAY

Speech and Language Therapy Group, Leeds Metropolitan University

INTRODUCTION

Many of the chapters in this book consider the potential for social disadvantage to cause language difficulties. In contrast, this chapter considers the potential for language and communication problems associated with learning difficulties to cause social exclusion and therefore social disadvantage. It sets out to explore the nature of learning difficulties, and show how being a member of a group labelled as suffering from learning difficulties can stigmatise young people and thus exclude them from everyday society. Finally, it discusses the extent to which language and communication problems can be said to be at the root of the social disadvantage experienced by people with learning difficulties.

Three models have been put forward as ways of understanding language and communication problems, and learning difficulties: the medical, the social, and the interactionist (Brechin, 1999). The medical model is impairment-based, seeing 'problems' as located within individuals. Sadly, this model led to some of the worst of human abuses; for example, people with learning difficulties were defined as 'patients' and incarcerated in mental hospitals where care was poor and regimes were harsh (French, 1999). The social model explains problems as creations of society, caused by lack of acceptance and understanding of difference. This model derives from the postmodern tradition, particularly social constructionism, which sees the individual as existing in interpersonal relationships within a social environment (Burr, 1995). Health and illness are thus socially constructed. The concept of discrimination is key to the social model. People with some kinds of impairment or illness are disadvantaged also by the attitudes of others. So, for example, someone in our society with a heart condition may receive emotional and financial support but be stigmatised for being mentally ill. At the same time, it is important to note that medical, or biological, factors may affect the behaviour of people with learning difficulties, exacerbating negative attitudes towards them. This being the case, an

Language and Social Disadvantage: Theory into Practice Edited by J. Clegg and J. Ginsborg
© 2006 John Wiley & Sons, Ltd

interactionist approach is needed to explore fully the relationship between biological and social factors affecting the language and communication of people with learning difficulties. Such an approach acknowledges that for biological reasons individuals may experience limitations on their ability to communicate, but they may also experience limited opportunities for interaction for social reasons. This is the approach that will be taken in this chapter.

WHAT ARE LEARNING DIFFICULTIES?

Over the years, terminology has played an important part in our understanding of and acceptance of people who are labelled in certain ways. We no longer describe those who are seen as different from the mainstream using terms such as 'idiot' and 'mongol', which carry highly emotionally charged, negative images. Instead, such people were said to suffer from 'mental retardation' and 'mental handicap'. These terms have in their turn been replaced, and we now refer to 'intellectual disability' or 'learning disability' (although 'mental handicap' is still found in much of the medical literature). There is still argument about these terms. Defining people in terms of their intellect can be misleading, as intellectual ability can be a poor predictor of social and functional coping strategies in life (Harris, 1995). Many people with learning difficulties are quite capable of managing their lives and do not come to the attention of professionals. The use of the word 'disability' focuses on the 'weaknesses' of an individual, suggesting that there is something wrong with him or her. Nevertheless, this is the term used by the UK Department of Health (2001, p. 14) in the government white paper *Valuing People*: 'Learning disability includes the presence of:

- a significantly reduced ability to understand new or complex information, to learn new skills (impaired intelligence), with;
- a reduced ability to cope independently (impaired social functioning);
- which started before adulthood with a lasting effect on development'.

The Department of Health also notes that 'learning disability does not include those who have a "learning difficulty" which is more broadly defined in education legislation' (Department of Health, 2001, p. 15). However, the people described as 'learning disabled' by the Department of Health prefer to be described as 'people with learning difficulties' (People First, n.d.). Harris (1995) argues that a 'fuzzy' term such as 'learning difficulty' is less open to having fixed boundaries around what is and isn't seen by society as part of the definition. It thus reduces the possibility of building negative stereotypes of the people who are given this label. For this reason, the term 'people with learning difficulties' will be used in this chapter.

As we have seen, the social perspective recognises that people with learning difficulties have to overcome a number of barriers, in order to live comfortably in society (Boxall, Carson & Docherty, 2004), and often need a great deal of support to do so. These barriers can be physical as well as intellectual, and also involve dealing with other people's attitudes. Clegg (1993) uses Doise's (1986) four levels of under-standing (intrapersonal, interpersonal, positional and ideological) to take a multi-faceted view of people with learning difficulties. At the intrapersonal level, the indi-vidual's specific strengths and difficulties are examined, and the ways in which these create barriers that need to be overcome. At the interpersonal level, the focus is on relationships with others, for example in the family, at school and in the workplace, and the communication difficulties that may arise. At the positional level, power in relationships, where the person with learning difficulties is almost always in the disempowered position, is addressed, as well as the effects that this may have on self-esteem and the competence to engage with others. Thompson (2003) reminds us that people with learning difficulties often lead lives surrounded by professional and paid workers rather than real friends. This puts them in a lower social posi-tion then those around them. Finally, at the ideological level, it is only possible to understand the issues faced by people with learning difficulties in relation to the attitudes and belief systems held by society, and the ways in which these impact not only on individuals but also on the decision-making processes and strategies employed by government and other agencies for people with learning difficulties.

ARE PEOPLE WITH LEARNING DIFFICULTY SOCIALLY DISADVANTAGED?

What do we mean by social disadvantage? To Oliver and Barnes (1998), it means the exclusion of people from participation in all aspects of daily living, social, educational and civil. Oliver and Barnes use the concepts of exclusion and inclusion to convey the reality of life for people with learning difficulties and they encourage us to consider the number of 'disabling environments' (p. 21) faced by such people. Over the years, people with learning difficulties have been excluded from education, from involvement in leisure and work activities and even from being cared for in the family home because they are perceived as 'deficient', less than 'normal'. Current government policy requires that education be inclusive but the move towards this position has been slow, with 'partial integration' being accepted even as recently as 1997 (Soresi & Nota, 2004). Worfensberger (1983, cited in Hickman, 2002, p. 3) introduced the idea of 'normalisation' to enable people with disabilities to lead a more 'normal' life, and the ideas of community presence, respect, and choice now enshrined in government policy (Department of Health, 2001) derive from this. However, as Oliver and Barnes point out, 'normalisation' is a word coined by, and used by, those who offer services to people with learning difficulties. Professionals hold the key roles in service organisations and make the important decisions, not the people with learning difficulties themselves. Their potential contribution is thus undervalued while the focus remains on changing them to make them more 'normal'.

It must be acknowledged that issues of informed consent, privacy and confi-dentiality have often hampered research to find out what people with learning difficulties need and want. However, denying people a voice in their own lives is a factor in the oppression of people with learning difficulties (Swain, Heyman & Gillman, 1998), and changes in the way people with learning difficulties are viewed have taken place since the mid-1990s, with the growth of pressure groups and self-advocacy. Booth and Booth (1994), for example, were influential in encouraging people with learning difficulties to act as informants and decision makers.

ACCESS TO LEARNING AND LEISURE ACTIVITIES

Valuing People sets out four key principles to improve the lives of people with learning difficulties: (1) legal and civil rights, which include 'the right to a decent education, to grow up to vote, to marry and have a family, and to express their opinions, with help and support to do so where necessary'; (2) independence, where public services are called on to provide the support needed to enable as much independence as possible, while 'independence in this context does not mean doing everything unaided'; (3) choice, which means having the 'help and support [to] make important choices and express preferences'; and (4) inclusion, which means helping people with learning difficulty 'to do . . . ordinary things, make use of mainstream services and be fully included in the community' (Department of Health, 2001, pp. 23–24).

To what extent have these principles been implemented, and what are the factors that might be standing in the way of achievement of such goals? There has been a definite shift away from a medical model when trying to understand the needs of people with learning difficulties. The social model of health care (as mentioned above) sees the needs of the individual less as situated within the person him- or herself, and more within interpersonal, social and societal relationships. It is based on the idea that what we are and how we feel about ourselves is constructed from our experiences and interactions. From such a perspective, it is obvious that, in order to feel valued and to learn how to live and cope in the world, the experience of being a part of the community and accepted by those around you is essential.

When it was first accepted that children with learning difficulties needed education, this took place in a range of special day and boarding schools (Soresi & Nota, 2004). Throughout the 1970s and 1980s, there was a move away from the institutionalisation of children with learning difficulties towards experimental models of inclusion in mainstream schools. Inclusion was shown to have positive outcomes, for example children with learning difficulties learning alongside typically-developing peers show higher ability and better learning overall (Buyesse & Bailey, 1993). Furthermore, they show more advanced social awareness and are better at relating to other people than children who attend special schools. Similarly, children without learning difficulties develop more positive attitudes towards disability, and interact with and become friendly with classmates with learning difficulties (Soresi & Nota, 2004).

Oliver and Barnes (1998) argue that one of the outcomes of exclusion is that people with learning difficulties can have an unrealistic understanding of their own abilities and fail to appreciate the challenges that have to be faced in order to cope in the 'real' world. This can have a negative effect on their developing self-esteem. Positive self-esteem and self-determination are linked to the ability to make choices and to have control over one's own life and decision making (Wehmeyer & Bolding, 2001).

Attempts to measure self-esteem in people with learning difficulties are fraught with methodological problems (Begley, 2000). Findings based on scales and ratings can be invalidated by arbitrary and variable responses. Engaging people with learning difficulties in open-ended interviewing has proved more effective but it requires interviewees to have reasonable language skills and researchers to have a good understanding of different communication modes (see further discussion below).

Although it is possible that belonging to a devalued group will have a negative impact on self-perception and self-esteem, there is no evidence that people with learning difficulties are either aware of being part of a group or are concerned by the possible stigma that is attached to the label given to the group. Finlay and Lyons (2000) found that people with learning difficulties compared themselves with others who were seen as worse than themselves, for example thieves, beggars and drunks, thus putting themselves in a positive light. It was the parents and professionals who held negative stereotypes associated with the label of learning difficulties, and its implications for reduced independence in adult life. Finlay and Lyons also discuss research suggesting that it is the able-bodied person who shows embarrassment and lack of ease when in the company of a disabled person, not the other way around.

However, whether self-esteem is affected or not, it is true that people with learning difficulties are excluded from many leisure activities, unless they are supported and accompanied by parents or professionals. Such exclusion is often related, not to the activity itself, but to difficulties of travel, of access and of language. For example, swimming may be a very enjoyable and appropriate activity for someone with learning difficulties, but getting to the pool, paying for a ticket, finding out how to use a changing room and open or close a locker may present insuperable stumbling blocks. The 'risks' involved in these activities may be seen as too great by parents and professionals. The trade-off between opportunity and risk needs to be acknowledged in order that opportunities to people with learning difficulties are not denied (Jupp, 1994). It may be necessary to establish support for people, for example by way of befriending schemes (Heslop, 2005), and making the time and effort to enable them to take their own decisions (Sanderson, 1998) and thereby become more independent. Another impediment to independence, however, is that people with learning difficulties often find that they are 'spoken for' by others. Thus, without the language and communication skills of the dominant culture or the opportunity to express themselves, people are disadvantaged in all areas of life from using public transport to accessing health care.

LANGUAGE AND COMMUNICATION AND PEOPLE WITH LEARNING DIFFICULTY

What level of language is necessary for people to be socially included? Is social inclusion dependent on language? Research with children who have language impairments shows that they are often excluded by their language-competent peers from taking part in games and social interaction. They are also more likely to be bullied than their language-competent classmates (Knox & Conti-Ramsden, 2003). Observation of children with Down syndrome in mainstream nurseries shows that they too are excluded from many of the activities by other children and, if included, are used as 'props' in the games of these children. Also, children who are unable to use verbal language and depend on augmentative and alternative communication devices become restricted to familiar patterns and routines of conversation (Pennington, Goldbart & Marshall, 2004), and they must therefore find it difficult to be accepted and to join in with the spontaneous give-and-take of language in interaction with peers. It appears that language, and particularly intelligibility, does matter when it comes to making friends and being accepted.

There is plenty of evidence to show that language and communication present ongoing problems for people with learning difficulties, and that certain aspects of language development level out when children are around 14 years of age. The most recent, thorough overview of the literature is provided by Rondal and Edwards (1997). Morphological and syntactic aspects of grammar fail to develop normally, with only simple sentences being produced even in adulthood. Word order seems to be used appropriately but few conjunctions and subordinate clauses are used. Markers for gender, number and tense are used rarely, and passives are never used. These kinds of problems with grammar are even more severe in young people and adults with Down syndrome. Their comprehension of language is in advance of their expressive abilities. Studies by Chapman, Schwartz, and Kay-Raining Bird (1991) and Chapman, Seung, Schwartz, and Kay-Raining Bird (1998) showed that syntax comprehension in people with Down syndrome was at the same level as that expected for their mental age, while vocabulary comprehension often accelerated and surpassed mental age by adolescence. At the same time, the syntactic complexity of the language they used, together with word frequency and word diversity, was below the level expected for their mental age.

The speech skills of people with learning difficulties differ from those of people with no learning difficulty. Evidence from a number of studies suggests that people with mild to moderate learning difficulties are very likely to experience both articulatory and phonological problems in their speech. Again, people with Down syndrome are particularly at risk. Stoel-Gammon (2003) reviews the literature on phonological development in children with Down syndrome, which shows that it is similar to that of children with delayed language development. However, it is suggested that speech production is widely variable in children with Down syndrome, and that inconsistent articulation produces high levels of unintelligibility (Dodd & Thompson, 2001). Hamilton (1993) used electropalatography to identify a number of articulatory features that contribute to unintelligibility in people with Down syndrome, such as the use of tongue blade to palate instead of tongue tip to alveolar region in order to produce sounds such as /t/ and /l/, longer durations of sounds and slower movements in transition from one sound to another and a tendency for articulators not always to reach their targets. Shriberg and Widder (1990) found that rate, volume and stress are also poorly controlled. All these factors lead to a loss of intelligibility, particularly in the context of connected speech, as opposed to single words.

On the whole, people with learning difficulties have fewer problems with pragmatic skills than with the computational aspects of language. However, competent interpersonal communication makes cognitive demands. Thus, the individual's developmental stage and mental age will strongly influence his or her ability to understand and use particular speech acts, to maintain topics and to infer meaning (Rondal & Edwards, 1997). People with learning difficulties often fail to make intended referents clear to listeners by providing them with a frame of reference or identifying the subject under discussion (Abbeduto & Keller-Bell, 2003).

COGNITIVE DIFFICULTIES, PRAGMATICS AND COMPREHENSION

It is important to understand in detail the language and communication problems experienced at all levels by people with learning difficulties, as their potential implications are far-reaching. To be competent communicators, people need to understand the language and speech of others, to infer meanings and intentions based on verbal and non-verbal information, to have self and other awareness and to be able to tune in to the emotional and contextual clues available.

Language is also necessary for problem solving. Baldo et al. (2005) showed that people who had comprehension and naming difficulties following a stroke were unable to respond flexibly to information and feedback provided by the researcher in a card-sorting task. Language is also dependent on short-term memory. Brock and Jarrold (2004) found that people with Down syndrome had particular difficulties in item and order memory linked to poor language ability, particularly poor phoneme recall, despite relatively good lexical knowledge. Numerous studies have demonstrated poor phonological working memory in people with learning difficulties, specifically Down syndrome (Hulme & Mackenzie, 1992; Jarrold, Baddeley & Hewes, 2000).

Intelligibility is closely correlated with communicative competence (Ball, Beukelman & Pattee, 2004). For an utterance to be intelligible, the contributions of both talker and listener are essential. The talker's contribution consists of articulating consistently and with as few errors as possible. Meanwhile the listener's contribution is to store the vocal characteristics of the talker in episodic memory in order to check the meaning of the utterance, and to recall specific articulations as they recur (Markham & Hassan, 2004). Markham and Hassan also show that the ability to interpret distorted messages and the vocal characteristics of talkers varies from one listener to another. Other factors influence intelligibility, such as the environmental context, the relationship between the talker and listener, and the topic of the utterance. Listeners' understanding can be affected by noisy environments, environments in which speech is subject to distortion, such as the telephone, the level of complexity of the message and the age and social standing of the speaker. Children younger than 12 years are less likely than older people to use contextual information to help them understand a message, nor do they use sensory information as efficiently (Markham & Hassan, 2004). Talkers' intelligibility can be affected when they speak to large groups of people, over a noisy background or in a highly emotionally charged situation.

For people with learning difficulties, the high cognitive demands associated with making themselves understood and of listening to others in any but the most optimal conditions, leads to regular breakdown in communicative effectiveness. They are likely to be inconsistent in their speech production and are unlikely to monitor their articulatory output. They may also find the attentional demands of listening and interpreting messages from other people difficult. As Rondal and Edwards (1997) point out, 'the more demanding the extralinguistic context, the nature of the speech act performed and the content and formal aspect of the utterance, the more likely some of the less firmly-established linguistic features will be lost or cause errors' (p. 199).

LANGUAGE AND POWER

Language is used to command and enquire, to explain and argue, to explore and to comment. Not only do we organise and manage our lives through language but we also use it to make social contact and to compare and contrast ourselves with others, thus developing our sense of self. There has been much discussion over the years as to the ways in which language is used by people to explain their environment, and also to constrain what they see or understand of it (Trudgill, 2000). People's social environments are reflected in the language they use. Thus, language changes and shifts as society changes. This is particularly true of the language used to express values that respond to changes in society but that can also be influential in forming the opinions and attitudes of the time, such as the terms used to describe and classify people with learning difficulties, which have changed over time, as discussed by Oliver and Barnes (1998). White and Epston (1990) point out that language is never a neutral activity; whenever people are engaged in discourse, they are sharing and exploring aspects of their own and other's experiences. Even a discussion about a topic as apparently benign as the weather can involve the participants in understanding a range of underlying meanings, from the function of the discussion as purely social intercourse to one that contributes to an assessment of the other person based on their accent, sentence structure and world knowledge.

People with language and communication problems are disadvantaged in many ways. They may experience difficulties in developing relationships and friendships, in making choices and in accessing community resources. Webb (1999) showed that friendships were difficult to initiate and maintain for adults with learning difficulties. They did not feel they had the language skills to initiate contact and to 'talk to people'. Also, as we have seen, people with learning difficulties often only have the opportunity to form relationships with the professionals who teach or work with them; these people often move on, leading to a lack of continuity in relationships. Gregory et al. (2001) argue that friendships require proximity, frequent interaction, time to discover similarities and differences, and to express liking both verbally and non verbally. Because of their lack of mobility and independence, people with learning difficulties are often unable to maintain friendships long enough to reach this point of mutual knowing and communicative understanding. Yet friendships are essential to our feelings of positive self-esteem, as they strengthen and confirm our sense of ourselves and our place in the community (Heslop, 2005).

Our culture, with its emphasis on verbal expression, places restrictions on people with limited verbal abilities. Bradshaw (2001) found that when people with learning difficulties tried to communicate with care workers, using modes of expression such as sign language and pointing at objects or pictures, they were ignored. The care workers, in turn, tried to communicate using complex spoken language. Interview data showed that the care workers were not trying to be awkward or cruel. Rather, they underestimated the extent to which they were using non-verbal communication, and overestimated the extent to which the people with learning difficulties could understand them. Law, Bunning, Byng, Farrelly & Heyman (2005) believe that effective communication is at the heart of access to healthcare. They interviewed people with a variety of communication problems, including people with learning difficulties. They reported that many health practitioners make no concessions to the particular communication needs of such patients. Rapid speech, use of unexplained terminology and pressure of time can all lead to a lack of comprehension on the part of the clients and a consequent lack of confidence in their ability to ask for what they need. Law et al. call for the construction of 'ramps', such as gesture, pictures, symbols and so on, to enable more effective communication.

As we have seen, 'choice' is one of the four key principles of government policy for people with learning difficulties (Department of Health, 2001). However, in order to make informed choices, we need to know what alternatives are available, and for this to be possible we need to be able fully to understand spoken and/or written language. Historically, knowledge and power have been linked, the dominant members of society denying knowledge to minority groups. Thus, black people were denied education during the apartheid era in South Africa. Until recently, many people with learning difficulties, too, were denied education. Full inclusion in mainstream schooling is still not totally accepted, because of teachers' attitudes and skills, lack of curriculum planning, access to schools, resources and so on (Parmenter, 2001). World knowledge develops as the result of experience and through the construction of narratives around that experience; people arrange their own experiences in sequences across time to form a coherent picture of themselves and the world around them (White & Epston, 1990, p.10). The dominance of written language in our society has led to people with learning difficulties being 'invisible', few of them believing that they have anything of value to say or contribute (Atkinson, 1998, p. 117). Townsley (1998) quotes one person with learning difficulties as saying 'big words keep us out' (p. 77). To enable people with learning difficulties to make choices, alternative means of communication need to be offered to them, and they may need additional support from advocates. Information needs to be provided in different forms, through symbols and simple language or through taped messages (Townsley, 1998) and their meanings need to be carefully constructed based on oral (Atkinson, 2004) or symbol (Pawson, Raghaven & Small, 2005) information. Caution must be exercised in the co-construction of meaning when information is provided by people with learning difficulties, as vocabulary and emphasis may be provided not by them but by the user of spoken and written language.

STORIES OF YOUNG PEOPLE WITH LEARNING DIFFICULTIES

What is the reality of life for people with learning difficulties? Can we say unequivocally that social disadvantage is a direct result of the language and communication problems they experience? Or are people with learning difficulties simply perceived as disadvantaged by the carers and professionals with whom they come in contact? The answers vary, as do people with learning difficulties themselves. As mentioned at the beginning of this chapter, the term 'learning difficulties' is deliberately loose. It pulls into its domain people with numerous strengths and difficulties. It includes those whose problems are related to medical conditions, and those whose problems are related to the way they are perceived by other people. For some people, the circumstances of their birth and upbringing may well have contributed to the social disadvantage evident in their lives. For others, social disadvantage may be at the root of the difficulties they currently face. The stories below show how varied people and their experiences are and lead to the conclusion that we cannot generalise about people and their abilities to cope with life.

ROB

Rob is currently 20 years of age. He was brain-damaged at birth and this has led to a lifetime of epilepsy and associated mild learning difficulties. Rob has difficulty with motor control leading to clumsiness, problems with fine control such as that needed in writing, and articulatory muscle weakness and slowness leading to slurred and sometimes unintelligible speech. However, he has good language skills and can understand and express a wide range of information. He has a very good long-term memory, especially for facts and information he enjoys and he is very keen to share this with listeners, often unaware that they may not share his enthusiasm.

Rob lives alone with his mother. He never goes out alone. He and his mother go regularly to the cinema and this is his major source of enjoyment. He has no special friends. He attends a further education course for people with learning difficulties where he is having difficulties conforming to the expected behaviour in the group. Whenever he goes anywhere, he is accompanied by a care worker, although he has been known to assert his independence by stepping off the kerb into the traffic. His mother claims that he needs supervision because of his poor road sense and his epilepsy, which can lead to temporary loss of awareness.

Rob's difficulties with his speech affect his relationship with his mother. She has only partial hearing and wants him to speak slowly and clearly for her. However, he often shouts to her from a distance, probably because of an inability fully to understand the implications of her hearing loss. He also has problems making his needs known in the community. Bus drivers particularly cause him frustration with their demand for clear and fast speech. He admits to finding them very difficult. He can become quite angry if misunderstood when he is trying hard to convey his message. His mother, although she tries to encourage him to be more independent, steps in if she sees him having difficulties.

AARON

At 26 years of age, Aaron has attained a minimal level of independence. He takes the bus to places alone. However, in order to do this, he needs his mother to write his destination for him and he needs someone to meet him at the other end. He also needs a tolerant bus driver who is not overwhelmed by his tendency to stand or lean a bit too close to people, his assertive noise-making and his enthusiasm to engage everyone in 'conversation'! Aaron has no intelligible speech. A traumatic birth following his mother's illness led to neurological damage, which has affected all areas of development. He too suffers from epilepsy. His primary area of difficulty is, however, language. He has learned to use some alternatives such as signing, picture pointing and a simple electronic voice-output aid, but his language difficulty is such that he cannot generate and formulate a message in any formal linguistic way. He is a good communicator but noise making, gesture and direct action (showing the thing he is talking about) are his main tools. If he is not understood, he persists and he may become quite distressed. This leads to more vigorous pointing and louder vocalisations, which can alienate his listeners.

Aaron's mother has worked hard to try and give him 'community presence'. She has used available advocacy groups, befriending services and social service provision to offer him opportunities to attend classes, develop skills and follow his own interests (train travel being his favourite occupation). Aaron has not had much success in developing any long-term relationships or attending any activities for extended periods. The relationships cease when people move on, when they find Aaron too demanding, and when Aaron's mother feels he is not being treated with respect by befrienders. Aaron's ability to attend for any length of time to an activity is limited and when he loses interest he is unable to control his need to walk away or become very vocal, sometimes inappropriately. This makes involvement in groups difficult. However, if he can be in control and take part on his own terms Aaron proves to be a positive member of a group and enjoys participating in and leading activities.

BOB

Bob has Down syndrome. He is now 21 and he attends a local college, belongs to a drama group, and enjoys sport and socialising. His family have given him a wide variety of experiences and he is well travelled. However he never goes anywhere independently and rarely moves outside his loving family's protective umbrella. He developed language very slowly and although he now has a lot to say, he stammers and is often unintelligible. His understanding of and use of grammar are limited to simple sentences, although he has a good vocabulary. He is very sociable, makes contact easily and is keen to talk to others. He has a number of friends but relies on his family to maintain these friendships by transporting him to clubs or homes and supporting him in maintaining contact.

Bob is beginning to be very aware of the opposite sex and is keen to sit near or make social contact with girls. He is able to initiate conversation by asking someone's name but is unsure how to proceed beyond this. When he is with his friends who also have Down syndrome or other learning difficulties, he will often simply tap someone or say 'hello' or smile and nudge. Very little language is used, or seemingly needed, to maintain these relationships.

While Bob can be a delightful and engaging young man, he can also be moody and belligerent. He can become frustrated if he is not understood and, although this has reduced considerably since he has begun using a 'conversation book', he sometimes withdraws and refuses to talk or participate for any length of time.

What are the similarities and differences between these three young people? They all have 'learning difficulties' and they are of a similar age. Are they disadvantaged by their language difficulties or simply by society?

The use of language is a barrier for all three young people. Getting information across to other people is not easy and all three show distress if they are not understood. Use of alternative means of communication such as written notes, conversation books, gestures and signing can help, but these all require support and interest from the listener.

Social disadvantage, if seen in terms of the opportunity to access and enjoy work and leisure pursuits, is definitely experienced by the young people. Both Aaron and Rob's mothers say that their sons want to work. But, as Aaron's mother points out, the choices are limited to mundane tasks such as pushing supermarket trolleys. Aaron does not choose to be interested in such work, but any alternatives would require much more effective language with better social and pragmatic awareness and control. All three are totally dependent on their families (mainly their mothers) for their leisure pursuits. They do not have the mobility and independence to form and develop relationships that could take them away from the home environment.

In relation to self-awareness and self-esteem, it is difficult to find out how each of these young people feels about himself. 'Challenging behaviour' in the form of angry outbursts, inappropriate social behaviour, and potentially dangerous activities have all been linked with frustration at not being understood and not being able to express needs as well as a lack of useful daily activity (Robertson et al., 2005). These three stories all contain evidence of frustration and anger leading to withdrawal or dangerous behaviour, such as stepping into traffic. Rob has said he knows he is different, and he sees himself as being part of a family with problems – a mother with hearing loss and a father with heart disease. Bob knows that he has Down syndrome but he shows no evidence at this point of being aware that this may be stigmatising. The probability is that all three have a sense of inability to deal with daily life events but there is no hard evidence that they have poor self-esteem as a result of this.

The future for these three young people is as yet hard to determine. How they will cope without their families is an issue that the mothers are only too aware of. It is easy to say that families should let go and encourage independence and risk-taking, but the reality is that they face many real dangers, from traffic to bus drivers who are prepared to put people off the bus if they are seen as awkward: this happened to Aaron. Society needs to be more open to difference in order to allow Rob, Aaron and Bob to lead their lives to the best of their abilities. Acceptance and understanding of different ways of communicating is at the heart of this willingness to tolerate difference. Once these three move into supported accommodation, there is the likelihood that, without much better education and awareness, care workers will discount their ways of communicating and thus limit their opportunities for making choices. The likelihood of their being able to work and earn their own money is limited by a range of social and pragmatic difficulties. These in turn are associated with their language and communication problems.

CONCLUSION

There is no doubt that social disadvantage is an on-going and as yet unresolved reality for a large majority of people with learning difficulties. There are still many barriers to inclusion. These are related to the lack of awareness shown by people without learning difficulties, their lack of time and commitment to helping break down or minimise the barriers to inclusion, and above all their unwillingness or inability to try to communicate effectively with people who do have learning difficulties. The three young people discussed above are still safe in the bosom of their families and are probably less aware of the extent to which they are excluded. However, as they get older, they will want more opportunities and they will find themselves living in community homes and hostels. Their needs for friendship, for participation and for communication will become more pressing as their ties with their families decrease. How will they fare? Will language barriers force them into isolation, into 'challenging behaviour' or into depression (Johnson, Mason & Withers, 2003), or will people who are more able language users be able to adapt and adjust to the communication needs of these and other people with learning difficulties?

REFERENCES

Abbeduto, L. & Keller-Bell, Y. (2003). Pragmatic development and communication training. In J. Rondal and S. Buckley (Eds.), *Speech and language intervention in Down syndrome* (pp. 98–115). London: Whurr.

Atkinson, D. (1998). Reclaiming our past. Empowerment through oral history and personal stories. In L. Ward (Ed.), *Innovations in advocacy and empowerment for people with intellectual disabilities* (pp. 115–126). Chorley: Lisieux Hall Publications.

Atkinson, D. (2004). Research and empowerment: involving people with learning difficulties in oral and life history research. *Disability and Society*, **19**, 691–702.

Baldo, J., Dronkers, N., Wilkins, D., Ludy, C., Raskin, P. & Kim, J. (2005). Is problem solving dependent on language? *Brain and Language*, **92**, 240–250.

Ball, C. Beukelman, D. & Pattee, G. (2004). Communication effectiveness of individuals with Amyotropic Lateral Sclerosis. *Journal of Communication Disorders*, **37**, 197–215.

Begley, A. (2000). The educational self-perceptions of children with Down syndrome. In A. Lewis & G. Lindsay. (Eds.), *Researching children's perspectives* (pp. 98–111). Milton Keynes: Open University Press.

Booth, T. & Booth, W. (1994). The use of depth interviewing with vulnerable subjects: Lessons from a research study of parents with learning difficulties. *Social Science in Medicine*, **39**, 415–424.

Boxall, K., Carson, I. & Docherty, D. (2004). Room at the academy? People with learning difficulties and higher education. *Disability and Society*, **19**, 99–112.

Bradshaw, J. (2001). Complexity of staff communication and reported level of understanding skills in adults with intellectual disability. *Journal of Intellectual Disability Research,* **45**, 233–243.

Brechin, A. (1999). Understandings of learning disability. In J. Swain and S. French (Eds.), *Therapy and learning difficulties: advocacy, participation and partnership* (pp. 58–71). Oxford: Butterworth and Heinemann.

Brock, J. & Jarrold, C. (2004). Language influences on verbal short-term memory performance in Down syndrome: Item and order recognition. *Journal of Speech, Language and Hearing Research.* **47**, 1334–1346.

Burr, V. (1995). *Social constructionism.* New York: Routledge.

Buyesse, V. & Bailey, D. B. (1993). Behavioral and developmental outcomes in young children with disabilities in integrated and segregated settings: a review of comparative studies. *Journal of Special Education*, **26**, 434–461.

Chapman, R., Schwartz, S. & Kay-Raining Bird, E. (1991). Language skills of children and adolescents with Down syndrome: I. Comprehension. *Journal of Speech, Language and Hearing Research*, **34**, 1106–1120.

Chapman, R., Seung, H-K., Schwartz, S. & Kay-Raining Bird, E. (1998). Language skills of children and adolescents with Down syndrome: II. Production deficits. *Journal of Speech, Language and Hearing Research*, **41**, 861–873.

Clegg, J. A. (1993). Putting people first: A social constructionist approach to learning disability. *British Journal of Clinical Psychology*, **32**, 389–406.

Department of Health. (2001). *Valuing people*. Retrieved 10 May, 2005, from http://www.valuingpeople.gov.uk/papers.htm

Dodd, B. & Thompson, C. (2001). Speech disorder in children with Down's syndrome. *Journal of Intellectual Disability Research*, **45**, 308–316.

Doise, W. (1986). *Levels of explanation in social psychology*. Cambridge: Cambridge University Press.

Finlay, W. & Lyons, E. (2000). Social categorizations, social comparisons and stigma: Presentations of self in people with learning difficulties. *British Journal of Social Psychology*, **39**, 129–146.

French, S. (1999). Learning Difficulties: a biological perspective. In J. Swain and S. French (Eds.), *Therapy and learning difficulties: advocacy, participation and partnership* (pp. 72–80). Oxford: Butterworth and Heinemann.

Gregory, N. Robertson, J., Kessissoglou, S., Emerson, E. & Halton, C. (2001). Factors associated with expressed satisfaction among people with intellectual disability receiving residential supports. *Journal of Intellectual Disability Research*, **45**, 279–291.

Hamilton, C. (1993). Investigation of the articulatory pattern of young adults with Down's syndrome using electropalatography. *Down's Syndrome Research and Practice*, **1**, 15–28.

Harris, P. (1995). Who am I? Concepts of disability and their implications for people with learning difficulties. *Disability and Society*, **10**, 341–351.

Heslop, T. (2005). Good practice in befriending services for people with learning difficulties. *British Journal of Learning Disabilties*, **33**, 27–33.

Hickman, J. (2002). Issues of service delivery and auditing. In S. Abudarham & A. Hurd (Eds.), *Management of communication needs in people with learning disability* (pp. 1–32). London: Whurr.

Hulme, C. & Mackenzie, S. (1992). *Working memory and severe learning difficulties*. NJ: Lawrence Erlbaum Associates.

Jarrold, C., Baddeley, A. D. & Hewes, A. K. (2000). Verbal short-term memory deficits in Down syndrome: a consequence of problems in rehearsal? *Journal of Child Psychology and Psychiatry*, **40**, 233–244.

Johnson, A., Mason, H. & Withers, P. (2003). 'I might not know what you know but it doesn't mean you can be awful to me'. *British Journal of Learning Disabilities*, **31**, 31–36.

Jupp, K. (1994). *Living a full life with learning disabilities*. London: Souvenir Press.

Knox, E. & Conti-Ramsden, G. (2003). Bullying risks of 11-year old children with specific language impairment (SLI): does school placement matter? *International Journal of Language and Communication Disorders*, **38**, 1–12.

Law, J., Bunning, K., Byng, S., Farrelly, S. & Heyman, B. (2005). Making sense in primary care: levelling the playing field for people with communication difficulties. *Disability and Society*, **20**, 169–184.

Markham, D. & Hassan, V. (2004). The effect of talker and listener related factors on intelligibility for a real-word open-set perception test. *Journal of Speech, Language and Hearing Research*, **47**, 725–737.

Oliver, M. & Barnes, C. (1998). *Disabled people and social policy: From exclusion to inclusion*. London: Longman.

Parmenter, T. R. (2001). The contribution of science in facilitating the inclusion of people with intellectual disability into the community. *Journal of Intellectual Disability Research*, **45**, 183–193.

Pawson, N., Raghaven, R. & Small, N. (2005). Social inclusion, social networks and ethnicity: the development of the Social Inclusion Interview Schedule for people with learning disabilities. *British Journal of Learning Disabilities*, **33**, 15–22.

Pennington, L., Goldbart, J. & Marshall, J. (2004). Interaction training for conversational partners of children with cerebral palsy: a systematic review. *International Journal of Language and Communication Disorders*, **39**, 151–170.

People First (n.d.). Retrieved 14 June, 2005, from http://www.peoplefirstltd.com/new_page_6.htm

Robertson, J., Emerson, E., Pinkney, L. Caesar, E., Felce, D., Meek, A., Carr, D., Love, K., Knapp, M. & Hallam, A. (2005). Treatment and management of challenging behaviour in congregate and non-congregate community-based supported accommodation. *Journal of Intellectual Disability Research*, **47**, 63–72.

Rondal, J. & Edwards, S. (1997). *Language in mental retardation.* London: Whurr.

Sanderson, H. (1998). A say in my future. Involving people with profound and multiple disabilities in person centred planning. In L. Ward (Ed.), *Innovations in advocacy and empowerment for people with intellectual disabilities* (pp. 161–182). Chorley: Lisieux Hall Publications.

Shriberg, L. & Widder, C. (1990). Speech and prosody characteristics of adults with mental retardation. *Journal of Speech and Hearing Research*, **33**, 627–653.

Soresi, S. & Nota, L. (2004). School inclusion. In J. Rondal, R. Hodapp, S. Soresi, E. Dykens & L. Nota (Eds.), *Intellectual disabilities: genetics, behaviour and inclusion* (pp. 114–156). London: Whurr.

Stoel-Gammon, C. (2003). Speech acquisition and approaches to intervention. In J. Rondal & S. Buckley (Eds.), *Speech and language intervention in Down syndrome* (pp. 49–62). London: Whurr.

Swain, J., Heyman, B. & Gillman, M. (1998). Public Research, Private Concerns: ethical issues in the use of open-ended interviews with people who have learning difficulties. *Disability and Society*, **13**, 121–136.

Thompson, J. (2003). *Finding things out.* British Association of Social Workers. Birmingham: Venture Press.

Townsley, R. (1998). Information is power. In L. Ward (Ed.), *Innovations in advocacy and empowerment for people with intellectual disabilities* (pp. 77–90). Chorley: Lisieux Hall Publications.

Trudgill, P. (2000). *Sociolinguistics.* London: Penguin.

Webb, T. (1999). Voices of people with learning difficulties. In J. Swain & S. French (Ed.), *Therapy and learning difficulties: participation and partnership* (pp. 47–57). Oxford: Butterworth and Heinemann.

Wehmeyer, M. & Bolding, N. (2001). Enhanced self-determination of adults with intellectual disability as an outcome of moving to community-based work or living environments. *Journal of Intellectual Disability Research*, **45**, 371–383.

White, M. & Epston, D. (1990). *Narrative means to therapeutics ends.* New York: Norton.

8 The Effects of Intervention on the Communication Skills of Socially Disadvantaged Children

JAMES LAW[1] **and FRANCES HARRIS**[2]

[1]*Centre for Integrated Healthcare Research, Queen Margaret University, Edinburgh, UK*
[2]*Sure Start Speech and Language Development Project, City University, UK*

INTRODUCTION

This chapter addresses the question of how far it is possible to promote the acquisition of communication skills in socially disadvantaged children. The chapter begins by providing a framework for describing different kinds of intervention. A historical overview of the child development literature relating to low-income groups reveals a gradual shift from thinking about the educational experiences of the individual child to thinking about the whole child, and then on to thinking about the family and the community in which that child grows up. Some examples of interventions are briefly described, and key historical exemplars of those types of intervention are outlined. Finally, a comparison is drawn with the literature on speech and language interventions for children who experience language-learning difficulties but do not come from socially disadvantaged backgrounds. Full reviews of the intervention literature can be found in Halpern (2000) and Farran (2000).

Many interventions designed for children from socially disadvantaged backgrounds focus on language and communication skills. In part this reflects the fact that language skills can be measured. But more importantly it reflects the aspirations of our highly communication-focused society. Children with better communication skills are likely to go on to cope better with both the academic and the social context of school, and subsequently find and retain employment. It could be argued that, while it is recognised that many children from socially disadvantaged families have lower levels of language in the preschool period and are vulnerable in terms of school readiness, their language skills may be one of the aspects of development that are most amenable to change. Furthermore, that change, while beneficial in its own right, is likely to have a mediating effect on the impact of social disadvantage by improving the child's ability to negotiate

Language and Social Disadvantage: Theory into Practice Edited by J. Clegg and J. Ginsborg
© 2006 John Wiley & Sons, Ltd

with peers and establish friendships, to create and retell stories and to contribute to the development of literacy and other more academic skills.

The link between limited communication skills and social disadvantage has been the subject of discussion for many years (Edwards, 1989; Puckering & Rutter, 1987; Chapter 1, present volume). One recent study found that more than half the children entering nursery schools in socio-economically deprived areas of the UK – all of whom had English as their first language – had significant language delays (Locke, Ginsborg & Peers, 2002). Interestingly, these difficulties appear to be specific to language, insofar as they were not reflected in performance on tests of non-verbal cognitive abilities. Furthermore, there is a literature to suggest that the verbal experience of such children can be qualitatively different from their more advantaged peers and, understandably, the explanation for these difficulties is often associated with the nature of the input that they receive (Hart & Risley, 1995). But this is not a simple matter of how much verbal input the children receive from their parents and carers. An extensive literature has developed in recent years about children who have poor language learning skills but who have not experienced high levels of social disadvantage. In such cases, the parental communication skills are considered to be qualitatively different from those of parents of so-called language normal children but these differences are not considered to be causing the difficulties that the child is experiencing (Conti-Ramsden, 1994). It is useful at this point to consider the difference between specific children with poorly developed language skills with and without social disadvantage.

Billy lives with his mother and three older siblings in a three-bedroom house, with a shared outdoor play area. His mother left school at 17, and dropped out of college when she became pregnant with her first child. She works as a cleaner during school hours while Billy is with his grandmother. Billy's dad takes casual work when available. At the age of 2½ years, Billy has yet to start talking. His mother describes him as an energetic strong-willed boy who likes to play with his cars or to watch children's videos. Billy does not have a nursery place planned.

Luke is the second child of university-educated parents. His father commutes daily to his office where he manages a personnel department. His mother works part-time in a local company's accounts department. Luke attends day care three days a week while his mother works. Their four-bedroom house has an attractive garden. Aged 2½ years, Luke has only just started talking. He would rather point to make his needs known, or rely on his 5-year-old sister. He is prone to colds and ear infections. His parents have already asked their health visitor for a referral to speech and language therapy, and they are awaiting an assessment appointment.

Luke and Billy come from very different backgrounds. Billy comes from a relatively disadvantaged, low-income household without the potential opportunities afforded by nursery, a healthy diet, a family car, outings, educational toys and so on. What would be the impact of adding positive factors to Billy's situation? A stable income for his father? A regular, good-quality nursery placement? Access to a toy and book library? A monthly parents' support group for his mother? Any one such action could be considered an intervention for Billy.

Luke does not apparently face economic or social disadvantage. However, like Billy he too may be at risk of poor communication skills as a result of reduced stimulation from significant adults and from a low-quality environment. He too may not be ready for school when the time comes. What would be the impact of speech and language therapy for Luke? How much would his spoken vocabulary expand by the age of 3? The lives of Billy and Luke are seemingly worlds apart. What unites them is their common experience of potential risks to their communication development.

UNDERSTANDING RISK

To say that a child is socially disadvantaged is not the same as saying that he will neces- sarily have communication problems. It may be more accurate to say that social disad- vantage puts a child at risk: it is a characteristic that may lead to an identifiable problem if the child encounters particular events or circumstances in the future (OECD, 1995). Billy lives in a poor household. The combination of adverse factors may have made him late to talk. Conversely, positive factors, which have potentially protective effects, are at work in similar households: a grandma who often visits the library with her grandson; an experienced childminder; a steady household income for a particular season. A child develops *resilience* to risks as a result of protective factors. Each stage of development will be affected by different risk and protective factors. Moreover, there is likely to be a dynamic relationship between the level and the range of risk and protective factors and this is likely to lead to a complex interaction rather than a simple linear or one-way relationship. This, in turn, has implications for the appropriateness of different inter- ventions at different stages and indeed intervention can itself be a protective factor. Yet children who appear to have comparable language skills may respond very differently to intervention, since different risk and resilience factors affect them. Furthermore, the relative influence of these factors is likely to change over time, providing different opportunities for effective intervention at different points in the child's development.

INTERVENTIONS TO ENHANCE COMMUNICATION SKILLS

This chapter reviews two bodies of information on interventions to enhance commu- nication skills. The case of children from socio-economically disadvantaged back- grounds, like Billy, is covered by a wide range of interventions often targeting language as one amongst many aspects of the child's development. Large-scale programmes, sometimes with follow-up over several years, have sought, since the 1960s, to alleviate the effects of social disadvantage. Outcomes may be in terms of IQ levels, job attainment or parental well-being, with language being measured indirectly or not at all. By contrast, children like Luke tend to be provided with specific speech and/or language interventions and these will tend to be published in the speech and language therapy literature. In such cases, specific language outcomes are often recorded over a relatively short-term, perhaps 6–12 months.

In judging the extent to which interventions are appropriate for any one group of children, it is clearly important to consider the value of specific intervention programmes. Increasingly this is also necessary for 'evidence-based practice'. The problem is, of course, that is there is often a tension between formal 'scientific' programme evaluation, on the one hand, where variables are controlled or children are allocated to treatment conditions and interventions are held constant, and more loosely defined community interventions, on the other hand, which pay due regard to the nature of the environment in which the child is developing, including familial experiences, but do not control variables and where it is difficult to distinguish the particular experiences of individual children or parents. The former may provide better-measured outcomes than the latter, but they often fail to reflect what commonly occurs in the routine experience of young children, and they may have limited validity.

A MODEL FOR CONCEPTUALISING INTERVENTIONS

It is helpful to describe different kinds of intervention using two different dimensions. One is concerned with the extent to which the intervention is focused on the individual child relative to the community at large; the other is concerned with the extent to which the intervention is delivered by individuals working within strict professional boundaries. These dimensions are described in detail by Tett, Munn, Kay et al. (2001).

Consider an intervention that tries to change a specific output from an individual, such as increasing the number of words spoken by a preschool child. Contrast this with an intervention that seeks to resource a community with low-cost or free access to books, toys and play experiences. Arguably, these are both interventions to enhance communication skills; they vary along the dimension of *individualism*. The former concentrates on changing the speech and language skills of the individual child, the latter on improving that child's access to resources. However, it also recognises the value of changing the broader environment of the child in order, indirectly, to change the experience of the child.

Consider now the kind of intervention where professionals such as doctors, speech and language therapists and clinical psychologists keep to their assigned roles and specialities. This is typical of conventional clinical and medical approaches to intervention. However, it contrasts strongly with the more systemic type of approach in which a team of professionals from different domains work together towards a common goal. This requires the attenuation of professional boundaries and a greater emphasis on team work in the interests of delivering high-quality, timely services to clients. Such interventions vary along the dimension of *professional boundaries*. The former focuses on the specific skills of the individual professional, the latter on the interaction between those of a number of people.

These dimensions are presented in Figure 8.1 as a model for conceptualising different types of intervention. The broader the scope of the intervention around the individual, the more the intervention is focused on the *systemic* or ecological aspects

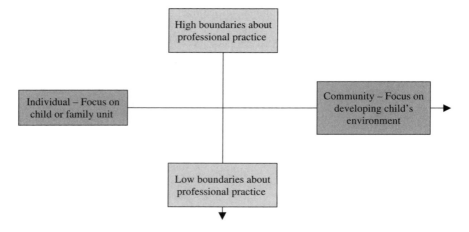

Figure 8.1. A model for conceptualising interventions

of a child's development (Bronfenbrenner, 1979). In broad terms, the literature related to children with identified speech and language difficulties tends to cluster towards the individualistic, clinical end of the spectrum, while the child development literature is more systemic.

UNDERSTANDING OUTCOMES

In discussing the impact of interventions it is important to pay close attention to the outcomes measured. Many of the child development programmes pay relatively little attention to the detail of children's language development, focusing instead on major social outcomes, or using language as a proxy for development in general. When language is assessed, measures are usually confined to the verbal component of an IQ scale or a widely recognised measure of receptive vocabulary such as the Peabody Picture Vocabulary Scale (Dunn & Dunn, 1997). Only rarely do we see a comprehensive assessment of expressive language or narrative skills, pragmatic language skills or parent–child interaction skills, which would traditionally be the focus of speech and language therapy interventions. So, while many of these studies are very sound from the perspective of their design or the way in which the intervention is delivered, they are often very limited in terms of the face validity of the language measures adopted.

The key question, of course, is what constitutes a good outcome for children. This question has been addressed comprehensively in a monograph by a team of researchers with extensive involvement in developing programmes for disadvantaged children (Moore, Evans, Brooks-Gunn & Roth, 1998). They conclude that it is most appropriate to see outcomes as stage-salient tasks of development; in other words, the goals of intervention should change according to the age of the child. But the authors argue that understanding needs to go beyond this to what they call the acquisition of *human capital* such as cognitive capacity, educational attainment, practical risk-taking and delayed gratification, and of *social capacity*, the ability to form close relationships and to demonstrate positive concern and caring in a larger social arena. Clearly, language is a part of the acquisition of human capital but investigators need to be aware that, while it has become relatively straightforward to measure language change, we are still left with the question of the social importance of treatment effects (Goldstein & Geirut, 1998). Only very rarely are broader measures of human capital or social capacity even hinted at in the evaluation of such interventions.

INTERVENTIONS FOR CHILDREN FROM SOCIALLY-DISADVANTAGED BACKGROUNDS

A review of the literature relating to intervention shows that there are three main approaches: (1) the child education strategy; (2) the whole-child strategy; and (3) the community strategy. Aspects of these interventions are outlined, with some key historical programmes described in more detail.

CHILD EDUCATION, *c*. 1962–1972

Intervention targeting the education of the individual child was underpinned by the assumption that it would be sufficient to provide an educational 'boost' to the child in the preschool period to enable him or her to be ready for school. The hope was that children could be lifted up out of poverty, mainly through accessing education and opportunity. Typically children aged 3 or 4 years old were given a year-long full- or part-time placement in childcare centres. Sometimes there was a parental education element. The original Head Start model focused principally on preschool child education. The very first Head Start initiatives run in 1965–1968 were summer programmes for 3–4-year-old children. From 1968 onwards, Head Start developed into a year-round preschool programme, and actively involved parents as participants.

The outcomes recorded were chiefly educational ones, such as IQ, reading and maths grade level, special educational services needed, and so on. This reflected the aim of bringing about educational readiness. There were no outcomes measured specifically for expressive language skills. IQ scores were indeed boosted for the children who received the intervention, but those in the control group had often caught up by the time they were 8 years old. However, the few programmes recording long-term follow-up noted important social benefits for the children in the intervention group. This phase of intervention is summarised in Table 8.1.

The Perry Preschool project (1962) is probably the most famous demonstration programme, although it was far from typical, since there were high resources for each child. A total of 123 children aged 3–4 years took part. A control group received no intervention; the intervention group received five half-days per week

Table 8.1. Characteristics of intervention programmes for disadvantaged children:
1962–1972

Intervention approach	Compensatory education
Description	Education programme for 3–4 year olds; parent guidance
Examples	Perry Preschool Project, Head Start, Abecedarian Project
Typical outcome indicators	IQ scores, reading and maths grade level, % kept down a year in school
Conclusions	Despite early gains in IQ scores seen by age 5 years, control children often caught up by about age 8. Longer-term follow-up for key demonstration projects shows promising social benefits.

of childcare for a whole year. Assignment was random, but with exceptions for siblings, who were placed together, and for employed single parents, whose children were placed in the control group. The intervention group children were taught a mainly Piagetian curriculum developed by the High/Scope Foundation for two and a half hours a day, five days a week. There were weekly home visits.

At age 5, the intervention group average IQ score was 94 compared with 83 for controls. At age 8, however, the intervention group average IQ of 88 was just one point ahead of the average IQ of 87 for controls. Follow-up at age 27 showed that the intervention group children had spent nearly an extra year in school (11.9 years compared to 11.0 years). Criminality and employment outcomes at age 27 favoured the intervention group. The control group had been arrested twice as often as the intervention group: 4.6 times compared with 2.3 times. Although the groups had similar levels of employment, those who had been in the intervention group had higher wages. Also, only 25% of the intervention group had spent time in jail, compared with 33% of the controls. The importance of this project, as a research study, is lessened by its small sample size. Rather, its historical impact lies mainly in the length of follow-up and in the social outcomes measured. It is clear from their monitoring of adult outcomes that the investigators expected broad and wide-ranging treatment effects. The actual IQ scores recorded are low average for both groups.

The 1972 Abecedarian project, which took children from the age of 6–8 weeks through to 8 years, was unusual in a time when not many infants were cared for out of the home. The 111 infants were divided into four groups: control (no intervention); preschool intervention only, up to the age of 5 years; school-age intervention only, from 5 to 8 years; and preschool plus school-age intervention, up to the age of 8 years. Assignment to groups was random, but exceptions were made for siblings to be together. The sample was 97% African American.

The preschool intervention consisted of day care for the infants in a child development centre from a mean age of 8 weeks, parental support, and sessions on parenting and child development. The school-only intervention comprised home-school coordination. From 18 months to 4½ years of age, the intervention group children had a lead of an average of 10 IQ points. From age 5 to 21, the gap in IQ narrowed, so that by age 21, the intervention group children had an average IQ of 90 compared with 85 for the controls (a lead of less than half a standard deviation). Reading and maths levels were higher for the preschool intervention group than for the controls at ages 12, 15 and 21 years, again by, at most, half a standard deviation. Absolute levels of reading achievement were below the population norm; for example, reading at age 15 was at the 31st percentile for the preschool intervention group (Campbell, Pungello, Miller-Johnson, Burchinal & Ramey 2001). However, more of the intervention group were enrolled in higher education, and fewer had become parents. Those in employment were working in better-rated jobs.

The school-only intervention was not effective. The majority of pupils at the receiving school for the intervention group children were from white, university-educated families, so the school may not have been well placed to meet the needs of poor African American children. Once again, IQ scores were shown to be at the low-average level when participants were followed up. As in the Perry Preschool project, the Abecedarian project sample was small. However, the study was well controlled, and follow-up took place over a considerable length of time. To summarise, the programme gave rise to improved social outcomes and more modest cognitive gains.

COMPREHENSIVE 'WHOLE CHILD' PROGRAMMES, c. 1972–1992

From about 1972, Head Start began to spearhead the move towards thinking about the whole child. At that time in the USA, medical and social services were often out of the reach of disadvantaged families. Head Start pioneered 'comprehensive' or 'integrated' services, which aimed to bring not just educational preschool care, but also basic healthcare, inoculations, developmental checks and social care for family crises. Interventions typically included home visits, parent groups, full or part-time childcare, as well as a range of other services, by referral or direct provision. Examples in the USA are the Comprehensive Child Development Programme (CCDP, 1989–1994, 21 sites) and the Infant Health and Development Programme (IHDP, 1990–1993, 985 low birth-weight babies). Recorded outcomes were parenting indicators (parent child-rearing attitudes, parent–child interaction, using the Home Observation for Measurement of the Environment (HOME) inventory (Caldwell & Bradley, 2003)) and child scores (Wechsler Preschool and Primary Scales of Intelligence (WPPSI), Peabody Picture Vocabulary Test (PPVT), behaviour ratings). The only language outcome was receptive vocabulary skills according to the PPVT. Table 8.2 provides a summary of the characteristics of these programmes.

The CCDP offered services from birth to the age of 5 years, although many families used services over one or two years only. Over the many sites, the consistency of services is likely to have varied and also the actual level of interventions

Table **8.2.** Characteristics of intervention programmes for disadvantaged
children: 1972–1995

Intervention approach	Comprehensive services
Description	Programmes provided a range of services for health, early development and social care for at-risk children. Home visits, parent groups, full- or part-time childcare
Examples	Comprehensive Child Development Programme, Infant Health and Development Programme
Typical outcome indicators	Parent-child rearing attitudes, parent–child interaction, HOME inventory, child scores on WPPSI, PPVT, behaviour ratings
Conclusions	No clear gains in child outcomes for the intervention groups at age 8 years.

received by families would have been very wide. In the CCDP, the intervention group children had equivalent outcomes to the controls, except that the intervention group mothers showed more sensitivity to their babies' cues, and spent more time with their babies.

The IHDP programme content drew on earlier programmes, Project Care and the Abecedarian programme, applying them to low birth-weight infants, most of whom were also from low-income families. The families were randomised to receive standard medical follow-up only (control group) or a programme of home visits from birth to age 3 years. These took place weekly, then fortnightly in the second and third years, with a half-day childcare element in the second and third years. There were also parents' groups every two months in the second and third years. At age 3 years, the intervention group mothers were more often employed, and had higher levels of mutuality during parent–child problem solving. By age 3 years, the children in the intervention group were ahead on receptive vocabulary (PPVT) and IQ scores (WPPSI). However, by age 8, the treatment and control groups had equivalent scores on WPPSI, PPVT, and on behaviour ratings.

It has been suggested that reasons for the lack of longer term effects could include the following: the intervention was not appropriate for multi-risk families (i.e. low income plus low birth-weight baby); the intervention was not long enough; or the attrition of families who could have responded well was disproportionately high.

THE WHOLE FAMILY, *c.* 1992–PRESENT

In 1995, the Early Head Start was launched in the USA, and was a downward extension of Head Start to children from birth to the age of 3 years. This represented a new, distinctive shift in emphasis on childcare, facilitating not only the child's development but also the carer's re-entry into the labour market. Parental needs for skills, training and work have been brought to the forefront, just as much as the child's developmental needs. This is the 'two-generation' approach, operating in the politically-motivated context of fewer 'handouts' for parents not employed out of the home, and the social context of greater flux in the family unit, and technological advances having raised the threshold of skills needed for entry to higher-paying jobs.

In the UK, Sure Start began in 1997 to focus on deprived neighbourhoods, often using a whole-child approach. Since 2002, programmes have been encouraged to take this two-generation approach, facilitating childcare to enable parents to work. It is too early yet to know if the approach is having the intended effect. The National Evaluation of Sure Start (NESS) team conducted more than 8000 observations in Sure Start households, and 3000 in non-Sure Start households, using a wide range of child, parenting and family measures (see next paragraph) and reported preliminary findings as to the impact of local Sure Start programmes (NESS Research Team, 2004). Their initial conclusion was that mothers and carers in programme areas were observed to treat their children in a warmer and more accepting manner than in comparison areas. As an early finding, the changes in parenting manner might be expected to improve family dynamics and have a follow-through effect on child development measures. Table 8.3 summarises the whole-family intervention approach.

It is not easy to measure the 'amount' of intervention received, nor its nature, when a programme is rolled out over more than 500 sites as in the case of Sure Start (UK), or 664 sites, as in the case of Early Head Start (USA) (Coote, Allen & Woodhead, 2004). Parent outcomes measured by NESS include malaise, parent–child conflict, parent–child closeness, home learning environment, support when needed and services used. Child outcomes include: measures of independence, cognitive functioning, verbal and non-verbal abilities, accidents and hospital admissions. The language measure is the verbal subscale of the British Ability Scales (Elliot, Smith & McCulloch, 1996).

Table 8.3. Characteristics of intervention programmes for disadvantaged children: 1995–present

Intervention approach	Whole-family approach; 'two generation'
Description	Meeting parental needs for skills and work combined with high-quality childcare opportunities
Examples	Early Head Start (USA), Sure Start (UK)
Typical outcome indicators	Child: measures of independence, cognitive functioning (e.g. British Ability Scales (BAS) (Elliot, Smith & McCulloch, 1996), Bayley Scales of Infant Development (Bayley, 1993)), verbal and non-verbal abilities (e.g. Peabody Picture Vocabulary Test (Dunn & Dunn, 1997)), accidents and hospital admissions. Parent: malaise, parent–child conflict, parent–child closeness, home learning environment, support when needed, services used

The history of the evaluation of Head Start follows these developments in intervention design. Head Start began as a summer child education programme (1965–1968), and then expanded to a year-long programme with parent participation. It was a pioneer of the delivery of comprehensive services and parent involvement. Since 1995, Early Head Start has expanded on the two-generation model of intervention.

Evaluation efforts have been refined, so that the evaluation of Early Head Start has used a wide range of measures to chart developments for the child, the family, the community and for the staff involved in the programmes. The impact study has looked at different types of programme, different degrees of implementation, different family subgroups and different levels of participation. Crucially, the Early Head Start Research and Evaluation (EHSRE) project has also included a control group of families who receive only standard services rather than specific Early Head Start services. Some 3000 families from among those enrolled in 1995–6 formed the cohort for the EHSRE project. The main report (EHSRE, 2002) found benefits at the level of the child, for parenting and for parental self-sufficiency (training and employment). Interestingly, the families rated at moderate risk demonstrated the most overall benefit. Families at high risk may have been 'overwhelmed' and unable to take advantage of new services. This indicates the importance of timing and the capacity of a family to benefit from an intervention. There were positive findings for each of the different programme types, but the best results are for mixed-approach programmes combining both home-based and centre-based childcare. A pre-kindergarten follow-up study of the Early Head Start cohort was conducted over 2001–2004, but the findings are not yet available. The language measures used were the MacArthur Communicative Development Inventories (MCDI) (Fenson, Pethick, Renda et al., 2000; MCDI Advisory Board, 1997) and the PPVT-III. Intervention group children scored higher at age 2 years on the MCDI measures of spoken vocabulary, combining words into sentences and sentence complexity score. At age 3 years, intervention group children scored higher on receptive vocabulary on the PPVT. The researchers note that the mean scores on the PPVT for both control and intervention children still fall below the norm. The mean standard score for intervention group children was 83.3, compared with 81.1 for the control children (with 100 as the population average standard score).

Longer term evidence for the usefulness of Head Start suggests that results are equivocal: modest gains are made initially but fade out later. The most famous preschool, the Perry Preschool, which was richly resourced and conducted under ideal conditions, found positive social results. The Perry Preschool sample of 123 is tiny, however, compared to the thousands of children going through Head Start under 'everyday' conditions. Reviews of the corpus of evidence relating to Head Start conclude that short-term gains in intelligence scores and learning skills disappear for most Head Start students after two or three years at school. Long-term evidence for social effects on employment, crime, high school graduation rates and teen pregnancy 'simply doesn't exist' (Hood, 2004, p. 502). Past approaches to evaluation and measures have not served well to capture the complexity of the many interventions called Head Start.

INTERVENTIONS DESIGNED TO ADDRESS COMMUNICATION SKILLS DIRECTLY

Children may experience language-learning difficulties either as a *primary* language impairment, in the sense that the language-learning difficulty is the most obvious area of concern for the child, or *secondary* to other conditions. In the main, studies of children with primary language difficulties either include children who are relatively advantaged or do not report details on the social background of the children in their studies. In such studies there is much more emphasis on capturing language variables than on characterising the sample using social markers. Nevertheless, a recent systematic review of the literature related to intervention for primary language impairment has indicated that positive results can be detected in the short term for expressive language, vocabulary and speech difficulties (Law, Garrett & Nye 2004). The two most prominent areas where there appears to be little evidence of treatment effects are in pragmatics and verbal comprehension. These two areas are often considered the strongest markers for negative outcomes and yet they have received least attention as far as intervention is concerned.

One important characteristic of these interventions is that they are mostly of relatively short duration. Rarely does intervention received by any individual child exceed 30 hours. This falls far short of the level of intervention commonly delivered by any of the more successful Head Start programmes, and sometimes this level is so low that it seems improbable that there could be any effect (Law & Conti-Ramsden, 2000). Studies that have specifically targeted children from socially-disadvantaged backgrounds with poor language skills have shown that standard, low-dosage speech and language interventions tend to have relatively little impact on the language skills of such children, especially if children experience both expressive and receptive language difficulties (Law, Kot & Barnett, 1999). Given what we know from the evaluation of early intervention programmes in the USA, this lack of impact is probably no surprise. Indeed, it provides a stark warning against assuming that a time-limited, clinical, model of service delivery is appropriate for children with a broad range of social and language difficulties.

In terms of our model, speech and language therapy interventions have tended to be on the individualistic end of the continuum commonly delivered by specialist professionals. There are moves for speech and language therapists to work indirectly through others, such as parents, carers, teachers and others with regular, direct contact with children, and there are now also many instances in practice of widened collaborations and skills sharing. However, where collaboration is difficult to initiate or sustain (such as through funding pressures, staff reluctance, lack of shared premises, etc.), the speech and language therapist may return to an individualised clinical model of therapy (Law, Lindsay, Peacey et al., 2002). In other words, there is a creative tension in the way in which speech and language therapists deliver their services to children. While they commonly recognise the need to engage with a wide range of people associated with a given child they often feel reluctant to commit to an indirect model unless they feel confident of the skills of the people with whom they are collaborating. In the event that this confidence declines the default is often to return to the individualistic model of service delivery.

SUMMARY

The overall picture is uneven. The quantitative evidence from the general child development literature for children from areas of socio-economic disadvantage is far from definitive. There are modest gains on selected dimensions of parenting, and 'intermittent effects' on child development (Halpern, 2000, p. 375). In terms of communication skills, there can be positive short-term gains, but there is still relatively little information on long-term benefits. At the practice level, the research supports intervention programmes that aim for early enrolment, integrated services, high-quality curricula delivered full-time by well-trained staff and which address the agenda of parents as well as children.

In terms of evaluation methodology, it is clearly difficult to measure the effects of variable-dosage multiple interventions for large cohorts of children. Within a framework of risk and resilience, it is plausible that valid interventions do not always produce developmental change in all the children studied. Intervention may, however, produce or increase resilience in a child, and thereby mitigate a range of risks. Programme goals could be rethought. Rather than seeking to effect specific changes in specific skills in individual children, goals could be reframed in

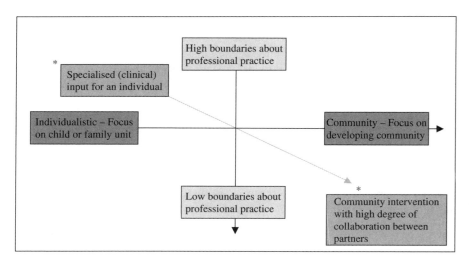

Figure 8.2. The relative positions of intervention programmes targeting the individual child and the community

Note: * The asterisks represent interventions in a two-dimensional space.

terms of developing resilience and capacity within communities so as to facilitate change within individuals. Developing (community) resources, rather than bringing in (expert) services, would be the medium- to long-term aim of interventions for children in areas of socio-economic disadvantage. This, in terms of the model in Figure 8.1, represents moving from one quadrant to another, as shown in Figure 8.2.

CONCLUSION

It has become clear since the 1960s that interventions aiming to address social disadvantage in general and communication skills in particular are difficult to implement; it is also hard to show that they work in more than the short term. Yet it would appear that the measurement tools used in many of these studies do not reflect our developing understanding of children's development, social well-being and communicative abilities. It is important that those seeking to promote children's communication skills do not focus exclusively on the measurement of speech, language and social skills. Our knowledge of risk and resilience remains imperfect and it is unclear to what extent, for example, that improved communication skills act as a buffer to underachievement in school. The key issue is the overall aims of the intervention programmes concerned and the outcomes that we seek for children.

Finally, there remains a gap between traditional evaluation research and 'real life' for many practitioners and families. We conclude with a metaphorical interpretation of the tensions associated with intervention research in this area.

> Rigour refers to the high hard ground where practitioners make use of rigorous research. In contrast the swamp is a lowland full of messy and confusing problems. Problems associated with life on the cliff are mostly of interest to researchers and research/practitioners who function as technical experts. The problems of greatest social concern and importance however, exist in the swamp. These are the most challenging and complex.
>
> (Schon, 1983, 1987, cited in Volpe, 1998, p. 153)

REFERENCES

Bayley, N. (1993). *Bayley Scales of Infant Development* (2nd edn). New York: The Psychological Corporation, Harcourt Brace and Company.

Bronfenbrenner, U. (1979). *The ecology of human development: experiments by nature and design*. Cambridge, MA: Harvard University Press.

Caldwell B. M. & Bradley R. H. (2003). *Administration Manual: Home Observation for Measurement of the Environment [HOME]*. Little Rock, AR: University of Arkansas.

Campbell, F. A., Pungello, E. P., Miller-Johnson, S., Burchinal, M. & Ramey, C. T. (2001). The development of cognitive and academic abilities: Growth curves from an early childhood educational experiment. *Developmental Psychology*, **37**(2), 231–242.

Coote A., Allen, J. & Woodhead, D. (2004). *Finding out what works: Understanding complex, community-based initiatives*. London: King's Fund. Available at www.kingsfund.org. uk/publications

Conti-Ramsden, G. (1994). Language interaction with atypical language learners. In C. Gallaway and B. Richards (Eds.), *Input and interaction in language acquisition*. Cambridge: Cambridge University Press.

Dunn, L. M. & Dunn, L. M. (1997). *Peabody Picture Vocabulary Test –III*. Circle Pines, MN: American Guidance Service.

Early Head Start Research and Evaluation project (2002). *Making a difference in the lives of infants and toddlers and their families: The impacts of Early Head Start*. Executive summary. Retrieved 28 January, 2005, from www.acf.hhs.gov/programs/core/ ongoing_research/ehs/ehs_intro.html

Edwards, J. (1989). *Language and disadvantage (2nd edn)*. London: Whurr.

Elliot, C. D., Smith, P. & McCulloch, K. (1996). *British Ability Scales Second Edition (BAS II)*. Slough: NFER-Nelson.

Farran, D. C. (2000). Another decade of intervention for children who are low-income or disabled: What do we know now? In J. P. Shonkoff and S. J. Meisels (Eds.), *Handbook of early childhood intervention (2nd edn)*. Cambridge: Cambridge University Press.

Fenson, L., Pethick, S., Renda, C., Cox, J. L., Dale, P. S., & Reznick, J. S. (2000). Short-form versions of the MacArthur Communicative Development Inventories. *Applied Psycholinguistics*, **21**, 95–115.

Goldstein, H. & Geirut, J. (1998). Outcome measurement in child language and phonological disorders. In C. M. Frattali (Ed.), *Measuring outcome in speech-language pathology*, pp. 388–406. New York: Thieme.

Halpern, R. (2000). Early intervention for low-income children and families. In J. P. Shonkoff and S. J. Meisels (Eds.), *Handbook of early childhood intervention (2nd edn)*. Cambridge: Cambridge University Press.

Hart, B. & Risley, T. R. (1995). *Meaningful differences in the everyday experience of young American children*. Baltimore: Paul Brookes.

Hood, J. (2004). Caveat emptor. The Head Start scam. In E. Zigler and S. J. Styfco (Eds.), *The Head Start Debates*. Baltimore, MD: Paul Brookes.

Law, J. & Conti-Ramsden, G. (2000). Treating children with speech and language impairments for six hours is not enough. *British Medical Journal*, **321**, 908–909.

Law, J., Kot, A. & Barnett, G., (1999). The efficacy of intervention for young children with severe language impairment: Report to North Thames Regional Health Authority. Available from the first author at Centre for Integrated Healthcare Research, Queen Margaret University College, Edinburgh EH12 8TS.

Law, J., Lindsay, G., Peacey, N., Gascoigne, M., Soloff, N., Radford, J. & Band, S. (2002). Consultation as a model for providing speech and language therapy in schools: a panacea or one step too far. *Child Language Teaching and Therapy*, **18**(2), 145–165.

Law, J., Garrett, Z. & Nye, C. (2004) The effectiveness of speech and language therapy interventions for children with primary speech and language delay or disorder. *Journal of Speech, Language and Hearing Research*. **47**, 924–943.

Locke, A. Ginsborg, J. & Peers, I. (2002). Development and disadvantage: Implications for the early years and beyond. *International Journal of Language and Communication Disorders*, **37**, 3–15.

MacArthur Communicative Development Inventories Advisory Board (1997). *MacArthur Communicative Development Inventories*. San Diego, CA: San Diego State University.

Moore, K. A. Evans, V. J., Brooks-Gunn, J. & Roth, J. (1998). *What are good child outcomes?* Washington: Child Trends.

NESS Research Team (2004). The National Evaluation of Sure Start Local Programmes in England. *Child and Adolescent Mental Health*, **9**(1), 2–8.

OECD (1995). *Our children at risk.* Report by the Centre for Educational Research and Innovation for the Council of the Organisation for Economic Co-operation and Development. Paris: OECD.

Puckering, C. & Rutter, M. (1987). Environmental influences on language development. In W. Yule and M. Rutter (Eds.), *Language development and disorders*. Oxford: McKeith Press.

Tett, L., Munn, P., Kay, H., Martin, I., Martin, J. & Ranson, S. (2001). Schools, community education and collaborative practice in Scotland. In S. Riddell and L. Tett (Eds.), *Education, social justice and inter-agency working: joined-up or fractured policy?* London: Routledge.

Schon, D. (1983). *The reflective practitioner*. New York: Basic Books.

Schon, D. (1987). *Education for the reflective practitioner: Toward a new design for teaching and learning in the professions*. San Francisco, CA: Josey-Bass.

Volpe, R. (1998). *Knowledge from Evaluation Research in Children and Families at Risk: New issues in integrating services*. OECD proceedings, Centre for Educational Research and Innovation. Paris: OECD.

II Research Reports

9 Interventions to Promote Language Development in Socially Disadvantaged Children

JAMES LAW

Centre for Integrated Healthcare Research, Queen Margaret University, Edinburgh, UK

The chapters in the first part of this book have shown that the level of risk experienced by socially disadvantaged children is now widely recognised, as is the central role of language in reducing or increasing risk. Given this recognition a key question is: what should we be doing about it? In this second part a number of different models of service delivery from the UK are described. They do not provide a complete picture, of course, but can be seen as snapshots of good practice. Decisions about how best to enhance children's well-being must now be informed by evidence-based practice, and one of the key features of the models that have been selected for inclusion in this book is that they are in the process of being evaluated. Together, they highlight the degree to which language development has become key to so many aspects of child welfare and some of these are picked out in the following overview.

LANGUAGE DEVELOPMENT IS A PUBLIC HEALTH ISSUE

At one level it is possible to derive some pretty simple messages from the chapters in Part I. Socially disadvantaged children tend to be at risk for all sorts of negative outcomes of which delayed or inadequate language competence is one. Given the generic nature of this statement, it is possible to argue that language-learning difficulties are a societal or even a public health issue requiring a public health response. The solution might be, then, for the state to provide people with better houses and employment opportunities and stop tinkering around the edges with educational programmes and humanistic notions of therapy directed at the child (and possibly the mother). Are we adopting a model of intervention rooted in the nuclear family that locates the problem within the individual? Of course, one answer

Language and Social Disadvantage: Theory into Practice Edited by J. Clegg and J. Ginsborg
© 2006 John Wiley & Sons, Ltd

is that it depends on how the child's needs are identified and what is being proposed in the way of intervention. As Pickstone (Chapter 9.1) suggests, formal language screening to identify children with language needs is not the most effective way of going forward. Rather, we should be trying to raise the level of participation in language-enhancing activities of the target populations, and not merely providing services for the usual suspects: parents, who are already actively searching out provision for their children. Similarly, messages about talking and listening to children and encouraging them to communicate should come within the remit of the public health authorities, and not be the sole province of one professional group or another.

LANGUAGE DEVELOPMENT IS AN EARLY YEARS ISSUE

To a certain extent this has been addressed by the promotion of early years provision for all children and increasing the skills levels of those providing such services. It is difficult to see how progress can be made unless all those who regularly interact with children value communication in and of itself and for what it can do to help them negotiate their way through their environment. A number of such programmes have been developed but all too often they get no further than the very earliest stages of development. Hobbs's description (Chapter 9.2) of an evaluation of the Teaching Children Talking programme for children in what is known in the UK as the Foundation Stage, that is, below 6 years of age, does just this, presenting outcomes from a treated and an untreated group. This report highlights the inevitable difficulties of working in the methodological swamplands of practice to which we refer in Chapter 8 in Part I.

LANGUAGE DEVELOPMENT IS AN EDUCATIONAL ISSUE

For many years, there has been a tension between 'clinical' and 'educational' models of service delivery. This is sometimes construed as a question of location: children may be withdrawn from school in order to receive an intervention provided in a *clinical* setting or the intervention may take place in an *educational* setting, such as the school classroom. However, it is probably more helpful to see the distinction between clinical and educational models in terms of whether children's difficulties are seen as originating primarily within the individual or if they are seen as arising from the environment in which the child is raised, including the school as well as the home. It could be argued that both options – clinical and educational – should be kept open at the start of any intervention, so that those carrying out the therapy or language support can address the needs of all parties. The critical issue is the extent to which the child is able to cope in the environments to which he or she is exposed. From an educational perspective it is essential that interventions reflect and enhance children's educational experiences, particularly in relation to the curriculum (see Joffe, Chapter 9.7), through which language is taught and learnt. And this needs to be true throughout the child's experience of school.

Clearly, as emphasised by several authors represented here, the key to effective provision in schools is the collaboration between all those involved in providing services to children: teaching assistants, speech and language therapists, special needs or classroom teachers or, indeed, students (see Leyden and Szczerbinski, Chapter 9.5). But it is sometimes easier to say that interested parties should collaborate than it is to achieve that collaboration. The devil is in the detail. The key is identifying how people collaborate and being honest about what works and what does not.

There is a need for those who work with children to be better informed about the relationship between language and academic achievement particularly insofar as it affects socially disadvantaged children. It is easy enough to say that people interacting with children need to 'do more' of whatever it is they already do. Yet the question remains as to why they were not doing more of it in the first place and whether it is simply a matter of providing information or a training programme for the scales to fall from their eyes and their behaviour patterns to change dramatically. In reality it is much more complex that this. As Farmer and Griffiths (Chapter 9.3) suggest, it may be necessary to develop methods for promoting the co-construction of meaning between children and adults; furthermore, a hands-on approach may be more effective than training for many early years workers. Again, professional practice only changes as the result of the day-to-day experiences of workers in the field. It is the grounded practice of professionals that determines whether practice really changes.

LANGUAGE DEVELOPMENT AS AN ECOLOGICAL ISSUE

What can be seen as an individual performance issue is, in fact, a complex interaction between the individual and the environment. It is helpful here to adopt the type of bio-ecological approach advocated by Bronfenbrenner (2005). The individual can only be seen within that broader context and interventions should pay attention to this. This is rare, Sure Start being one of the only major initiatives in the UK, although there are others in other countries, that have specifically included community development in their targets. The way in which children become members of their communities is central to this. Language can often play an important role here but to date very little attention has been paid to this issue in terms of intervention. Key here is the reciprocal nature of the interaction between the child's skills and the environment. It is tempting to see the effect of the environment on the child as essentially one-way: the more you speak to children, the more they speak back. However, the relationship between children and the environment works both ways. As children start to speak more they make more demands – verbal and otherwise – on parents and caregivers. Schoon, Brynner, Joshi et al. (2002) have shown that the extent to which adults are able to respond to children's changing demands may reflect their beliefs about child development, their social network and the availability of local resources to help them meet their own needs. Little is known, however, about the role of these factors in children's language development.

LANGUAGE DEVELOPMENT AS A SET OF DIFFERENTIATED SKILLS

The extent to which an intervention can be said to be successful is all too often measured in terms of generic, standardised, 'composite' language measures. This is sensible enough if it is generic composite language skills that we are trying to improve. However, there is a risk that such an approach does not help us to see where particular interventions are most effective. In other words, the effects on individual skills get lost in the melting pot of the composite measure. Dockrell, Stuart, and King (Chapter 9.4) suggest, in their analysis of the effects of the Teacher Talking programme, that it may be useful to be clearer about which language skills we are actually aiming to enhance in our interventions. Specifically, they recommend the separation and individual targeting of vocabulary, narrative and inferencing skills. Similarly, Leyden and Szczerbinski (Chapter 9.5) suggest that the key variables are listening and conversational skills, more generally, while Joffe (Chapter 9.7) emphasises the need to improve vocabulary and narrative skills.

It would seem that young children's language development is particularly susceptible to environmental pressures. That said, it is important to see language difficulties in the context of other problems experienced by children. So, for example, many children with language learning difficulties also have behaviour problems. Irrespective of the mechanism proposed to explain the relationship between the two, the findings of Stringer's study (Chapter 9.6) suggest that socially disadvantaged children with language and behaviour difficulties should be prioritised for intervention.

LANGUAGE DEVELOPMENT INTO ADULTHOOD

Language is often construed as something that develops in the early years and at one level this is obviously true. However, as our knowledge of the course of language development improves, so it becomes clear that, a few late bloomers aside, children with difficulties developing language often go on to experience all sorts of problems in school both academically and socially. In the UK, services for such children have tended to stop at the end of the primary school period, when children are about 11 years old. The rationale for this is unclear but researchers and practitioners are becoming increasingly aware that many children experience difficulties with language and literacy in high school or secondary school. As Stringer demonstrates (Chapter 9.6), it is likely that links between language and behaviour may be a key determinant of such problems in this older age group. It is almost certainly true that intervention studies need to monitor changes in both domains, perhaps specifically examining the effect of interventions targeting speech and language on behaviour over time. These may be most effective for older children when the focus is on their verbal interactions with their peers, as Joffe suggests (Chapter 9.7). Ultimately, however, young people leave school and look for work. They may well come up against economic and employment policies limiting prospects for people with communication difficulties.

So what do we do about it? Data from relatively large-scale intervention programmes in the USA suggest that, despite very limited language outcomes, enough of the right sort of intervention can be effective in other ways, such as greatly improved life chances. But how does this map onto practice in the UK? This volume, and in particular Part II, aims to answer this question.

LANGUAGE DEVELOPMENT AS AN ISSUE OF EFFICACY

The first stage in the development of any intervention study is the proper development of the intervention itself. This needs to start with an understanding that there is something that educational and health services can do to address a difficulty that the child is experiencing. But this is just the start of the process of moving towards evidence-based intervention for these children. These research reports demonstrate the awareness that intervention, once developed, needs to be evaluated. Whether or not this involves 'manualising' the intervention, the fact is that, whatever activities are involved, they need to be sufficiently well specified for someone else to use them. As Dockrell and her colleagues suggest (Chapter 9.4), we need go beyond 'best practice' or consensus guidelines to pay attention to both the 'what' and the 'how' of intervention. We have moved beyond describing good practice. We need to know how these interventions affect the child's performance and we need to be as clear as we can that the intervention must do substantially more than that which would be achieved simply over the course of time, especially against the background of normal language development.

REFERENCES

Bronfenbrenner, U. (2005). *Making human beings human: bioecological perspectives on human development.* London: Sage.

Schoon, I., Brynner, J., Joshi, H., Parsons, S., Wiggins, R. D. & Sacker, A. (2002). The influence of context, timing and duration of risk experiences for the passage from childhood to mid-adulthood. *Child Development*, **73**(5), 1486–1504.

9.1 Participation in Sure Start: Lessons from Language Screening

CAROLINE PICKSTONE

Institute of General Practice, University of Sheffield

BACKGROUND

SURE START

There has been growing concern that many disadvantaged children enter nursery and school with inadequate skills in language and that these hamper their ability to access the curriculum (Baird, 2001; Kelly, 1998). It may be possible to identify these children during their preschool years and provide early intervention to improve their skills. Screening all preschool children for language delay is not indicated (Law, Boyle, Harris, Harkness & Nye, 1998), because – aside from the financial cost – the predictive validity of such screening tends to be low (Klee, Carson, Gavin et al., 1998) and screening on a single occasion cannot capture the patterns of change inherent in developmental difficulties (National Screening Committee, 2001). However, it is worth screening populations thought to be at increased risk for developmental delays; this is consistent with targeting for health interventions, based on the presence of known risk factors marking out individuals more likely to have particular disorders. Targeted screening is expected to be more cost-effective than mass screening, should have a higher predictive value in areas of increased prevalence (Rose, 1992) and should identify individuals with reversible risk factors, which can then be the focus of intervention (Gordis, 1996). This report focuses on participation in a language-screening programme in the light of these predictions, rather than on the detail of the programme itself (see Pickstone, 2003, for details of the full research study).

Sure Start consists of a range of early childhood programmes, funded and established following the Comprehensive Spending Review of 1997 (Her Majesty's Treasury, 1998), in which the UK government identified children in poverty as a major area of investment. Early intervention programmes of this type were new in the UK but drew on lessons learned from years of experience and research in the USA. Sure Start programmes all emphasise the intergenerational nature of poverty and disadvantage, aim to strengthen local communities, reduce inequality

Language and Social Disadvantage: Theory into Practice Edited by J. Clegg and J. Ginsborg
© 2006 John Wiley & Sons, Ltd

and improve children's health and learning (Blunkett, 1999). The programmes serve families who live in areas of disadvantage, based on geographical targeting using mean income levels. Such families may be socially excluded or marginalized; this means that, hitherto, they may have been 'hard to reach', and it can be quite challenging to engage them, for example, in health- and childcare services. The research described below was carried out in a Sure Start 'trailblazer', part of the first wave of programmes set up in 1999 to develop practice and test new models.

THE IMPORTANCE OF ENGAGING FAMILIES

Although Sure Start programmes are given considerable flexibility in responding to local needs, a set of Public Service Agreement (PSA) targets provide a common framework for measuring change (Sure Start Unit, 2000). The PSA targets for language development required programmes to survey the language attainments of children in the community, and to carry out screening in order to identify children who needed referral for specialist assessment. Two sources of evidence suggested that a high level of language needs would be found in the local area. First, services appear to be under-used based on the numbers of referrals to speech and language therapy (SLT). Local audit data (unpublished) revealed that only 10% of the expected number of children was referred for assessment. Second, the proportion of children with language delay on entry to school was high: 65% of girls and 80% of boys scored one or more than one standard deviation below the mean on standardized tests of language skills (Locke, Ginsborg & Peers, 2002).

The current project aimed to screen and survey the language attainment of preschool children in the area, involving the maximum number of children so that an accurate picture could be obtained overall, and to ensure that children requiring referral were not missed. The term 'screening' is used here in the loosest sense as it is well known that screening for language delay cannot fulfil the classical criteria for screening programmes (see National Screening Committee, 2001, for a discussion; Wilson & Jungner, 1968).

The use of both survey and screening methods made it possible to determine the percentage of children who were:

1. showing signs of language delay (on the basis of observations by parents and others);
2. showing signs of clinically-significant language delay (in this case defined as being below the level of the 10th centile);
3. at risk for long-term problems with language development, literacy or learning.

The first group may benefit from opportunities for language learning in preschool settings but do not need clinical services. The second group is a clinical population whose skills in language are at the low end of the range for their age; they may therefore benefit from specialist assessment and early therapeutic intervention. Research suggests that the group of 'late talking' children performing at or below the level of the 10th centile at 24 months of age will include about 50% who are likely to experience subsequent language disorders, although the remainder will improve spontaneously (Kelly, 1998).

INVOLVEMENT OF SUPPORT WORKERS

In common with many Sure Start programmes, support workers took front-line roles. Locally, the support workers were trained nursery nurses who offered home visits to parents of children under the age of 2 years, to increase their knowledge and confidence about parenting and provide a link with health- and childcare provision. Typically, little systematic effort had been made previously in many disadvantaged communities to increase the use of health- and childcare services. Thus, the programme needed to find ways of measuring attainments to monitor change and to identify the subgroup of children who needed specialist assessment from SLTs and access to early intervention, encouraging families to use these services quite possibly for the first time. Since home visiting was carried out by support workers, and they would have access to all the families in the Sure Start area, it made sense for them to carry out both the survey and the screening for language delay. When the programme began in 1999, however, the Sure Start Language Measure (Sure Start Unit, 2001), a language skills survey, was not yet available and there were few instruments suitable for the purposes of survey and screening. The support workers already had knowledge of child development, in relation to children aged 3 years and above, but lacked the skills to carry out developmental assessments. In order to maximise consistency between assessments, it was decided to use a standardised test. A review was therefore undertaken of all the instruments that might prove suitable (Pickstone, Hannon & Fox, 2002). The criteria for selection were UK standardisation on a sample including disadvantaged groups, receptive and expressive language norms and suitability for use in homes by support staff. Although none of the instruments available at the time met all of these requirements, the First Words Test (Gillham, Boyle & Smith, 1997) was selected and has proved to be highly suitable. It uses an appealing picture book to test single word use, and a structured parental report to determine children's expressive vocabulary and sentence length.[1]

BRIEF SUMMARY OF METHODS

SETTING

The research took place between November, 2000 and March, 2003 (see Pickstone, 2003, for a full account). A brief summary is offered here to provide the reader with enough detail to inform the discussion of targeted screening that follows.

---

[1] The UK standardisation included children from disadvantaged groups but did not include black and minority ethnic (BME) groups of children for whom English is not a first language. In the case of the local programme this was not a drawback because fewer than 1% of the local population are from BME groups.

Demographic information about the local area at the start of the Sure Start local programme provides some information about the setting:

- Population 12,140, including 920 children under the age of 4 years
- 96% white British; 1.2% mixed ethnic group; 1.8% Asian; and less than 1% black or black British
- Unemployment 11.2% (30% if those excluded because of incapacity and illness are added)
- In lowest 1% of wards using Index of Multiple Deprivation (IMD), 2000, and in lowest 2% using IMD child poverty index
- 70% children under 16 years live in homes receiving means-tested benefits

SUPPORT WORKERS

Support workers had had two years' training in child development, and a local two-day training course covering language development in the 18- to 30-month period, risk factors for language disorders and the use of the First Words Test. An additional day was used to establish inter-judge agreement between the support workers and the researcher (a qualified SLT).

PARTICIPANTS

Children in the area between 20 and 24 months of age were identified from the local Sure Start database. This uses notification data for all new births in the area by postcode, and information from the child health database of all children registered with a GP. The database is updated weekly to show families moving into and out of the area. There were no exclusion criteria. All the parents of such children ($n = 525$) were offered a home visit to check their child's language. Contact to arrange a visit was made by letter or telephone. In some cases, as many as seven visits were offered to ensure that a maximum of two visits took place. A random sample of the screened children ($n = 68$) was visited by the researcher to carry out more in-depth tests for comparison with the results of the screening.

RESULTS

Selected results are presented to highlight themes relating to targeting, including the participation of eligible families, the positive predictive value (PPV) of the screening (which gives the percentage of the children detected by the test who are language delayed) and the prevalence of language delay in 20- to 24-month-old children in the community.

PARTICIPATION

Although support workers made extensive efforts to contact families, and reached a large number of them, the level of participation was still comparatively low: 49%.

In some cases, this was because families had left the area; in other cases, repeated attempts to visit were unsuccessful. Of the 525 children whose parents were contacted and offered a 'Talking Check', 251 were visited and screened by support workers. There were no significant differences in birth weight or maternal age between those who were and were not screened. This proportion was similar to families reached by health visitors in the same area, however. A comparison with the percentage of children receiving developmental checks by health visitors was made using a secondary data source, the Child Health Database, showing all children in the area registered with a GP. Health visitors carried out 18-month to two-year developmental checks with 55.8% of local children; this is consistent with earlier findings showing that 54.2% of children received developmental checks at 24–30 months (Law, 1994). All 251 children screened by support workers in the present programme, however, had had at least one recorded contact with a health visitor during the first year of life. This indicates that support workers were reaching a group who had previously used health services, if only once.

THE POSITIVE PREDICTIVE VALUE OF THE SCREENING

There was good inter-judge agreement (Cohen's $\kappa = 0.7$–1.0) between the support workers and the researcher on the children's language skills measured by the First Words Test. Scoring was carried out in all cases by the researcher in order to maximise consistency.

The test was shown to be sensitive: using the 10th centile as the cut-off point, 95% of children with delayed language would have been identified. It was shown to be specific: 81% of children with 'normal' language skills would have been identified. The PPV of 68% was within the range expected when whole populations of children are screened (Law et al., 1998) whereas, if the risk factor was a strong basis for targeting language delay, the figure should have been higher.

PREVALENCE

The level of prevalence of language delay ($<$10th percentile) by sex is summarised in Table 9.1.1, below. Overall, the local population scored one standard deviation below the reference sample used in standardising the test despite the UK reference population having included disadvantaged groups.

Table 9.1.1. Mean percentages of children scoring at or below the level of the 10th centile at 20–24 months

	Boys	Girls	Mean
Parent report	35%	17%	26%
Direct testing	45.9%	25%	36%

DISCUSSION

In comparison with the general population, the population targeted in this Sure Start programme are at higher risk of language delay. The screening carried out by support workers successfully identified language-delayed children, the results of the First Words Test being confirmed by the in-depth testing carried out by the researcher with a small sample of those screened. It is thus possible to identify children with clinical language delay and those at risk of longer term language problems at an early stage so that they can be assessed further and receive appropriate intervention. However, although the programme engaged 49% of families, this figure was much lower than was expected or desirable. It is thus possible that the children who were screened differed in some way from those who were not screened, and that this could have affected the results. This possibility is being explored in the course of follow-up research.

TARGETING ON THE BASIS OF POVERTY

Sure Start used the principles of geographical targeting to identify areas with high levels of poverty. Not all disadvantaged children live in Sure Start areas and not all children who do live in Sure Start areas are disadvantaged. There is a trade-off, for the organisers of programmes, and indeed researchers, between efficiency and completeness. The risk factors for targeting are poverty and its correlates but the pathways whereby poverty leads to poorer outcomes are still not fully understood (Duncan & Brooks-Gunn, 2000). Figure 9.1.1 provides a diagram of some of the pathways between poverty and early brain development. In discussing the likely benefits of targeting, Rose (1992) notes that the relationship between the risk factor and the outcome of interest should be known. If this is the case, PPV should be higher in high-risk populations than in the general population. As we have seen, however, when the PPV of the present screening was compared with population screening for delayed language (Law et al., 1998), the PPV was within the same range as mass population screening. This suggests that targeted screening using Sure Start boundaries may not be more effective than mass screening because poverty is not a discrete risk factor.

PARTICIPATION

Sure Start communities may have had few services prior to the introduction of the programmes. While communities are likely to include a mix of families (Salmond & Crampton, 2002) some families in Sure Start areas will be hard to reach, tending not to use health services for themselves or for their children (Hall & Elliman, 2003). The families who did not take up the offer of screening probably included this group. Other factors preventing engagement may include perceived stigma

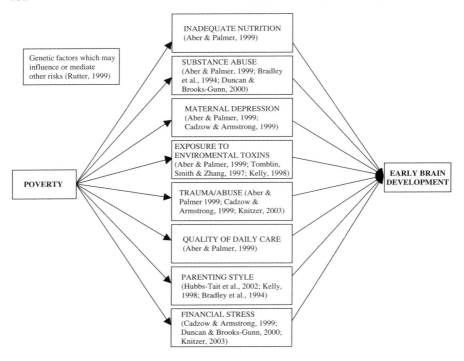

Figure 9.1.1. Examples of possible pathways whereby poverty may influence early brain development and child outcomes

(Glogowska & Campbell, 2000), lack of awareness of what was available and the mobility of the local population: 9–18% of families move from, or into, this area each year; the city-wide average is no more than 10%. This impacts on survey and screening in two ways: it is difficult to check children's language in the first place, and then to follow them up subsequently if they need referral for more in-depth assessment. The larger the number of children who are not reached, the more it is likely that there are systematic differences between those reached and not reached. Any differences between these two groups will also impact on the level of prevalence for language disorders in the local population of children.

As we have seen, no differences were found in the present study between the children who were and were not screened, in terms of their maternal age and birth weight, both of which are sometimes used as a proxy variable for poverty (Spencer, 2000). However, this finding is counter-intuitive. To reiterate: there may well be differences between families who take up the offer of screening and those who do not, and, furthermore, that the same factors that preclude families from screening may well preclude them from taking up any interventions that may be offered (Barnes, 2003).

INTERPRETING SCREENING RESULTS

When disadvantaged children are screened, how should the results be interpreted? Clearly they need to be interpreted in context (Lindsay, 1984; Meisels & Atkins Burnett, 2000), but which one: that of the local population, based on figures for prevalence, or the normative context using the data on which the instrument was standardised? As we have seen, one criterion for choosing the First Words Test was standardisation using a UK sample including disadvantaged groups. The local population was disadvantaged (albeit on the evidence of average income rather than income for each individual household) and, as predicted, the scores were positively skewed with more children scoring at the low end of the distribution for their age. The prevalence of delayed language, represented by a score of 1.25 SD below the mean, was higher in boys (35% according to parental report, 45.9% according to direct testing), but it was still high for girls (17% according to parental report, 25% according to direct testing). Screening requires a cut-off point to distinguish those children who need assessment and intervention from those who do not. The results of the present study showed that up to 45.9% of those screened would be referred for assessment. The use of a cut-off point, however, forces a binary decision, to define children as 'at risk' or 'not at risk'. Most practitioners would agree that this is an over-simplification and that interpretation of results needs to take into account patterns of change, the home environment and other risk factors as described above. As we have seen, screening should identify children on the basis of reversible risk (Rose, 1992). Sure Start interventions are designed to address reversible risk factors to improve readiness for school. Such interventions are therefore likely to be of value both to the group with clinically significant language delay and the group where there is parent or carer concern. Some researchers argue that the whole of the lowest quartile of the population distribution in a community is likely to derive benefit from early childhood programmes (Glascoe, 2001). Indeed, in some cases intervention is offered to all those in the lower 50% of the local population distribution (see Barlow, Shaw & Stewart-Brown, 2004, for a review).

Finally, we need to be realistic about reaching and engaging families. Despite extensive efforts by support workers in the local programme to contact families and maintain their involvement, many families did not take up the offer of screening. This suggests that securing the participation of some disadvantaged groups may not necessarily be more cost-effective than screening the wider population, and that engaging the harder-to-reach groups will take much effort and expenditure. As suggested above, the same factors precluding involvement in screening might well preclude take-up of interventions (Barnes, 2003). Sure Start programmes thus need to make provision for later intervention with children who present with language difficulties later, even as late as on school entry. Furthermore, interventions at every stage need to be diverse, allowing for those families who may not be able to engage at all, and those who engage with the programme to a limited degree but cannot take an active role in intervention themselves.

REFERENCES

Aber, L. & Palmer, J. (1999). *Poverty and brain development in early childhood*. New York: National Center for Children in Poverty.

Baird, G. (2001). Speech and language problems in preschool children. *Current Paediatrics*, **11**, 19–27.

Barlow, J., Shaw, R. & Stewart-Brown, S. (2004). *Parenting programmes and minority ethnic families*. Oxford: National Children's Bureau for the Joseph Rowntree Foundation, University of Oxford.

Barnes, J. (2003). Interventions addressing infant mental health problems (Research review). *Children and Society*, **17**, 386–395.

Blunkett, D. (1999). *Ministerial opening address by Rt Hon David Blunkett MP, Secretary of State for Education and Employment*. Paper presented at the Sure Start Trailblazer Conference, July.

Bradley, R. H., Whiteside, L., Mundform, D., Casey, P. H., Kelleher, K. J. & Pope, S. J. (1994). Early indications of resilience and their relation to experiences in the home environments of low birth weight, premature infants living in poverty. *Child Development*, **65**, 346–360.

Cadzow, S. P. & Armstrong, K. L. (1999). Stressed parents with infants; reassessing physical abuse risk factors. *Child Abuse & Neglect*, **23**(9), 845–854.

Duncan, G. J. & Brooks-Gunn, J. (2000). Family poverty, welfare reform and child development. *Child Development*, **71**(1), 188–196.

Gillham, B., Boyle, J. & Smith, N. (1997). *First Words and First Sentences Test Manual*. London: Hodder & Stoughton Educational.

Glascoe, F. P. (2001). Are over referrals on developmental screening tests really a problem? *Archives of Pediatrics and Adolescent Medicine*, **155**(1), 54–59.

Glogowska, M. & Campbell, R. (2000). Investigating parentals views of involvement in preschool speech and language therapy. *International Journal of Language and Communication Disorders*, **35**(3), 391–406.

Gordis, L. (1996). Assessing the validity and reliability of diagnostic and screening tests. *Epidemiology* (pp. 58–76). Philadelphia, PA: W.B. Saunders.

Hall, D. M. B. & Elliman, D. (2003). *Health for all children* (4th edn). Oxford: Oxford University Press.

Her Majesty's Treasury (1998). *Comprehensive Spending Review (CSR); The cross departmental review of provision for young children*. Available from the Public Enquiry Unit, HM Treasury, Parliament Street, London, SW1P 3AG. Retrieved 13 September, 1999, from http://www.hm-treasury.gov.uk/pub/htlm/csr/401122.htm

Hubbs-Tait, L., McDonald Culp, A., Huey, H., Culp, R., Starost, H. J. & Hare, C. (2002). Relationship of Head Start attendance to children's cognitive and social outcomes; moderation by family risk. *Early Childhood Research Quarterly*, **17**, 539–558.

Kelly, D. (1998). A clinical synthesis of the 'Late Talker' literature; implications for service delivery. *Language, Speech and hearing Services in Schools*, **29**, 76–84.

Klee, T., Carson, D., Gavin, W. J., Hall, L., Kent, A. & Reece, S. (1998). Concurrent and predictive validity of an early language screening programme. *Journal of Speech, Language & Hearing Research*, **41**, 627–641.

Knitzer, J. (2003). Social and emotional development in young low income children: What research tells us and why it matters for early school success. *Testimony presented at the Mailman School of Public Health, Columbia University New York, January*.

Law, J. (1994). Early language screening in City and Hackney: the concurrent validity of a measure designed for use with 2½ year olds. *Child: care, health and development*, **20**, 309–322.

Law, J., Boyle, J., Harris, F., Harkness, A. & Nye, C. (1998). Screening for speech and language delay; a systematic review of the literature. *Health Technology Assessment*. Winchester, England.

Lindsay, G. (Ed.). (1984). *Screening for children with special needs*. Kent: Croom Helm.

Locke, A., Ginsborg, J. & Peers, I. (2002). Development and disadvantage: Implications for the early years. *International Journal of Language and Communication Disorders*, **37**(1), 3–16.

Meisels, S. J. & Atkins Burnett, S. (2000). The elements of early childhood assessment. In S. J. Meisels (Ed.), *Handbook of early childhood intervention* (2nd edn, pp. 231–257). Cambridge: Cambridge University Press.

National Screening Committee (2001). *Recommendations of the National Screening Committee – Speech and language delay*. National Screening Committee – Children's sub-group. Retrieved 28 October, 2003, from http://www.nelh.nhs.uk/screening/child_pps/speech_chsgr.html

Pickstone, C. (2003). A pilot study of paraprofessional screening of child language in community settings. *Child Language Teaching and Therapy*, **19**(1), 49–65.

Pickstone, C., Hannon, P. & Fox, L. (2002). Surveying and screening preschool language development in community-focused intervention programmes: a review of instruments. *Child: Care, Health and Development*, **28**(3), 251–264.

Rose, G. (1992). *The strategy of preventive medicine*. Oxford: Oxford University Press.

Rutter, M. L. (1999). Resilience concepts and findings: implications for family therapy. *Journal of Family Therapy*, **21**, 119–144.

Salmond, C. & Crampton, P. (2002). Heterogeneity of deprivation within very small areas. *Journal of Epidemiology and Community Health*, **56**, 669–670.

Spencer, N. (2000). *Poverty and child health* (2nd edn). Oxford: Radcliffe Medical Press.

Sure Start Unit (2000). *Annexe B, PSA targets for 2001–02 or earlier*. London: Sure Start Unit.

Sure Start Unit (2001). *Sure Start Language Measure (SSLM) Information Pack*. London: Sure Start Unit.

Tomblin, J. B., Smith, E. & Zhang, X. (1997). Epidemiology of specific language impairment: prenatal and perinatal risk factors. *Journal of Communication Disorders*, **30**, 325–344.

Wilson, J. M. G. & Jungner, G. (1968). *Principles and practice of screening for disease*. Geneva: World Health Organisation.

9.2 The 'Teaching Children Talking' Project

LINDA HOBBS

East Riding of Yorkshire Council, Children Family and Adult Services

INTRODUCTION

The 'Teaching Children Talking' project was designed to facilitate improvement in the speech and language skills of children in mainstream nurseries and primary schools in the East Riding of Yorkshire including areas of low socio-economic status (SES). In contrast to some of the other interventions described in research reports presented in this volume, this project was developed to train the professionals (nursery nurses, teaching assistants and teachers) directly involved in teaching. It was designed and implemented by practitioners lacking the expertise of professionals trained in research design and delivery. Rather, teaching professionals and speech and language therapists (SLTs) collaborated to design, implement and evaluate the project. This report presents the rationale for the development of the project, the design, implementation and evaluation, and finally, the impact of the project on the teaching professionals.

Although the East Riding of Yorkshire is a predominantly rural county with areas of rural deprivation, a high level of socio-economic deprivation is recorded in several towns. Recent statistics confirm that the number of households experiencing income deprivation in the county stands at 31,888 and some of the county's schools are situated in the 10% most deprived areas of the UK, with over 30% of the children eligible for free school meals (Noble, Wright, Dibben et al., 2004). In 2001, the regional education and health services, in response to the *Report of the Joint Working Group* (Law, Lindsay, Peacey et al., 2000), recognised the need to enhance the provision for local children with speech and language difficulties (SLD). Across the UK, SLT services have recently moved towards a consultancy approach in the delivery of services to such children, advocating greater collaboration between SLTs and teaching professionals in recognising and improving the speech and language abilities of children.

In 2001, a teacher and an SLT (referred to here as the project workers) were seconded to the 'Teaching Children Talking' project initially for two days per week over two years. The primary aim of the project was to develop and implement a course, delivering specialist training to teaching professionals in how to facilitate the learning of children with SLD in the Foundation Stage. The funding for this came initially from the SEN Standards Fund, which supports school and local authority strategies to remove barriers that prevent children from achieving their potential. One area that the grant covers is the provision of therapies. Together, the local authority and the local SLT service collaborated to develop the 'Teaching Children Talking' project and delivered this during the first year to staff in one partnership of schools. The first stage of the project involved designing the two-year training course. The aim of the second stage was to deliver the course to the teaching professionals and then to evaluate the training. Evaluation formed an important component of the project, as it was imperative to assess the impact of the project on both the children's speech and language development and the skill levels of the teaching professionals receiving the training. A combination of quantitative and qualitative measures was employed to achieve this.

The aims of the 'Teaching Children Talking' project were to:

- provide the teaching professionals with knowledge about children's speech and language development;
- enable the teaching professionals to learn strategies for increasing the speaking and listening skills of the children that could be incorporated into everyday nursery and classroom activities;
- determine the extent to which the training delivered through the project improved children's speech and language abilities;
- ascertain the views of the teaching professionals regarding the effectiveness of the project.

METHOD

PARTICIPANTS

In 2001, when the project began, training was offered to all the schools in a partnership. In 2002, the project workers decided to offer the training only to Foundation Stage practitioners in the schools as it was felt that the project would be most effective with the youngest children. Between 2002 and 2004, the project workers worked with a further two partnerships. In these two partnerships, 53 teaching professionals participated in the project (16 nursery nurses, 13 teaching assistants and 24 teachers) from 21 schools. Each year, 20 children from the Foundation Stage in the partnership took part in the evaluation. These children were each matched with children that had not participated in the project and could therefore act as controls. Between 2002 and 2004, therefore, 40 children from two partnership schools were recruited to an experimental group and 40 children from two non-partnership schools were recruited to a control group matched on size, free school meals and Foundation Stage Profile outcomes for communication, language

Table 9.2.1. Mean ages of children in the control
and experimental groups at the start of the intervention

Group	Mean age
Experimental 1 (2002–3) ($n = 20$)	4 years 6 months
Control 1 (2002–3) ($n = 20$)	4 years 10 months
Experimental 2 (2003–4) ($n = 20$)	4 years 4 months
Control 2 (2003–4) ($n = 20$)	4 years 6 months

and literacy (see Table 9.2.1). The children in both groups were in Foundation Stage classes but the control group did not receive the training component of the project.

ASSESSMENTS

The *CELF-Preschool^{UK}* (Wiig, Secord & Semel, 2000) and the *Bus Story Test* (Renfrew, 1997) were used to assess the children's speech and language skills at the beginning of the academic year when the project began. These measures provided baselines from which to assess any improvement after the project had taken place. To complete the evaluation of the programme, children in the experimental and control groups were then re-tested at the end of each academic year (the first group in June, 2003 and the second group in June, 2004). Twenty-nine nursery nurses and teaching assistants who took part in the training during 2002–2004 also completed a questionnaire, both pre- and post-training in order to measure its impact. The questionnaire consisted of 21 statements to assess the nursery nurses' and teaching assistants' confidence in areas from their knowledge of language and communication to designing and delivering intervention programmes. The 24 teachers with whom the nursery nurses and teaching assistants worked also completed the questionnaires.

PROCEDURE

All the children in the experimental and the control groups were first tested at the beginning of the academic year of the first year of the project. After the baseline measures had been taken, the project was implemented by teaching professionals in the partnership schools. Supply cover was paid for one teaching assistant or nursery nurse and one teacher from each school to attend training sessions during the school day. The project workers felt that it was important that the teachers were involved in supporting the nursery nurses and teaching assistants in the training so that the project could be embedded in the planning for the classes. It was stressed from the beginning of the course that the project should be seen as integral rather than additional to the curriculum in the Foundation Stage. The course was structured so that the nursery nurses and teaching assistants were supported throughout the two years of training. It began with an induction day at the beginning of the first year to introduce the nursery nurses and teaching assistants to the course, and to train them to use an initial speech and language screen with their class. This was also an opportunity to invite members of other services who were working in the partnership, such as the SLT and the Special Educational Needs (SEN) support service to join in with the training and support the work in the schools. The nursery nurses, teaching assistants and teachers then met together with the project workers every six weeks throughout the first year of training. At each session, the next assessment or intervention sheet was explained and any problems that may have arisen since the previous session were discussed and addressed. The project workers also visited the schools to work with the children identified by the screen as having particular speech and language needs, and to model lessons. The post-intervention measures were administered at the end of the academic year in June and July.

CONTENT OF THE 'TEACHING CHILDREN TALKING' PROJECT

The training course and classroom intervention were based upon the *Teaching Talking* programme (Locke & Beech, 1991) and the SENA + T module *Speech and Language* (Caswell & Pinner, 1995). The SENA + T materials were developed in Northumberland as a joint venture between education staff, advisers, SLTs and educational psychologists working with children with statements of SEN. Each school was provided with a copy of these resources, along with the necessary screening and assessment sheets. As the programme developed, lesson-plan sheets making links to Foundation Stage and National Curriculum documents were provided at the request of the nursery nurses and teaching assistants. Other resources introduced to the schools throughout the year included *Time to Talk* (Schroeder, 2001), *Developing Baseline Communication Skills* (Delamain & Spring, 2001) and *Speaking and Listening through Narrative* (Shanks & Rippon, 2001).

During the first term, the teaching professionals were trained to make observations and assessments and to group the children who had been identified by the initial screening process as having speech and language needs. The children were grouped according to their need for play, social and emotional experiences, or the development of listening and understanding. General strategies to improve the children's language skills were also introduced in the partnership schools and used with the whole class throughout the first term. During the second and third terms of the academic year, the nursery nurses and teaching assistants in the partnership schools were trained to deliver small-group activities targeted at the children's needs. These training sessions took place every six weeks.

A basic training in speech and language was provided by the SENA + T module, covering the use of language, listening to and understanding language, speech skills and expressive language, and links with reading and written language. These materials remained in the schools so that they could be used for future in-house training when needed. The nursery nurses and teaching assistants read one chapter of the SENA + T module every six weeks. At the end of the first year they were asked to produce a portfolio that included all the SENA + T activities, the completed *Teaching Talking* assessment sheets and a short case study. Each nursery nurse and teaching assistant also delivered a 10-minute oral presentation to the rest of the group, based on a resource that they had made. In the second year, they and the teachers were required to attend a half-day refresher session at the beginning of each term. The nursery nurses and teaching assistants then produced a second portfolio showing how they had implemented *Teaching Talking* over the course of the year, in collaboration with the class teacher.

RESULTS

The *CELF-Preschool*^{UK} and the *Bus Story Test* were used as pre- and post-intervention measures of language ability. The *CELF-Preschool*^{UK} results are presented in Table 9.2.2. At baseline, the control and the experimental groups had very similar receptive and expressive language scores, indicating a similar profile of abilities for the two groups. The mean scores of both groups were within the range considered normal. The evaluation of the project took place during the first year of the training course. Between baseline and follow-up, eight to nine months later, the experimental group showed a mean increase of nearly six points in receptive language and a mean increase of nearly five points in expressive language. In contrast, the control group showed no improvements in receptive language and a drop of approximately 3 points in expressive language.

The *Bus Story Test* was used to measure expressive narrative skills (see Table 9.2.3).

The baseline assessment showed that the experimental group had poorer language skills than the control group on measures of information provided, sentence length and use of subordinate clauses. At follow-up, the experimental group showed greater gains in language ability than the control group. There were mean increases of 12

Table 9.2.2. Mean standard scores for receptive and expressive language as measured by *CELF Pre-school*^{UK}

	Receptive Standard Scores		Expressive Standard Scores	
	Baseline	Follow-up	Baseline	Follow-up
Experimental	101.4	107.1	103.5	108.2
Control	99.7	99.7	103.3	100.5

Table 9.2.3. Mean scores for the *Bus Story* narrative assessment

	Information		Sentence Length		Subordinate Clauses	
	Baseline	Follow-up	Baseline	Follow-up	Baseline	Follow-up
Experimental	14	26	6.5	10	0.5	2.5
Control	21	17	8	7	1.5	1

points for information, 3.5 for sentence length and 2.0 for subordinate clauses. In contrast, the mean scores of the control group on the three measures fell.

Although the quantitative results from the *Bus Story* measures are interesting in themselves, qualitative data from the transcripts of the children in the experimental group provides us with more information as to the nature of the increase in their language production. For example, the transcripts of one little girl, aged 4;1 at baseline and 4;10 at follow-up, read as follows:

Pre-Intervention	Post-Intervention
bus	*there was a bus*
naughty	*he was naughty*
the policeman blowed a whistle	*when the driver was trying to fix him*
fell into the pond	*he runned away*
	he went really fast
	he saw a train
	but the train went into a tunnel
	he saw a policeman
	he blowed his whistle and
	he said 'Stop'

The transcripts of a little boy, aged 4;11 at baseline and 5;07 at follow-up, read as follows:

Pre-Intervention	Post-Intervention
there was a very naughty bus	*there was a naughty bus*
was on the road	*the driver was trying to mend him*
stop	*but he run away*
the bus driver	*the bus and the train pulled funny faces at*
he raced him and	*each other and*
they gone on the road and	*the train went into the tunnel and*
the policeman said 'Stop'	*the bus went into the city*
	the policeman blowed his whistle

All the children in the experimental group who did not show improvements in expressive language (as measured by the *CELF-Preschool*[UK]) did show an improvement in their narrative abilities (as measured by the *Bus Story*). In contrast, only three children in the control group showed improvement in all three areas of the *Bus Story* assessment, while 12 showed improvement in some areas and seven had lower scores for all three parts of the assessment.

QUESTIONNAIRE DATA

Questionnaires were completed by the nursery nurses and teaching assistants before and after the training to measure their confidence in working with children with speech and language difficulties. The results show that the project had the most impact on confidence in the areas of 'assessment' and 'appropriate teaching approaches'. The greatest increase in scores was found in the following seven areas:

1. Selecting and using appropriate assessment techniques to identify the needs of children with SLD.
2. Recommending appropriate teaching approaches for pupils with SLD.
3. Evaluating a child with SLD's readiness for reading and writing and identifying approaches.
4. Current developments and innovations in the field of SLD.
5. Devising relevant individual programmes.
6. Designing, reviewing, modifying and evaluating individual education plans.
7. Participating in programmes of work for children with SLD.

The results of the teachers' questionnaires show that, although they only attended the training sessions to support the nursery nurses and teaching assistants, their confidence in working with children with SLD also increased.

DISCUSSION

The 'Teaching Children Talking' project was designed to teach nursery nurses and teaching assistants about children's speech and language development and to enable them to deliver activities aimed at facilitating speech and language abilities. The teaching assistants, nursery nurses and teachers in the partnership schools spent the first term of the academic year observing, assessing and grouping the children, while learning how to implement general strategies to improve the children's language skills. In the second term, the intervention was carried out, primarily through small-group activities. Although the results show that the children in the experimental group made some improvement in their language skills, in comparison with those in the control group, this finding needs to be interpreted within the methodological limitations of the study (see below).

The nursery nurses and teaching assistants who took part in the project reported that the children's expressive language had benefited from intensive small-group work. One of the partnership schools was inspected by OFSTED in the summer of 2004 as the nursery nurses and teaching assistants completed the first year of their training on the project. In their report about the school, the OFSTED inspectors reported the following:

Children make very good progress in their communication, language and literacy through the highly skilful teaching they receive in nursery and in the reception classes. The staff training on talk, in which the nursery nurses are involved, is contributing very well to children's development in language. The impact of this is seen in the way that children confidently communicate across all areas of their learning. Teachers and staff seize numerous opportunities to extend children's speaking and listening skills.

Office for Standards in Education, 2004, © Crown Copyright, July 2004

METHODOLOGICAL LIMITATIONS

The strengths of this project are that an intervention was designed that has the potential to improve the knowledge and skills of professionals who work with children on a daily basis, incorporating a research design where an experimental group is compared with a control group and collecting both qualitative and quantitative data. However, some methodological issues compromise the findings of the 'Teaching Children Talking' project. The *CELF-Preschool^{UK}* was used as a pre- and post-intervention measure of receptive and expressive language and a small improvement in the language of the experimental group compared to the control group was detected. However, the primary aim of the project was to develop the knowledge of nursery nurses and teaching assistants in children's speech and language as well as increasing their strategies for working with children with SLD in the classroom. It could be argued that the *CELF-Preschool^{UK}* was not an ideal measure of improvement as the intervention did not specifically target the specific linguistic structures measured by the *CELF-Preschool^{UK}*. More useful qualitative information was yielded by the *Bus Story*, where increases in language production were observed. Furthermore, the intervention was broad; this made it difficult to quantify and measure outcomes. For example, the nursery nurses and teaching assistants did not necessarily deliver the same activities at the same intensity so there were differences in the quality of the intervention received by the children. In addition, the project workers had little influence over how many small-group sessions actually took place each week, or if the general strategies were incorporated into the daily curriculum. In addition, both the partnership schools had staff changes during the year but despite this, the teaching professionals did continue to implement the programme. In summary, the project raised the profile of speaking and listening in the Foundation Stage within the East Riding of Yorkshire and enabled a partnership of schools each year to facilitate the speech and language development of children.

REFERENCES

Caswell, J. & Pinner, S. (1995). *SENA + T Unit 4 Speech and Language*. Morpeth: Northumberland County Council Education Department.
Delamain, C. & Spring, J. (2001). *Developing Baseline Communication Skills*. Bicester: Winslow Press.

Law, J., Lindsay, G., Peacey, N., Gascoigne, M., Soloff, N., Radford, J., Band, S. & Fitzgerald, L. (2000). *Report of the Joint Working Group on the Provision of Speech and Language Therapy Services to Children with Special Educational Needs*. London: Department of Education and Employment/Department of Health.

Locke, A. & Beech, M. (1991). *Teaching Talking*. Windsor: NFER Nelson.

Noble, M., Wright, G., Dibben, C., Smith, G., McLennan, D., Anttila, C., Barnes, H., Mokhtar, C., Noble, S., Gardner, J., Braswell, S., Covizzi, I. & Lloyd, M. (2004). *The English Indices of Deprivation*. London: Office of the Deputy Prime Minister.

Office for Standards in Education (2004). *www.ofsted.gov.uk/reports*. Retrieved 16 June, 2005.

Renfrew, C. (1997). *The Bus Story Test*. Bicester: Winslow Press.

Schroeder, A. (2001). *Time to Talk*. Wisbech: Learning Development Aids (LDA).

Shanks, B. & Rippon, H. (2001). *Speaking and Listening through Narrative*. Louth: Black Sheep Press.

Wiig, E., Secord, W. & Semel, E. (2000). *Clinical Evaluation of Language Fundamentals-Preschool^{UK}*. London: The Psychological Corporation.

9.3 The Talking Table

MARION FARMER[1] and **FLEUR GRIFFITHS**[2]

[1]*Division of Psychology, School of Psychology and Sport Sciences, University of Northumbria*

[2]*Educational Consultant, Hartlepool Local Educational Authority*

INTRODUCTION

The Talking Table intervention was devised in response to a request from the Principal Educational Psychologist of an urban area in the North–East of England concerned about low levels of language use and development in early years settings. In setting up this intervention, it was considered that more emphasis was needed on the intrinsic value of conversation between adult and child as a means of cognitive and language development. The need for and benefits of this type of approach have recently been demonstrated in research carried out by Siraj-Blatchford and Sylva (2004) who report that 'conversations in which the adult and child co-construct an idea or activity' (p. 724) provide for optimum developmental outcomes for children. The aim of the Talking Table, therefore, was to raise the profile of talking and listening in early years settings. The purpose of the current research was to investigate (1) the feasibility and acceptability of the use of this approach and (2) the perceptions of the staff involved of its effects on children's communication skills and staff methods of developing skills in this area.

THE INTERVENTION

The principles underlying the development of the Talking Table come from the social constructionist model of language learning. This model suggests that language is a sociocultural tool which develops out of social encounters as a consequence of human motivation to interact with others and to develop a concept of self (Bruner, 1968; Vygotsky, 1962). A key underlying principle is the idea that we only speak if we have something pressing to say to someone who cares to listen closely. The Talking Table aims to provide a context in which children's talk is valued, the conversational principles of listening and turn-taking are fundamental

Language and Social Disadvantage: Theory into Practice Edited by J. Clegg and J. Ginsborg
© 2006 John Wiley & Sons, Ltd

and meaningful communication takes place. For a review of this model and related research see Farmer (2002). Box 9.3.1 provides a summary of the key conversational principles employed.

The Talking Table itself consisted of a round table with four chairs set up, one day a week for six weeks, alongside the usual activity areas in nursery settings, with the Talking Table Instigator (TTI) available as a conversational partner. During each session the TTI (having been introduced to the children) was reliably to be found at her Talking Table. She was always dressed in a blue tunic with colourful pockets, with enticing objects peeping out. These were chosen to spark off different experiences to share: a toy spider in a box; a sparkling jewel; a spinning top; a magnifying glass; a mirror or a chime. Children were also encouraged to bring a small pocket-size treasure to 'show and tell'. Large pieces of paper covered the surface of the table and felt-tipped pens were available to allow each child in turn to choose a colour and make expressive marks. The watchful TTI then put words to these. What might appear to be scribble came to represent pathways, journeys, mazes, enclosures, anger, fire, speed – all ingredients of a possible narrative. 'Once upon a time' openings were sometimes used to create a story to include each child's contribution. The TTI joined in with pen and voice of her own, partnering the child and mediating the process of using language to make and impart sense. Children saw their ideas represented visually and in the writing of key words; they heard the accompanying commentary and assented to their story as it was told (for a fuller account see Griffiths, 2005). Children were able to use this opportunity merely to watch, or to investigate the small objects, draw them, and develop stories about them with help from the TTI.

The role of the TTI, then, was to be a conversational partner for the children and also to provide a model for staff of good practice: turn-taking, courtesy and the building of emotional rapport. Circle-time strategies promoted the pattern of watch/do, the forerunner to the listen/speak alternation of conversational exchange. The TTI attended to the full range of children's communication, non-verbal as well as verbal, since non-verbal communication provides the basis for communicative relationships. The aim was 'only connect' in order to provide each child with confidence that her contribution was valued. In short, the TTI and a changing series of four children round the table shared the same experience, exchanged meaningful communications about it and concentrated together to make articulate sense of it. Some adaptations of this basic set-up were made in settings for older children where activities were more constrained by curricular demands. In a reception class, the table was available one afternoon a week; in a nurture group for older children, the whole group of seven children took part; and in Personal, Social, Health and Citizenship Education (PSHCE) work in an early years setting, a class was divided into two Talking Table groups (see below).

Before the Talking Table was introduced in each setting, a preliminary visit was made to agree practical details with staff and to provide handouts about conversational principles, mediational strategies, techniques for extending oral language and the role of the adult in promoting talk. These were based on guidelines provided by various authors, reproduced with their permission: Duffy (1998, in Griffiths, 2002,

p. 19), Tough (1997, in Griffiths, 2002, p. 34) and Webster (1987, in Griffiths, 2002, p. 17) and summarised in Box 9.3.1. Thereafter, the TTI visited each setting six times, on the same day each week.

Box 9.3.1. Conversational principles for facilitating child talk

1. Create a context for conversation
2. Comment on the child's play and activity
3. Talk with, not at the child
4. Be patient
5. Don't overload conversation
6. Be personal
7. Don't cross-examine, ask open, genuine questions
8. Avoid correcting
9. Listen attentively to the child
10. Extend the child's utterances and reflect back what the child has said
11. Offer your own speculations and reasons
12. Ask questions that offer a choice of answers
13. Contribute information when asked to do so
14. Provide a model of high-quality spoken language
15. Speak quietly

The Talking Table was designed to be inclusive, open to all children who chose to take part. They varied in the frequency with which they participated (see below), but generally all the children in each setting chose to come to the Table and indeed were anxious to join in. Nursery staff explained the intervention to parents, who were invited to meet the TTI half an hour before home time to talk about the day's happenings and the progress of their children.

During the six-week period in which the Talking Table was established in each setting, the intervention was subject to action-research evaluation with a plan/do/review cycle. At the end of the intervention, the staff and TTI met to discuss its perceived benefits and shortcomings, and to agree on pointers for future action.

METHOD

In order to assess the longer term effects of the Talking Table, an independent researcher, acquainted with its history and methods, visited six settings where it had been used and interviewed staff one to six terms later. In two of the settings, the Talking Table was used in the nursery, and also with older children in a reception class and nurture group (a small special class providing a safe and predictable structured environment in which children with behavioural and

Table 9.3.1. Summary of characteristics of settings, roles of interviewees, current use and organisation of the TT

ID	Setting	Age of children	Time since TT intro	Interviewee/s	Continued use of TT?	Current format and organisation
A	Nursery school	3–4 years	2 years	1.HT 2.NT 3.NN	Discontinued TT but continues to use some of the methods	Methods continued: bringing in an item. Small group opportunities for talk for newcomers to the nursery. Drawing method used as adjunct or stimulus for talk
B	Nursery class	3–4 years	1 year	NT	Continued original format	Uses original format of TT one day a week but also extended the use into other areas of the nursery such as the construction area
B	Reception class	4–5 years	1 year	RT NN	Continued original format, changed organisation	Original format used in structured groups of six, once a week focused on literacy activities: story-telling and writing
C	Reception class	4–5 years	3 terms	PSHCE coordinator	Continued, changed organisation	Continued, using a large group organisation for PHSCE work.
C	Nurture class	6–7 years	3 terms	1. Nurture CT 2. Deputy HT	Continued original format	Continued, once a week, but also used as an approach in other areas of the curriculum such as Maths and writing
D	Nursery class	3–4 years	3 terms	NT	Continued original format	Keeps original format, one day a week. Uses drawing as stimulus/adjunct to talk on other days.
E	Nursery class	3–4 years	2 years	1. NN 2. NN	Continued original format	Continued one morning a week in original format.
F	Nursery school	3–4 years	2 years	NT	Discontinued the TT itself but continues to use the approach	Has a round table to promote interaction. Has taken on board that 'natural genuine talk' should be used everywhere. Alters her language to match the child's level. Uses mark making now in all areas. Intention to reinstate TT

Key to interviewees: HT = head teacher, NT = nursery teacher, NN = nursery nurse, RT = reception teacher, CT = class teacher, PSHCE = personal, social, health and citizenship education

emotional problems are given opportunities to revisit early missed 'nurturing' experiences). Interview data were gathered, then, from staff working with eight groups of children.

SETTINGS

Information relating to settings is summarised in Table 9.3.1. All settings were in a metropolitan borough in an area of the North-East of England with generally high levels of unemployment and social deprivation (for example, unemployment rates among men were twice the national average in 2004). All the settings except Setting A were in wards within the borough with high levels of social deprivation: figures obtained from local statistical deprivation analyses indicated levels of deprivation 50% higher than the national average. Setting A was in a ward within the borough with levels of deprivation similar to the national average for England, where it was possible to consider the role of the intervention in a setting where speech and language development issues were not considered to be a major concern for the children. A short video was made in this setting of the Talking Table approach, which was then used as an illustration in later training events for early years staff.

PROCEDURE

Interviews were carried out with individual staff members in their settings, in a staff room or separate quiet area. They were advised beforehand of the purpose of the interviews, which lasted between 30 and 45 minutes, were recorded with a portable tape recorder and later transcribed in full.

Box 9.3.2. Protocol for the semi-structured interview

1. Have you continued to use the TT in your setting?
2. If you have continued to use the TT, how is it organised?
3. What benefits are there from using the TT approach?
4. Do you think the TT has affected the way the children talk?
5. Do you think the TT has affected the way that staff talk to children?
6. What are the drawbacks/problems in using the TT approach?
7. How often do children come to the TT?
8. Are there some children who you think would benefit from the TT who do not come to it?
9. Are parents involved in the TT?
10. Would you recommend the TT to other early years settings?

INTERVIEW PROTOCOL

A semi-structured approach to the interview was used (see Box 9.3.2 for questions asked). All the themes addressed in these questions were covered in each interview, but the questions were not necessarily presented in the order shown. The interviewer also provided support to the interviewee in terms of conversational reflecting back and rephrasing of her words in order that the interviewee should be at ease and the interview should have, as far as possible, a conversational format.

RESULTS AND DISCUSSION OF ANALYSIS OF INTERVIEW DATA

Information relating to the interviewees is summarised in Table 9.3.1. The interviews were analysed primarily using content analysis relating to the responses to the questions in Box 9.3.2. The content sought for the purpose of this report consisted of references to the following topics:

1. Continuation/discontinuation of use of the Talking Table approach
2. Current organisation of the Talking Table
3. Benefits of the Talking Table approach for the children, their attitudes to and use of the Talking Table
4. Benefits of the Talking Table approach for the staff
5. Drawbacks/problems associated with the Talking Table approach.

The content identified in the analysis is summarised in Tables 9.3.1, 9.3.2 and 9.3.3, and comments on the information provided in the tables are made below.

TOPIC 1: CONTINUATION/DISCONTINUATION OF USE OF THE TALKING TABLE APPROACH

Staff working with six of the eight groups of children in the six settings where the Talking Table had been introduced had continued to use the Talking Table in a format similar to that originally demonstrated by the TTI (see Table 9.3.1). Setting A, where speech and language development issues were not a major concern, had not continued to have a Talking Table as such, but had benefited by absorbing the principles of the approach, and had adopted and adapted some of the methods used (see below). Setting F had also not continued to use the Talking Table as such, much to the regret of the nursery teacher. This was largely because there had been a major organisational change in the nursery: a complete transfer of the setting into a new building, during which there had been many issues around multiple demands on personnel. The teacher concerned explained: 'It just sort of went a bit flat. Even when it worked, even when we didn't get pulled away. I don't know why because I really liked it and I thought it was a brilliant idea and we wanted it to keep going, and didn't . . . But this term we're going to start it again.'

TOPIC 2: CURRENT ORGANISATION OF THE TALKING TABLE

The variety of approaches to the organisation of the Talking Table illustrates its flexibility and adaptability, described as valuable by several interviewees (see Table 9.3.1). Some kind of Talking Table continues to be set up once a week in most settings, usually covered with a large piece of paper, and coloured pens provided for mark making with an adult in constant attendance. In one of the nursery settings, however, the teacher found that it was mainly girls who came to the table while boys tended to stay in the construction area, making models and playing with toy cars without adult supervision. Following consultation with the TTI, she now takes the Talking Table into the construction area once a week, as well as having a Talking Table in the mark-making area. In this way, the boys are also drawn into talk. This teacher also intends to use the same approach in other activity areas of the nursery.

An interviewee in another setting explained how the Talking Table approach had influenced the way she talks with the children in other contexts. She said: 'you can use the Talking Table anywhere . . . We were talking about the Mulberry Bush and drew pictures . . . And then we started walking round the pathway. We had lovely stories. . . There's a story about a crocodile in one part. Stories about different fruits in another . . . a story about Mum and Dad going walking round the bushes . . . And then . . . there was a dog in the park and he was chasing people. So there are at least five or six different stories.'

The interviewees who worked with older children had adapted the basic intervention in a variety of ways. One was the PSHCE Coordinator in Setting C, who used an adapted Talking Table approach with reception class children. She divided a class of 20 children into two groups. She worked with one group, and another staff member worked with the other, both of them taking the role of TTI. The two groups then worked separately on developing a story with characters selected from a storyboard set. The children drew on paper and whiteboards to help them develop the story. At the end of each session, the two groups would come together to narrate their stories to each other. This approach was also used in the afternoons for other story work. The Talking Table was also used in the same setting, regularly and very successfully, with a small nurture group that had been established to foster the social and academic development of a group of 6- and 7-year-old children in Year 2 who presented with behavioural and attention problems that prevented them from progressing in school.

TOPIC 3: BENEFITS OF THE TALKING TABLE APPROACH FOR THE CHILDREN

As can be seen in Table 9.3.2, all the interviewees reported perceived benefits of the Talking Table, either in terms of improved communication and social interaction skills generally, or specific aspects of communication such as turn-taking and story-telling. They saw the Talking Table as an opportunity for children to express their ideas and feelings and to be heard; they believed this gave the children increased confidence in their communicative competence and thus raised their self-esteem. Shy children, and children who needed a place to talk, were drawn to the Table. Sometimes they communicated only non-verbally at first through their drawings. These communications were validated by the TTI and laid the foundation for verbal communication. Some children's behaviour improved, and they developed more respect for each other. An interesting perceived benefit for older children related to the transition from oral to written communication. Staff involved with older children found that their activities at the Talking Table provided inspiration for stories – 'something to say' – and helped them structure their writing.

TOPIC 4: BENEFITS OF THE TALKING TABLE APPROACH FOR THE STAFF

As can also be seen in Table 9.3.2 the Talking Table was perceived not only to benefit children, but also staff. Perhaps this is a key to the success of any curricular activity. Classrooms are workplaces for children and staff. If activities are found to have shared benefits then it seems likely that they will be more readily accepted and continued with enthusiasm. Staff noted that the experience of using the Talking Table had made them more aware of the ways in which they communicated with children and their effects on the children. They reported that it had enabled them to develop their own communication skills with children. They also noted that it gave them an opportunity to develop their knowledge of individual children's communicative competencies and evidence for use in profiling. As noted above it was also considered to be an excellent intervention to develop writing skills. Some commented on the value of the Talking Table in calming children. And finally, perhaps most important, staff enjoyed the activity.

TOPIC 5: DRAWBACKS OF THE TALKING TABLE APPROACH

As can be seen in Table 9.3.3, several interviewees found no drawbacks in or problems associated with the Talking Table approach. Of the problems that were mentioned, the most frequently reported was the difficulty of balancing the Talking Table's demand that an adult should provide children with undivided attention with the many other demands made on staff working with young children. In two of the settings where this comment was made the Talking Table had been discontinued (the first being the nursery where speech and language development were not a major concern, the second was the nursery that had suffered severe disruption from the transfer to a new site). The third interviewee continued to maintain a Talking Table despite this perceived difficulty; she had clearly understood the message that the Talking Table approach to encouraging children's talk did not need to be tied to a particular table and time but could be employed in any area at any time. Indeed, this particular interviewee had found that the principles and ideas behind the Talking Table approach enabled her to find intrinsic value in

Table 9.3.2. Summary of benefits of TT for children and staff

ID	Staff	Benefits for children	Benefits for staff
A	Nursery HT	Communication skills. Social and personal skills. Sustains children's attention	
	NT	Communication skills. Self confidence	Awareness of importance of listening to children Opportunity to develop knowledge of children's communicative competence. Enjoyment of process
	NN	New experience. Extension of children's language	Enjoyment of process
B	NT	Draws much language from them. Gives children confidence in speaking. Opportunity for communication of feelings.	Gives a great deal of easily captured evidence for the new early years profile. Versatility and adaptability
B	RT & NN	Encourages speech work. Confidence to speak in small group Social skills in turn-taking and questioning. Respecting each other. Benefits all children Leads into writing	Skills in listening to children and drawing them out. Evidence for foundation stage profile. Evidence for individual education plans (IEPs). Sharing children's interests with parents
C	PSHCE coord.	Communication skills. Story narration. Confidence. Self-esteem/self-worth. Opportunity to be heard	The approach fits well with the area of personal, social and citizenship education
C	Nurture group teacher	Opportunity for self-expression. Opportunity to be heard Overcomes hurdle of not having anything to say when asked to write. Self-confidence. Chance to talk without fear of not having anything to say. Children are enthusiastic about it	Aid to development of writing. Model of turn-taking, listening and how to listen useful in many areas of the curriculum. Awareness of steps children need to go through in the development of conversation skills
	Deputy HT	Social skills. Self-esteem. Development of writing skills. Increase in SATs scores. Enjoyed and valued by children	Improvement in behaviour/manageability in nurture group. Excellent intervention to develop writing skills
D	NT	Withdrawn children open up. Children know they will be heard. Children who need to talk go there. Development of story-telling abilities	Alters way staff talk to children. Increases awareness of the effect of the way they talk on children's talk and self-expression
E	NN	Turn-taking and listening. Opportunity to be heard	Valuable to have the time set aside for talk with children Opportunity to listen to children and their ideas. Teaches you to listen to children. Increases awareness of effects of the ways
	NN	Children's enjoyment. Ability to express themselves	in which you encourage children to talk
F	NT	Language, personal and social skills. Confidence. Behaviour	Enjoyment. Affected the way staff talk to children

Table 9.3.3. Drawbacks and problems relating to the TT approach identified by interviewees

ID	Staff	Drawbacks/Problems
A	Nursery HT	None identified
	NT	Identifying a quiet area not secluded from main activities
	NN	Finding the time for staff to be 'tied to' the TT. Not all staff have the skills to draw children out
B	NT	Boys prefer construction to mark making Knowing how to support a child with ESL at the TT
B	RT & NN	None
C	PSHCE coord.	None
C	Nurture group T	Larger group of seven children means that they have to be more patient in listening and waiting for their turn
	Dep. HT	None
D	NT	If children bring things from home they can get lost Other demands on staff make it difficult to stay at TT
E	NN	Regular TT may become a bit 'flat'. Children may save their talk for the TT
	NN	Sometimes it is difficult to find ways of encouraging the children's talk if you have a quieter or younger group. Sometimes need to rekindle the children's interest in the TT
F	NT	Other demands on staff make it difficult to stay at TT. May need a different character there to stimulate the children. The TT adult needs to have appropriate skills

conversations with the children at other times. This enabled her to value some of the work she did that did not have measurable outcomes in terms of children's outputs.

The other frequently mentioned problem was the concern that not all the adults in each setting had the skills to provide the 'right' conversational environment at the Talking Table. This may seem a little odd since the idea of the Talking Table is that it should provide an opportunity for naturalistic two-way, equal conversation, rather than pedagogic dialogue. However, it may be a valid concern. The Talking Table approach can be seen as a challenge to pedagogic strategies relying on teacher/adult control of communication and behaviour. Adults in educational settings are expected to manage and organise access to materials and resources, control behaviour, find out how much children know and what they can do, and give them information. Siraj-Blatchford and Sylva (2004) investigated practice in 12 preschools in the UK that had been selected from 141 preschools as showing the best developmental outcomes for children. Their research showed that in these settings there were frequent communicative interactions that showed 'sustained shared thinking', which provided optimum developmental outcomes for the children. These were defined, as noted in the Introduction (see above) as 'conversations in which the adult and child co-construct an idea or activity'. Siraj-Blatchford and Sylva's findings suggest that in the remaining 129 preschools – representing 85% of the whole sample – it is possible that many interactions between adults and children in nurseries did not facilitate the same level of co-construction and sharing of meaning and ideas. Furthermore, studies of talk in preschools in the USA (reviewed by Massey, 2004) also suggest that teacher–child conversations during free play tend to centre around providing children with assistance in obtaining items, managing behaviour, supporting children in peer relationships, praising children for appropriate behaviour and providing instructions to children. In book-reading with groups of children, the majority of teacher talk deals with organisation of the reading task, simple feedback and naming activities. A shared conversation model of interaction between adult and child does not appear to be prevalent in preschools. It may be that this model of interaction is not provided during basic training and has therefore to be explicitly described and promoted in the training of teachers and others who work in early years settings.

CONCLUSION

As this summary of interview data suggests, the Talking Table approach was perceived in a highly favourable light by staff in the early years settings investigated. Their response to the question as to whether they would recommend it to colleagues in other early years settings (see Box 9.3.2) was unanimous, and unequivocally positive. Although some drawbacks and problems were mentioned, these were relatively few and on the whole thought to be surmountable. All but one setting had continued to use the Talking Table approach in some form; this indicates that it was regarded by all the interviewees as an effective way of developing children's communication skills. These data are, nevertheless, limited in terms of their support for the usefulness of this method in achieving its aims for the children. Further research using observations of adult–child conversations and assessment of children's language skills is now needed.

REFERENCES

Bruner, J. (1968). *Processes of cognitive growth: infancy (Vol. III Heinz Warner lecture Series)*. Worcester, MA: Clark University Press.
Duffy, B. (1998). Talking with and listening to young children. In S. Smidt (Ed.), *The early years: a reader*. London: Routledge.
Farmer, M. (2002). Social interactionism in practice: a review. In F. Griffiths (Ed.), Communication counts. London: David Fulton.
Griffiths, F. (2002). *Communication counts*. London: David Fulton.
Griffiths, F. (2005). The art of conversation. *Times Educational Supplement Teacher*, **11 February**, 6–7.

Massey, S. L. (2004). Teacher–child conversation in the preschool classroom. *Early Childhood Education Journal*, **31**(4), 227–231.

Siraj-Blatchford, I. & Sylva, K. (2004). Researching pedagogy in English pre-schools. *British Educational Research Journal*, **30**(5), 713–730.

Tough, J. (1977). *Talking and learning: a guide to fostering communication skills in nursery and infant schools*. London: Ward-Lock Educational/Drake Educational Associates.

Vygotsky, L. S. (1962). *Thought and language*. Cambridge, MA: MIT Press.

Webster, A. (1987). Enabling language acquisition: the developmental evidence. *British Psychological Society. Division of Educational and Child Psychology Newsletter*, **27**, 25–31.

9.4 Implementing Effective Oral Language Interventions in Preschool Settings[1]

JULIE E. DOCKRELL, MORAG STUART and DIANE KING

Psychology and Human Development, Institute of Education, University of London

INTRODUCTION

Concern about the oral language skills of a significant minority of the preschool population is widespread; explanations are variously made at child, parent or school level (see Chapter 1, present volume). Two groups of children appear particularly vulnerable in this context: those from disadvantaged backgrounds and those for whom English is an additional language. Meanwhile, there is a growing awareness that formulaic interventions are unlikely to address the range and variety of the children's language needs or be sensitive to the variety of contexts in which children are learning. Suggestions for quick-fix solutions are not uncommon (see Riley, Burrell & McCallum, 2004) but these are rarely adequately evaluated. Detailed analyses of interventions are central to developing theory and practice as 'the more implementation and process data that are collected, the better the chance of explaining why interventions work relative to comparison conditions, when they do, and why they fail when they do not' (Pressley, Graham & Harris, 2006). We consider here the issues raised in devising and implementing oral language interventions in preschool contexts. Problems encountered in the design, execution and analysis of the study we describe are used to provide a framework for the development of future studies that can contribute to our understanding of evidence-based practice.

Our focus is an inner-city multilingual environment where the development of oral language skills in the language of the education system (English) is often compromised. Early work in the area had established that oral language skills were reduced for a significant minority of children in the primary schools (Stuart, 1999). Our aim was to offer targeted oral language support prior to school entry with the

[1] We are grateful to the funding provided by the Esmée Fairburn Trust and the schools and children for their participation in the study.

Language and Social Disadvantage: Theory into Practice Edited by J. Clegg and J. Ginsborg

aim of minimising later effects of language disadvantage. The first step was to identify the nature and the extent of the problems.

LANGUAGE LEARNING AND INTERVENTIONS

Valid and reliable interventions in preschool settings should be based on an understanding of (1) the children's personal and social contexts, (2) the processes involved in language acquisition, and (3) a rigorous evaluation of the efficacy of the intervention. We examined the children's personal and social contexts by collecting baseline measures that examined the opportunities that children had to acquire English in the nursery context and to provide a profile of their oral language skills in English.

Observations in a sample of nursery settings across the LEAs indicated that while there were opportunities to engage in oral language activities these were, typically, only used by a minority of children. Moreover, there were few opportunities for small-group work that built on oral language skills. Language modelling occurred in teaching and small group activities, whereas both outdoor and unstructured activities were dominated by language that was used to control behaviour. Measures of the children's language skills revealed low levels of both expressive and receptive language. Comprehension levels were significantly different to the children's non-verbal abilities, indicating that the children were not generally delayed. Vocabulary and narrative skills were specifically limited. These two components of the language system in conjunction with the development of the children's comprehension skills served as the basis for our intervention.

THE CONTENT AND PROCESS OF THE INTERVENTION

Vocabulary can be conceptualised as the building block of language (Anglin, 1993) and thus is central to the production and comprehension of language (Dockrell & Messer, 2004). Vocabulary knowledge is also a strong predictor of academic success, and plays a central role in cognitive development, especially in relation to literacy and learning (Cunningham & Stanovich, 1997; Stanovich & Cunningham, 1993). Vocabulary is learnt in context and children 'capitalize effectively on the information-rich social context within which word learning occurs' (Baldwin & Moses, 2001, p. 318). Developing the children's lexical knowledge was, therefore, identified as a key component of the current intervention.

Effective language use depends on being able to link words in meaningful grammatical constructions to produce narratives. The ability to narrate emerges in the preschool years and by the time children enter school, a majority possess a basic repertoire of narrative abilities (Wolf, 1985). Children who enter school without basic narrative abilities are at risk; both language and literacy development are compromised (Bishop & Edmundson, 1987; Feagans & Appelbaum, 1986; Michaels, 1981). There are clear developmental changes in both the form and the content of narratives beginning in the early preschool years (age 3) and continuing across the lifespan (e.g. Applebee, 1978; Berman & Slobin, 1994; Chafe, 1980).

Early narratives are often concerned with dramatic personal events, such as illness or injury (Miller & Sperry, 1988; Sutton-Smith, 1986). Importantly, children's narratives can be enhanced by opportunities to engage in the retelling of familiar materials (McGregor, 2000). Thus, the ability to produce oral narratives is an important skill for preschool children, a competence that was lacking in the current participants, and therefore constituted the second component of the intervention.

Finally, we considered the importance of comprehension and children's abilities to draw inferences. Inferences are based on the integration of world knowledge and text knowledge and are important precursors to the production of oral and written text. Inferences in a narrative are based on three identifiable sources of information including the why or how; the who, what, when and where; and the understander's world knowledge about information that was specified in the narrative (Warren, Nicholas & Trabasso, 1979). The ability to draw inferences is central to development of reading comprehension (Cain & Oakhill, 1999; Cain, Oakhill, Barnes & Bryant, 2001; Cornoldi & Oakhill, 1996; Oakhill & Garnham, 1988). Previous research with a similar population in primary classes highlighted problems with reading comprehension despite adequate decoding skills (Stuart, 2004). The third element of the intervention, therefore, focused on developing children's abilities to draw inferences in narrative contexts, thus supporting comprehension.

Our initial review of the literature and analysis of the skills of the children from the locality identified three components of oral language that were compromised in the current cohort: vocabulary, narrative and inferencing skills. These three dimensions comprised the content (the WHAT) of our intervention. We used two distinct sets of evidence to develop a rationale for how the development of children's language skills was to occur (the HOW). One set of evidence relates to adults' use of language during interaction with children, and the factors associated with increases in children's language development. These factors include the expansion of children's utterances into well-formed equivalents, the recasting of children's utterances into other grammatical forms or using other lexical items, commenting on the child's actions and focus of attention and following the child's lead. Thus, the ways in which adults talked with the children in the course of the intervention was seen as central to its success.

The second set of evidence relates to the organisation of the nursery setting. In preschool contexts the nature of language interactions is influenced by the size of the group. The larger the group taking part in the interaction, the less linguistic production there is and the simpler the structure of the utterances made (Pellegrino & Scopesi, 1990). However, it would be wrong to assume that interventions are best provided one-to-one. Peer interactions enhance language abilities in preschoolers (Goldstein, English, Shafer & Kaczmarek, 1997; Robertson & Ellis Weismer, 1977) and preschoolers' narratives are influenced by what they hear from their peers (McGregor, 2000). Our intervention therefore involved working with children with differing language abilities in small groups in a linguistically responsive manner using materials that were related to familiar activities and local contexts.

EVALUATING AND MEASURING CHANGE

Identifying valid and reliable effects of interventions is problematic; methodological and statistical issues are paramount. To identify an intervention-specific effect it is important to have both a control group and a 'realistic' comparison group (Pressley & Harris, 1994). Moreover, within the skills measured, a distinction needs to be drawn between specific effects and general effects. Obtaining positive effects on the specific variables and no effect on the general or untargeted variables permits confidence that the positive outcomes are not due to Hawthorne or other general effects (Campbell & Stanley, 1966).

For the majority of children, some change will occur in test performance in the absence of any targeted intervention. Analysis must control for this; scores can be analysed in at least three different ways, for example, t tests based on gain scores (normalised gain score, Hake, 1998), ANCOVA or split-plot. Some statisticians argue that 'in most cases you should analyse the data in several ways' (Wright, 2003, p. 130), although these comparisons are virtually never published outside the statistical literature. The current project addressed these methodological pitfalls by including a realistic comparison group that offered children all the features of the main intervention except the key linguistic components. Both targeted and non-targeted language skills were measured and analyses were carried out using more than one statistical approach.

METHOD

PARTICIPANTS

One hundred and forty-two children participated in the study. Fifty-three children were exposed to the 'Talking Time' (TT) intervention, 41 children were exposed to story reading (SR) and 48 children attended the nursery that served as a comparison.

STUDY DESIGN

To evaluate the impact and efficacy of TT, children's progress in the target nursery was compared with two other groups. To compare children's progress with typical developmental trajectories for the population, a successful nursery with a strong oral language philosophy was identified and served as a comparison nursery (C). To contrast the specific effects of the TT activities and staff training, a second nursery was identified where children were exposed to additional oral language – small-group story telling sessions (SR), effectively a comparison intervention. The variables common to both TT and SR were small groups (maximum size five), regular activity, minimum period of 10 minutes and group membership remaining constant.

'TALKING TIME'

Table 9.4.1 presents each area of language competence and the ways in which these were translated into developmentally-appropriate activities. These activities

Table 9.4.1. Target language skills and supporting activities

Target	Talking Time activity	Aims
Development of core vocabulary	Acting out	Develop core vocabulary through play-acting around themes. Data from parental questionnaires and age of acquisition norms were used to help identify target vocabulary
Ability to use language to predict and infer	Story talk	Develop the children's abilities to hypothesise about objects and activities and to draw literal and inferential conclusions by structuring discussions around pictures in books
Production of narrative text	Hexagon game	Support narrative development by using photographs of common activities in the child's environment. The pictures were chosen following consultation with the staff and piloting in a nursery not involved in the study. The photographs (on hexagonal cards) can be connected to form a series of narrative stories

typically occur in preschool provision, are consistent with and complement the Stepping Stones outlined for the Foundation Stage curriculum (QCA, 2000).[2] The intervention was carried out over two terms; vocabulary development and inference activities occurred in the first term while the narrative activities were introduced in the second term when children had acquired greater levels of oral language competence.[3] Children took part in the activities twice a week. The activities lasted for approximately 10 minutes.

TALKING WITH YOUNG CHILDREN

Talking with young children whose language skills are limited is both difficult and demanding. Staff discussions were held about understandings of language development and particular emphasis was placed on the ways in which language models provided by adults and peers have a significant impact on a child's developing oral language skills. Staff were provided with a number of training sessions both to familiarise themselves with the activities but also to highlight and discuss the specific types of language that supports children's communication skills. The importance of adult recasts of children's utterances and the drawing of appropriate contrasts between words and grammatical constructions while retaining the child's basic meaning were seen to be central to such activities. Staff were encouraged

---

[2] It was important that the staff saw the intervention as consistent with but extending current government guidelines.
[3] Details of the intervention are available from the authors.

to avoid direct questions and demands, following an inflexible script or forcing the child to repeat what was said. Children's language skills were assessed at the beginning and end of the intervention. Fidelity of the intervention was ensured by weekly visits to the nursery.

'STORY READING'

A comparison intervention was developed. This condition exposed children to language but did not necessarily require them to use language. Age-appropriate stories were identified and stories were repeated as appropriate to ensure familiarity with content and language. Children took part in the story reading situation twice a week. Staff were trained in story-telling techniques but no specific information about language development was provided. The story lasted for approximately 10 minutes. Children's language skills were assessed at the beginning and end of the intervention, and fidelity of the intervention was ensured by weekly visits to the nursery.

EFFICACY AND IMPACT

All children were expected to improve over time but no specific or differential effect was expected for non-verbal abilities or tasks tapping phonological skills, as these were not targeted in the intervention. We predicted that both intervention groups (I) would improve in their comprehension abilities, but that the TT group would demonstrate greater gains. In addition, we predicted that the TT group would demonstrate an enhanced ability to produce oral language as measured by vocabulary, sentence repetition and narrative skills.

RESULTS

Table 9.4.2 presents the measurements used to assess baseline performance and changes following the intervention.

As predicted, there was a general increase in performance over time. As a group at the end of the intervention the children were producing sentences with an average length of three words, their naming vocabulary was at the 19th centile and their comprehension skills were at the 11th centile. This contrasted with non-verbal abilities, 29th centile, which continued to be in the average range.

The results indicated that while both interventions supported children's performance on tasks that drew on language skills. TT had a direct impact on four of the tasks that assessed language competencies that were targeted in the intervention: comprehension, naming vocabulary, narrative length and sentence repetition. These skills underpin oral language competence. The limited improvement in children's oral narratives was a source of significant concern.

Table 9.4.2. Baseline measurements and change overtime

Competence		Change predicted from comparison groups	Overall improvement	Differential improvement between groups*	Comment
Non-verbal	Block building	X	Yes	No group differences	
	Picture similarities	X	Yes	I > C	It can be argued that
Language contribution	Early number	?	Yes	I > C	both these tasks draw on
Core language skills	Non-word repetition	X	Yes	No group differences	semantic knowledge
	Sentence repetition	√	Yes	TT > SR	and are thus associated
	Comprehension	√	Yes	TT > SR	with language
	Naming vocabulary	√	Yes	TT > SR	level
	Narrative length	√	Yes	TT > SR	
	Narrative information	√	Yes	No group differences	

* Significant differences at the 0.05 level controlling for baseline performance

GENERALISATION

Baseline data examining teachers' talk with children had indicated that nurseries provided few opportunities for language modelling or facilitative use of language. Analysis of the teacher talk data following the intervention indicated that there were no changes in the level or type of oral language produced in the control nursery in terms of language modelling or overall facilitative language. In contrast, there were highly significant positive changes in the nursery that had implemented the TT intervention. Some changes were noted in the SR nursery but these were not statistically significant. These data indicate that the intervention and training provided with TT had generalised to interactions throughout the nursery.

DISCUSSION

PROBLEMS, LESSONS LEARNED AND FUTURE DEVELOPMENTS

The current project demonstrated that it was possible to facilitate language development by means of a systematic programme based on current understanding of language development. Intervention research also provides the opportunity to raise questions about the application of theory to practice in an evidence-based fashion.

In this final section, we consider five aspects of the intervention implementation that should inform the development of future studies in the area.

CHILDREN'S NEEDS

The levels of oral language skills of the children in the current study raised considerable challenges for the staff. A large proportion of the children were functioning at the very early stages of language development, with many children at the beginning the study producing only one- and two-word utterances in English. Such needs were difficult to address; staff had not been provided with the appropriate training in oral language development during their initial training and regular informed support was not available. As a result there was not a principled understanding of the language skills that needed to be acquired, how this might be facilitated and the long-term nature of the task. This resulted in an idealised and simplified notion of how language is acquired. Indeed, at the end of the study staff felt that the children's oral language skills were appropriate for school entry. This perception contrasted with objective measures of language performance. Staff did not use difficulties and problems to develop subsequent changes in the curriculum; rather such problems allowed the inference that the problem was inherent within the child. There is a clear need for concrete guidance in turning objectives into practice.

CHILDREN'S PROGRESS

The length of the current intervention was insufficient to support the development of expressive language as measured by the children's narrative production. There are empirical and theoretical reasons to believe that understanding precedes expression. As such, the gains in comprehension should be viewed as a positive first step. However, the current cohort of children will require additional support to develop these skills in the primary classroom. Given the intransigence of expressive language development there is a need to extend these principles into reception and KS1 classes and provide a systematic evaluation of their efficacy. Supporting oral language development is a long-term activity.

The analysis of data at the group level over the period of time has inevitably meant that group results on standardised assessments have been reported. It has not been possible to profile changes in individual students. An important further question is how different types of students fared in the intervention. This requires data collection from naturalistic communication over longer time periods.

TRAINING

The pilot work and intervention identified a number of specific training issues. The realities of the preschool setting placed limitations on the staff's ability to organise the nursery programme in such a way that all children would be provided with the opportunity to engage in the activities. The significant demands in meeting government targets reduced time for more flexible individually-tailored activities. Indeed, this meant that when the intervention project was finished, staff felt that the maximum time available for oral language work in groups was 10 minutes a week. The role of the head teacher in supporting the work was paramount.

FIDELITY

An important dimension of the present study was the researcher's presence in the nurseries on a weekly basis. This ensured that the interventions were implemented as intended and allowed monitoring of the difficulties in intervention. These observations played a central role in understanding the difficulties staff had in eliciting narratives. We are therefore confident that this is an area in need of further work.

VIABILITY

The two interventions presented served to enhance the children's oral language skills, both had strengths and weaknesses. These contributed to the staff decisions as to their viability for supporting children's early language development. TT had the more powerful effect on the children's language and generalised to oral language input throughout the nursery. However, the staff found it difficult to programme the activities and considerable amounts of external training and support were required. For this reason, staff did not continue with the programme at the same level of intensity at the end of the intervention period. In contrast, although SR provided some improvement in oral language, it did not generalise. SR highlighted the importance of oral language while placing fewer demands on the staff, and the school intended to continue with the activity at the end of the intervention period.

CONCLUSION

Our study indicates that interventions need to be systemic. Firstly, they need to consider both the what and the how of the intervention. Both aspects should be based on current best evidence about language learning for preschool children. It is no longer acceptable to devise interventions on what is thought to work or what is thought to be 'good practice'. However, in addition, it is critical to address the wider context and needs of both the learners and the teachers. Failure to address the former will mean that materials and procedures will be ineffective, whereas failure to address the latter will mean that the intervention does not happen as planned or does not continue after the initial implementation phase. As we have shown, when these factors are addressed even preschool language support that happens twice weekly for short periods can enhance comprehension. Extending these results to narrative language and evaluating the longer term effects of such programmes requires further work.

REFERENCES

Anglin, J. M. (1993). Vocabulary Development: A Morphological Analysis. *Monographs For The Society For Research In Child Development*, **58** (10 Serial No. 238).

Applebee, A. (1978). *The child's conception of story: Ages two to seventeen.* Chicago, IL: The University of Chicago Press.

Baldwin, D. A. & Moses, L. J. (2001). Links between social understanding and early word learning: Challenges to current accounts. *Social Development*, **10**(3), 309–329.

Berman, R. A. & Slobin, D. I. (1994). *Relating events in narrative: A crosslinguistic developmental study.* Hillsdale, NJ: Lawrence Erlbaum.

Bishop, D. V. M. & Edmundson, A. (1987). Language impaired 4-year-olds: Distinguishing transient from persistent impairment. *Journal of Speech and Hearing Disorders*, **52**, 156–173.

Cain, K. & Oakhill, J. V. (1999). Inference making ability and its relation to comprehension failure in young children. *Reading and Writing: An Interdisciplinary Journal*, **11**, 489–503.

Cain, K., Oakhill, J. V., Barnes, M. A. & Bryant, P. E. (2001). Comprehension skill, inference-making ability, and their relation to knowledge. *Memory and Cognition*, **29**, 850–859.

Campbell, D. T. & Stanley, J. C. (1966). *Experimental and quasi-experimental designs for research.* Chicago, IL: Rand-McNally.

Chafe, W. (Ed.) (1980). *The pear stories: Cognitive, cultural, and linguistic aspects of narrative production.* Norwood, NJ: Ablex.

Cornoldi, C. & Oakhill, J. (1996). *Reading comprehension difficulties: processes and intervention.* Mahwah, NJ: Lawrence Erlbaum Associates.

Cunningham, A. E. & Stanovich, K. E. (1997). Early reading acquisition and its relation to reading experience and ability ten years later. *Developmental Psychology*, **33**, 934–945.

QCA (2000). *Curriculum guidance for the foundation stage.* London: QCA Publications.

Dockrell, J. E. & Messer D. (2004). Later vocabulary acquisition. In R. Berman (Ed.), *Language development across childhood and adolescence: psycholinguistic and crosslinguistic perspectives. Trends in language acquisition research 3* (pp. 35–52). Amsterdam: John Benjamins.

Feagans, L. & Appelbaum, M. (1986). Validation of language subtypes in learning disabled children. *Journal of Educational Psychology*, **78**, 358–364.

Goldstein, H., English, K. Shafer, K. & Kaczmarek, L. (1997). Interaction among preschoolers with and without disabilities: Effects of across-the-day peer intervention. *Journal of Speech, Language, and Hearing Research*, **40**, 33–48.

Hake, R. R. (1998) Interactive engagement versus traditional methods: A six-thousand-student survey of mechanics test data for introductory physics courses. *American Journal of Physics*, **66**, 64–74.

McGregor, K. (2000). The development and enhancement of narrative skills in a preschool classroom: Towards a solution to clinician-client mismatch. *American Journal of Speech and Language Pathology*, **9**(1), 55–71.

Michaels, S. J. (1981). 'Sharing time': Children's narrative styles and differential access to literacy. *Language and Society*, **10**, 443–487.

Miller, P. J. & Sperry, L. L. (1988). Early talk about the past: The origins of conversational stories of personal experience. *Journal of Child Language*, **15**, 293–315.

Oakhill, J. & Garnham, A. (1988). *Becoming a skilled reader.* Oxford: Blackwell.

Pellegrino, M. L. M. and Scopesi, A. (1990). Structure and function of baby talk in a day-care centre. Journal of Child Language, **17**, 101–114.

Pressley, M. & Harris, K. (1994) Increasing the quality of educational intervention research. *Educational Psychology Review*, **6**(3), 191–208.

Pressley, M., Graham, S. & Harris, K. (2006). The state of educational intervention research as viewed through the lens of literacy intervention. *British Journal of Educational Psychology*, **76**, 1–19.

Riley, J. Burrell, A. & McCallum, B. (2004). *Developing the spoken language skills of reception class children in two multicultural, inner-city primary schools. British Educational Research Journal*, **30**, 657–672.

Robertson, S. B. & Ellis Weismer, S. (1997). The influence of peer models on the play scripts of children with specific language impairment. *Journal of Speech, Language, and Hearing Research*, **40**, 49–61.

Stanovich, K. E. & Cunningham, A. E. (1993). Where does knowledge come from? Specific associations between print exposure and information acquisition. *Journal of Educational Psychology*, **85**, 211–229.

Stuart, M. (1999). Getting ready for reading: Early phoneme awareness and phonics teaching improves reading and spelling in inner-city second-language learners. *British Journal of Educational Psychology*, **69**, 587–605.

Stuart, M. (2004). Getting ready for reading: A follow-up study of inner city second language learners at the end of Key Stage 1. *British Journal of Educational Psychology*, **74**, 15–36.

Sutton-Smith, B. (1986). The development of fictional narrative performances. *Topics in Language Disorders*, **7**, 1–10.

Warren, W. H., Nicholas, D. W. & Trabasso, T. (1979). Event chains and inferences in understanding narratives. In R.O. Freedle (Ed.), *New directions in discourse processing* (pp. 23–52). Norwood, NJ: Ablex.

Wolf, D. (1985). Ways of telling: Text repertoires in elementary school children. *Journal of Education*, **167**, 71–87.

Wright, D. B. (2003). Making friends with your data: Improving how statistics are conducted and reported. *British Journal of Educational Psychology*, **73**, 123–136.

9.5 Working and Learning Together: An Evaluation of a Collaborative Approach to Intervention

JENNY LEYDEN and MARCIN SZCZERBINSKI

Human Communication Sciences, University of Sheffield

BACKGROUND

This study was commissioned by an Education Action Zone (EAZ) in a city in the north of England. The Indices of Deprivation (Noble et al., 2004) indicate that the EAZ covers some of the most socio-economically deprived wards in the country. Staff report that the vocabulary skills of a vast number of children at nursery school are poor, their sentence construction is restricted and their conversational skills are limited. Empirical support for this anecdotal evidence was reported in a study conducted by Locke, Ginsborg and Peers (2002). They discovered that 54% of their sample of 240 three-year old children from low-SES backgrounds were language-delayed despite having cognitive skills within the normal range. At follow-up, two years later (Locke & Ginsborg, 2003), the number of children presenting with delayed language had decreased only minimally to 48%, and the proportion of children with severe language delay had increased from 9% to 26%.

A number of longitudinal studies have demonstrated that young children with speech and/or language impairments are at are greater risk of literacy difficulties (e.g. Nathan, Stackhouse, Goulandris & Snowling, 2004). This is hardly surprising, since spoken and written language share many common processes, including metaphonological, semantic and syntactic systems (Catts & Kamhi, 1999), and there is a strong interplay between them. Moreover, Stackhouse and Wells (1997) suggest that spoken language supports the development of written language, particularly during the early years of literacy acquisition.

Although there is a large body of research in the USA that has investigated language, literacy and educational outcomes of children from low-SES backgrounds, there is a dearth of British studies in this field. Nevertheless, teachers, head teachers and Ofsted inspectors all express concern at the lower levels of attainment (particularly in literacy) within the EAZ schools, compared with national norms. The EAZ in which the present research was carried out established a Foundation Stage Project to address this problem. Its primary aim was to improve the spoken language skills of children in nursery and reception classes. The key objectives were: (1) increasing the staff's knowledge and skills of early language development; (2) recording and assessing the extent of the children's learning; and (3) increasing the involvement of family members in the development of the children's communication skills.

The Foundation Stage Project, however, drew on expertise beyond that of teachers alone. Speech and language therapists (SLTs) play a critical role in the management of children with language delay. This role can take a number of different forms, including face-to-face contact in a clinic setting, home/school programmes and in-service training for teaching staff.

The need for increased collaboration between teachers and SLTs in an educational context is widely acknowledged and recommended (Law, Lindsay, Pearcey et al., 2000; McCartney, 1999; Tollerfield, 2003; Wright & Kersner, 2004). The sharing of knowledge and skills is more likely to ensure that children's needs are met more comprehensively. In addition, communication is best learnt in a real-life context, where newly acquired skills are more easily generalised (Davies, Shanks & Davies, 2004).

Although initiatives involving collaborative work in schools have been reported, it is recognised that more work of this nature needs to be done (Law et al., 2000; Locke et al., 2002). This would help to ensure that the language skills of all children who attend nursery school are developed to a more competent level, facilitating both their access to the curriculum and subsequent acquisition of written language.

AIMS/RATIONALE

The overall aim of this project was to evaluate the outcome of small-group intervention with children presenting with language delay, but who were not speech and language therapy clients, involving student SLTs and nursery staff. Small-group learning provides enhanced opportunities for children to develop confidence, acquire new skills and practise those they have already learnt. The staff–child ratio is higher (e.g. 1:4) than in the larger nursery group (1:13). Small groups provide a supportive learning environment that can easily be adapted to the needs of the children. Moreover, monitoring progress is also facilitated.

The specific aims of the project were to:

1. Gather assessment information and establish baselines relating to the children's listening or conversational skills.
2. Provide an effective intervention programme that would improve these skills.
3. Encourage collaborative practice between the student SLTs and nursery staff throughout the assessment/intervention/evaluation process.
4. Develop the nursery staff's knowledge and skills so that they are better able to observe, assess and use specific techniques that are conducive to language learning.
5. Evaluate the outcome for the children.
6. Evaluate the outcome for the nursery staff.

The focus on listening and conversation was based on Locke and Beech's (1991) programme 'Teaching Talking'. The authors argue that it is important that these rudimentary skills are established in nursery-age children, since they provide the foundation for higher-level spoken language skills such as narrative and discussion, which are vital for children to access the primary school curriculum successfully.

METHOD

DESIGN

There were two intervention groups: listening, and conversation. Each intervention group was matched to its own control (no intervention) group. Baseline and outcome measures were obtained for all children.

PARTICIPANTS

Children: Children in the intervention groups attended five nurseries. The control groups were drawn from five different nurseries within the EAZ. The children were recruited and allocated to the groups by language coordinators (see below). The intervention groups and control groups were very closely matched on age, sex and length of time in nursery. Details are given in Table 9.5.1 below. Written, informed consent was obtained from the parent/carer of each child.

Student SLTs: Student SLTs in their final year of the post-graduate qualifying course at a local training establishment assessed and worked with the intervention groups. Second-year undergraduate SLT students assessed the control groups.

Staff: Nursery staff worked alongside the student SLTs. Each of the five intervention nurseries had a self-selected teacher or nursery nurse who had acted as a language coordinator for the previous 12 months. Language coordinators had only just been assigned to three of the five control group nurseries.

MATERIALS

Listening: The listening assessment used an unfamiliar, simple nursery rhyme. A vocabulary check of the target words was conducted first using a picture booklet. In addition to the target, there were three other pictures on each page that were

Table 9.5.1. Intervention and control groups

Group	Listening	Conversation
Intervention	$n = 19$ 6 girls, 13 boys mean age 3;7	$n = 20$ 6 girls, 14 boys mean age 3;7
Control	$n = 17$ 8 girls, 9 boys mean age 3;7	$n = 16$ 8 girls, 8 boys mean age 3;9

either semantically or phonologically related to the target, or unrelated. The child was required to listen while the student SLT said the rhyme twice. On the third occasion the student SLT missed out the last word in each line, and the child was required to point to the target picture or say the missing word.

Conversation: The conversational skills assessment was carried out by two student SLTs as follows: having establishing rapport, and after a five-minute settling-in period, one student SLT played with the child for 10 minutes in the home corner 'making dinner for Teddy', talking about what they were doing. The other recorded the child's utterances. The components of conversation to be assessed were:

- evidence of greeting/recognition
- number of responses
- number of initiations
- number of turns on same topic
- inappropriate topic changes
- conversational repair
- ending conversation appropriately.

Mean length of utterance was also calculated.

Additional materials: A group rating form was used to provide information about the progress made by the children receiving intervention that could not be captured in the individual follow-up assessments. A questionnaire was used to establish what, if anything, the staff felt they had gained from the experience of working with the students. Questions related to knowledge, skills, confidence, perceived impact on the children, perceived impact on the staff and collaborative practice.

PROCEDURE

The student SLTs were fully briefed about the project before it began. Baseline measures were collected in week 1 of the placement followed by seven weekly group intervention sessions. Targets were set for each group as a whole and for the each child within the group. Each group followed a similar structure: first, a 'hello' song, followed by two 'hands-on', traditional, fun, learning activities based on the current theme in the nursery. Materials included everyday objects, toys, pictures, games and songs. The activities were designed to engage the children while they were helped to achieve their target, employing a range of facilitative techniques. The group ended with a 'bye-bye' song, and the children often took an activity home to do with their parents. There were three to four children in each of the groups, which lasted for approximately 20 minutes.

The language coordinator and student SLTs worked collaboratively, discussing background details regarding the children, planning the sessions, recording the children's responses and discussing children's performance. Student SLTs left their session plans and materials so that staff could repeat the activities during the week.

All children in the intervention groups were rated on the group rating form after the second and final group intervention sessions. Children in both the intervention groups and control groups were reassessed using the same listening or conversation assessment tool during the last week of the placement.

Questionnaires were sent to the five intervention nurseries after the children had been reassessed. To maximise the numbers available for analysis, they were also sent to the nursery staff that had been involved with the previous cohort of student SLTs. Finally, a sample of the staff involved attended a discussion group after the project had finished.

RESULTS

LISTENING

Statistical analysis of children's performance on the listening assessment indicated that both intervention and control groups improved significantly over time. The improvement was greater for the intervention group than the control group but the difference was small and not statistically significant (see Table 9.5.2).

Analysis of the group rating forms (collected for the intervention group only) showed that all ratings improved over time and differences between the second and last intervention sessions were statistically significant. Clearly, the children's

Table 9.5.2. Listening assessment: mean scores (standard deviations)

	Baseline	Outcome	ANOVA
Intervention ($n = 19$)	3.47 (1.58)	4.53 (1.84)	Time: $F(1,34) = 5.79$, $p = 0.022$
Control ($n = 17$)	4.82 (2.01)	5.24 (1.86)	Group: $F(1,34) = 3.84$, $p = 0.058$
			Time × Group: $F(1,34) = 1.11$, NS

Note: The possible range of scores was 0–8. The data were analysed using mixed-design analysis of variance (ANOVA) with a within-subject factor of Time (baseline vs outcome) and a between-subject factor of Group (intervention vs control).

Table 9.5.3. Students' ratings for listening intervention group: mean scores (standard deviations)

	Baseline	Outcome
Amount of encouragement required to come to group	3.00 (1.41)	4.08 (1.11)
Child's responses during session	2.95 (1.28)	3.84 (1.11)
Level of participation in group	3.03 (1.34)	3.58 (1.04)
Level of success on tasks	2.79 (0.95)	3.55 (0.94)
Amount of spontaneous interaction with peers in group	2.18 (0.87)	2.74 (0.99)
Amount of spontaneous interaction with students in group	2.89 (1.34)	3.42 (1.30)
Listens appropriately in nursery	2.26 (0.98)	3.26 (0.81)
Spontaneous interaction with peers in nursery	2.76 (1.40)	3.45 (1.14)
Spontaneous interaction with staff in nursery	2.89 (1.52)	3.55 (1.26)

Note: The possible range of scores was 1–5. All baseline-outcome differences are significant ($p < 0.05$) on Wilcoxon test.

listening skills, as perceived by the students, had improved (see Table 9.5.3). Moreover, almost two-thirds of children achieved 75–100% of their intervention targets.

CONVERSATION

The conversation intervention was effective, insofar as the MLU scores of the intervention group improved significantly, while in the control group they stayed virtually the same. That difference was statistically significant (see Table 9.5.4). The differences between the two groups in the amount of improvement on the other measures were not statistically significant, although on some dimensions (number of initiations, number of responses, conversation repair) the trend was in the expected direction.

As with the listening intervention group, all group ratings improved significantly over time: in the student SLTs' judgement, the children had made good progress (see Table 9.5.5). Just over half of the children achieved 75–100% of their intervention targets.

The nursery staff also reported that both types of intervention had a positive impact on the children's spoken language: the children were more confident and

Table 9.5.4. Conversation assessments: mean MLU scores (standard deviations)

	Baseline	Outcome	ANOVA
Intervention ($n = 20$)	1.93 (1.07)	2.57 (1.27)	Time: $F(1,34) = 4.54$, $p = 0.04$
Control ($n = 16$)	3.99 (1.06)	3.97 (0.91)	Group: $F(1,34) = 26.21$; $p < 0.001$
			Time × Group: $F(1,34) = 4.93$, $p = 0.03$

Note: The data were analysed using mixed-design analysis of variance (ANOVA) with a within-subject factor of Time (baseline vs outcome) and a between-subject factor of Group (intervention vs control)

Table 9.5.5. Students' ratings for conversation intervention group: mean scores (standard deviations)

	Baseline	Outcome
Amount of encouragement required to come to group	2.78 (1.52)	3.97 (1.29)
Child's responses during session	2.42 (1.26)	3.44 (1.14)
Level of participation in group	2.19 (1.02)	3.36 (1.01)
Level of success on tasks	3.06 (1.00)	3.81 (0.93)
Amount of spontaneous interaction with peers in group	1.58 (0.60)	2.56 (0.64)
Amount of spontaneous interaction with students in group	2.39 (1.42)	3.42 (1.09)
Child initiates and maintains conversation appropriately in nursery	2.19 (1.02)	2.86 (0.72)
Spontaneous interaction with peers in nursery	2.50 (0.92)	3.17 (0.92)
Spontaneous interaction with staff in nursery	2.58 (0.81)	3.28 (0.73)

Note: The possible range of scores was 1–5. All baseline-outcome differences are significant ($p < 0.01$) on Wilcoxon test.

their communication skills had improved. For example, some children were now initiating conversation in the larger nursery group, taking part in role-play, and approaching staff, e.g. to ask for their shoelaces to be tied; other children were now concentrating for longer on one task. Staff also reported that the children enjoyed the intervention sessions: they liked the routine that the groups provided, having new people in the nursery, and feeling 'special'. Moreover, they enjoyed having something to take home from the group.

OUTCOMES FOR NURSERY STAFF

Thirteen nursery staff, working in seven different nurseries, completed the question-naire. Twelve reported successful collaboration with the student SLTs. Observing the intervention sessions was thought to be most useful, followed by participating in the intervention sessions, and discussing children's performance. They said that they thought the experience of working with the student SLTs would impact on their day-to-day work through improved knowledge and skills. According to the vast majority of staff, the best thing about working with the students was gaining new ideas for activities, new strategies and/or new techniques to enhance language development that could easily be transferred to the larger nursery setting. Reported problems relating to working with the student SLTs were lack of a suitable space and the shortage of time to establish rapport with the children before the assess-ment sessions. Nevertheless, the staff felt that working alongside the student SLTs had been a valuable experience. These themes were also reiterated in the group discussion with the nursery staff at the end of the project.

DISCUSSION

This study aimed to evaluate a collaborative approach to intervention with language-delayed children, involving student SLTs and nursery staff. Baselines were estab-lished in relation to listening and conversation skills. For the latter group, the MLU was below the expected age norms, both before and after intervention. This provides further evidence for the incidence of language delay in children from socio-economically deprived backgrounds in this part of the country (Locke & Ginsborg, 2003), justifying the need for intervention. Since the assessments used were informal and experimental, normative data are not available for any of the other measures.

OUTCOMES FOR CHILDREN

In relation to baseline and outcome assessments, the intervention was to some extent effective, insofar as the conversation group had significantly improved MLU whereas the control group had not. However, the seven-week intervention period was relatively brief: had the intervention been twice as intensive or continued for twice as long, then it may be that there would have been significant improvement on the other conversation and listening measures. Furthermore, the children varied in their attendance at nursery and therefore the amount of intervention they received. This may have influenced the amount of progress they made.

Both student SLTs and nursery staff reported that the children had improved particularly in areas that had not been assessed in the listening and conversational assessments. Questionnaire data included the following comments: 'some children who used little spoken language in nursery have now begun to communicate more verbally with staff'; 'another child who responded mainly by grunts began talking more'; 'listening is improved'.

More than half the staff commented on the benefits of small-group work for the children: 'the small numbers in the groups helps the children stay focused and develop within the group'; 'small groups encouraged speech'. Many staff in the discussion group commented on how difficult it is to address the language and social communication needs of children in the usual nursery group of 13, because they lack the confidence to interact in larger groups. Such comments support the questionnaire data relating to children's confidence, e.g. 'regular structured sessions which every week follow a similar format helped the children to grow in confidence within the groups'; 'the small groups gave the children confidence'.

The children enjoyed attending the groups each week, which was very evident both to the students and the nursery staff. Their increased confidence is likely to impact positively on their self-esteem.

COLLABORATIVE WORKING

The evaluation of collaborative working was crucial since one of the key aims of the study was to provide nursery staff with skills so that they felt better equipped to support and develop children's spoken language in the day-to-day nursery setting.

Impact on knowledge: The majority of the staff felt that the student assessments provided them with new information regarding individual children's listening/conversational skills, and that as a result they had a better understanding of the processes involved in listening, and of the components of conversation. This was further confirmed in the discussion group, and one member of staff will continue using the listening assessment in her nursery following the intervention sessions. In the questionnaire data, staff reported: 'better knowledge of children's stages of development'; '[it has] given me a better understanding of listening skills'.

Impact on skills: The majority of staff felt that they were better able to observe children's listening ability and conversation skills. More strikingly, they felt that they had learnt useful techniques for developing both listening skills and conversational skills. In the questionnaire data, 12 respondents reported improved skills, e.g. 'I have acquired lots of techniques for developing conversational skills'; 'practical ideas that are workable during a normal working day'. Two members of staff have continued to run each of the groups, finding the overall structure useful.

Impact on confidence: All but one member of staff felt that they were now better able to set targets for individual children. This seems to relate to increased knowledge of individual children's spoken language abilities. The vast majority now feel more confident in trying to achieve those targets, probably because they feel better equipped, both in terms of knowledge and skills.

Impressions of the student SLTs: The staff were very positive about the student SLTs, and this was a recurrent theme in both the questionnaire and the group discussion. They were particularly impressed with their professional approach and their high levels of preparation and organisation throughout the placement. Comments were also made about the 'fresh' ideas they brought with them, as well as their competence in interacting with and engaging the children.

LIMITATIONS OF THE STUDY

Although the listening and conversation assessments provided baseline and outcome measures of these language skills, the assessments themselves were problematic. The listening assessment relied heavily on short-term auditory memory and should also, perhaps, have included following instructions and story comprehension. These were avoided originally since children with receptive language difficulties would have been penalised. Notwithstanding, the latter tasks more accurately reflect the listening/processing demands of a reception classroom.

The conversational assessment consisted of a single 10-minute sample of the child talking. While this snapshot view may well be typical, it is quite possible that on a different occasion, in a different context, or even in the same context, there would be considerable differences due to normal variability. An alternative method of assessing conversation would be to ask one or two members of staff who know the child well, to rate the child on how he or she typically performs on the dimensions of conversation included in the current assessment. This would go some way to improving reliability.

FUTURE DEVELOPMENTS

In this study, the children were reassessed immediately following intervention. It would be useful to assess them again three months later, to see if progress is maintained. Moreover, gains in communication skills are often apparent some weeks after terminating intervention.

There was discussion with the nursery staff about the benefits of a single staff member working alongside the students, or whether to rotate the staff involved, so that new knowledge and skills could cascade throughout the nursery. As a group, they thought this could be valuable but some were cautious about the experience becoming 'too watered down'. It was also agreed that parents should be involved.

CONCLUSIONS

It was felt that this project has gone some way towards fulfilling the three key objectives of the Foundation Stage Project outlined at the start of this report:

student SLTs working collaboratively with nursery staff had positive outcomes on children's confidence and communication skills. Moreover, the benefits extended to the nursery staff, who reported that their knowledge and skills had increased as a result of working with the student SLTs. They were better able to observe children's listening and conversational skills and learnt useful facilitative techniques that could easily be used on a day-to-day basis. Nursery staff felt that it had been an informative and useful experience and would like it to be repeated again, incorporating a parents' workshop and rotating the members of staff involved.

ACKNOWLEDGEMENTS

We would like to thank Margaret Booth, Project Director of the Education Action Zone, for her enthusiasm and support throughout, and enabling this study to take place. Thanks are also extended to Sue Baxter, Joy Stackhouse, and Ann Locke for their role in managing the project.

REFERENCES

Catts, W.W. & Kamhi, A.,G. (1999). *Language and learning disabilities*. London: Allyn & Bacon.

Davies, P., Shanks, B. & Davies, K. (2004). Improving narrative skills in young children with delayed language development. *Educational Review*, **56**, 271–286.

Law, J., Lindsay, G., Peacey, N., Gascoigne, M., Soloff, N., Radford, J., Band, S. & Fitzgerald, L. (2000). *Provision for children with speech and language needs in England and Wales: Facilitating communication between education and health services*, Research Report No. 239, London: DfEE.

Locke, A. & Beech, M. (1991). *Teaching talking*. Windsor: NFER Nelson.

Locke, A. & Ginsborg, J. (2003). Spoken language in the early years: The cognitive and linguistic development of three-to five-year old children from socio-economically deprived backgrounds. *Educational and Child Psychology*, **20**, 68–79.

Locke, A., Ginsborg, J. & Peers, I. (2002). Development and disadvantage: Implications for the early years and beyond. *International Journal of Language and Communication Disorders*, **37**, 3–15.

McCartney, E. (1999). Barriers to collaboration: An analysis of systemic barriers to collaboration between teachers and speech and language therapists. *International Journal of Language and Communication Disorders*, **34**, 431–440.

Nathan, L., Stackhouse, J., Goulandris, N. & Snowling, M. (2004). The development of early literacy skills among children with speech difficulties: A test of the 'critical age hypothesis.' *Journal of Speech, Language, and Hearing Research*, **47**, 377–391.

Noble, M., Wright, G., Dibben, C., Smith, G.N.N., McLennan, D., Anttila, C. et al. (2004). The English Indices of Deprivation (revised). Wetherby: Office of the Deputy Prime Minister Publications.

Stackhouse, J. & Wells, B. (1997). *Children's speech and literacy difficulties: a psycholinguistic framework*. London: Whurr.

Tollerfield, I. (2003). The process of collaboration within a special school setting: An explanation of the ways in which skills and knowledge are shared and barriers overcome when a teacher and speech and language therapist collaborate. *Child Language Teaching and Therapy*, **9**, 1–67.

Wright, J.A. & Kersner, M. (2004). Short-term projects: The Standards Fund and collaboration between speech and language therapists and teachers. *Support for Learning*, **19**, 19–23.

9.6 Facilitating Narrative and Social Skills in Secondary School Students with Language and Behaviour Difficulties

HELEN STRINGER
School of Education, Communication and Language Sciences, University of Newcastle upon Tyne; Newcastle upon Tyne Hospitals NHS Trust

INTRODUCTION

At secondary school, the adolescent student with persisting language difficulties (LD) experiences subsequent difficulties in meeting the demands of the educational curriculum. In addition to the increasing language demands of the classroom, the role of language in establishing peer group acceptance and personal identity becomes equally important. Not only are adolescents with LD at an increased risk of literacy, educational and behavioural difficulties (EBD) (Baker & Cantwell, 1983; Beitchman, Brownlie & Wilson, 1996; Bishop & Adams, 1990; Stothard, Snowling, Bishop, Chipchase & Kaplan, 1998; Tomblin, Zhang, Buckwalter & Catts, 2000), they are also more vulnerable to social difficulties, rejection from peers and associated problems in self-esteem and self-image (McAndrew, 1999; Nelson, 1993).

Differentiating between the emotional and behavioural difficulties associated with the student's LD and those associated with the usual process of adolescent development is complex. Over time, symptoms of LD become less obvious as the student grows older and progresses through school. Initial speech and language difficulties often improve, leading others to assume that the student has developed adequate language abilities. However, these students can be left with unresolved and unrecognised LD. This places the student at greater risk of educational, behavioural and social problems. Speech and Language Therapy (SLT) services generally target preschool and early school-age children, with additional resources only for those older children who have Statements of Special Educational Needs. The paucity of SLT services available to secondary school-aged children is well

Language and Social Disadvantage: Theory into Practice Edited by J. Clegg and J. Ginsborg
© 2006 John Wiley & Sons, Ltd

documented (Lindsay, Soloff, Law et al., 2002). Until recently, there has been insufficient evidence relating to this population to justify such provision. Yet Leahy and Dodd (2002) and Joffe (Chapter 9.7) have shown that SLT can help secondary school-aged students make significant progress.

Given that poor educational attainment may well be the result of undiagnosed LD in secondary school-age students with EBD, the present study aimed to investigate the efficacy of speech and language therapy with this group of students, particularly in facilitating improvements in expressive language skills. The secondary school that participated in this study is situated in an area of high socio-economic deprivation: approximately 62% of the students attending the school are entitled to free school meals. In terms of GCSE results, the students perform well below the national average. In 2002, 14% achieved five or more GCSEs graded A*–C, compared with the national average of 52%. Recently, a project was conducted in the school to determine the prevalence of LD. A sub-sample of students from Year 7 was randomly selected ($n = 127$) and screened for LD using a range of language measures. The results indicated that a significant proportion of the sample showed LD with performance on standardised language measures at least one standard deviation below the mean. The participants in this study presented with behaviour as well as language difficulties. Due to the heterogeneous nature of the LD in the study group, disorder-based intervention and individual intervention were considered inappropriate. Instead, an emphasis was placed on oral narrative competency and social skills training. Narrative skill development was included to evaluate its impact on the development of language skills in general, rather than on narrative development per se. Social skills training has been shown to have a long-term effect on the behaviour of children with conduct disorder (Webster-Stratton, Reid & Hammond, 2001). However, the effect is small and not dependent on the content or length of the programme, or the age of the participants (Kavale, Mathur, Forness, Rutherford & Quinn, 1997). The teachers in the school had commented on the poor social skills and high level of aggression of some of the participants involved in the study. Therefore, an element of social skills development was included in the intervention with a focus on the development of assertive behaviour and communication skill as an alternative to aggressive or passive behaviour.

METHOD

PARTICIPANTS

The participants in the study were 12 boys with LD and behaviour difficulties. The ages ranged from 11;8 to 13;2 with a mean age of 12;4. Seven of the boys were already known to local SLT services, but only two had received treatment previously. The remaining five were selected from the Year 7 language screen project (see above) as having scored at or below the fifth percentile on two receptive language measures. All the participants scored below the 10th percentile on at least two measures of expressive or receptive language and exhibited difficulties in at least two areas of behaviour as measured by either teachers, parents or self report on the Strengths and Difficulties Questionnaire (SDQ) (Goodman, 1997). Of the two participants who had previously received SLT, one had generalised learning difficulties and additional LD, the other had been referred at preschool with LD and continued to have residual expressive and receptive difficulties, following several years of varying levels of intervention. Seven of the participants had ADHD, one with co-morbid Asperger's syndrome, diagnosed by medical practitioners specialising in child and adolescent mental health. Five were taking Ritalin (methylphenidate) at the time of the study. The participants were randomly assigned following the baseline assessments into two intervention groups (Groups 1 and 2). This was not for the purpose of comparison but to make the numbers in the groups more manageable. Due to constraints imposed by the school calendar, it was necessary to begin intervention with Group 1 before Group 2.

ASSESSMENT MATERIALS

The Raven's Coloured Progressive Matrices (CPM) (Raven, 1962) was used to assess cognitive skills pre-intervention even though some of the participants were older than the recommended upper-age limit. The following measures were taken pre- and post-intervention:

- *the Strengths and Difficulties Questionnaire* (SDQ) (Goodman, 1997): self, parent and teacher forms
- four subtests of the *Clinical Evaluation of Language Fundamentals* (CELF-3^{UK}) (Semel, Wiig & Secord, 2000): (1) concepts and directions (CD), (2) word classes (WC), (3) formulated sentences (FS), (4) listening to paragraphs (LtP)
- two subtests of the *Test of Word Knowledge* (TOWK) (Wiig & Secord, 1992): (1) expressive vocabulary (EV), (2) receptive vocabulary (RV).

PROCEDURE

The researcher and another experienced speech and language therapist delivered the intervention to both groups. This consisted of a twice-weekly one-hour session. It was planned to give each group 10 sessions. However, due to unforeseen circumstances including staff training days and difficulties with room bookings, Group 1 received nine sessions and Group 2 received seven. The content of the sessions, however, was the same for the two groups. The two strands of narrative and social skills intervention were delivered separately and then integrated together in other activities. For example, problems familiar to the participants were discussed, such as bullying, being blamed for things they did not do and disagreements with peers. A theme was then developed as a narrative with the protagonists behaving in an assertive rather than aggressive way. Narratives were composed as a group using the questions 'who?', 'where?', 'when?' and 'what happened?' as prompts throughout the sessions. The narratives were introduced following a developmental pattern (Westby, 1999), from descriptive sentences through to stories with sequences of episodes. The social skills intervention was modified from existing resources (Hutchings, Comins & Offiler, 1991; Kelly, 2001; Michelson, Sugai, Wood & Kazdin, 1983; Rustin & Kuhr, 1999). The focus of the social skills work was to develop assertiveness as opposed to passive or aggressive behaviour. The participants were asked to role-play situations, such as being blamed by another student for something they had not done, and being unable to communicate their innocence. The role-plays were presented to the rest of the group, and video-recorded to enable self-evaluation and further discussion – although participants were, understandably, reluctant to engage in this. The vocabulary and some set phrases for the role-play were modelled by the authors, and the participants were given further models on an individual basis as required. A snack break and an informal activity were incorporated into each session to develop informal conversation, reinforce the overall objectives of the group and promote interaction between the participants. Behaviour was a secondary aim of the intervention and was not therefore targeted unless there were episodes of physical aggression. Behaviour difficulties were nevertheless evident and included inattention and impulsiveness (e.g. prowling round the room, fiddling with pencils and distracting one another) and inappropriate social behaviour (e.g. making 'farting' noises, grunting and shouting). Although the participants appeared not to be listening, they consistently complied with all the instructions, except for one occasion when a participant admitted to 'not listening'.

RESULTS

Pre- and post-intervention measures were administered six months apart for Group 1 and five months apart for Group 2. The shortened interval for Group 2 arose due to constraints imposed by the school calendar. The group results of the pre- and post-intervention measures are set out in Table 9.6.1. The converted Raven's CPM score is a percentile score, as standard scores are not available for this assessment; other scores are standard scores (mean standard score for all measures = 10). Mean scores and standard deviations (SD) are given for all measures except the CPM.

Table 9.6.1. Pre-intervention measures for Group 1 and Group 2

Group			Cognition	Receptive measures			Expressive measures		
			CPM	CD	RV	LP	WC	FS	EV
1	Pre-intervention	Mean (SD)	< 5 > 50	5.7 (1.37)	6.8 (4.11)	6 (1.67)	5.7 (2.16)	4.5 (2.35)	6.3 (1.75)
	Post-intervention			6.2 (1.72)	7.3 (3.98)	7.5 (2.07)	6(2)	5.2 (2.71)	5.3 (1.5)
2	Pre-intervention	Mean (SD)	10–75	5.5 (1.64)	7.2 (3)	5.6 (4.41)	5.5 (1.64)	4.3 (1.75)	5 (2.1)
	Post-intervention			8.7 (3.55)	7.8 (1.72)	7.8 (2.79)	6.7 (1.97)	6 (2.97)	6.2 (1.83)

Small increases in the mean standard scores were evident across both groups except for Group 1 on the Expressive Vocabulary subtest from the TOWK. The combined group data from the pre- and post-intervention language measures were analysed using a Wilcoxon Signed Ranks Test. This analysis showed that significant improvements were made on the concepts and directions (receptive) subtest of the CELF-3^{UK} ($z = 2.33, p = 0.02$) and the formulated sentences (expressive) subtest of the CELF-3^{UK} ($z = 2.39, p = 0.017$). There were no significant improvements on any of the other measures. Further analysis revealed that there were no significant differences between the performance of Group 1 and Group 2 on these two subtests either pre- or post-intervention.

Pre- and post-intervention differences on the CELF-3^{UK} listening to paragraphs subtest did not reach significance due to two participants performing significantly lower at post-test compared to pre-test. However, nine of the participants did increase their performance on this subtest.

Differences in behaviour, pre- and post- intervention, were measured by the *Strengths and Difficulties Questionnaire*. However, only three post-intervention questionnaires were returned from teachers and parents and therefore it was not possible to evaluate the effect of the intervention on the participants' behaviour as perceived by teachers and parents. Anecdotal reports from the participants' teachers indicated that the boys were participating in class more appropriately. Eleven of the boys completed two self-report versions of the SDQ with the researcher. Table 9.6.2 shows the pre- and post-intervention self-report SDQ scores of the participants. No significant difference was found between the pre- and post-intervention assessments (Wilcoxon Signed Ranks Test, $p > 0.40$). However, six boys rated themselves as having worse behaviour overall. Descriptive analysis showed that the self-report scores did not correlate with the scores from teachers or parents.

Table 9.6.2. SDQ Self-report scores pre- and post-intervention

	Total		Emotional		Conduct		Hyperactivity		Peer		Prosocial	
	Pre	Post	Pre	Post	Pre	Post	Pre	Post	Pre	Post	Pre	Post
1	A	A	A	A	A	A	A	A	B	A	N	N
1	A	A	B	B	B	A	A	A	N	N	N	N
1	B	A	B	B	A	A	A	A	N	N	N	N
1	A	A	A	N	A	A	N	N	B	A	N	N
1	A	–	N	–	A	–	A	–	N	–	B	–
1	A	A	N	N	A	A	A	A	N	N	N	N
2	N	N	N	N	A	A	A	N	N	N	A	N
2	N	N	N	N	N	N	N	B	N	N	N	N
2	B	N	N	N	A	A	A	N	N	N	N	B
2	N	N	N	N	N	N	N	N	N	N	B	B
2	B	B	A	A	N	N	N	N	N	B	B	N
2	N	B	N	N	N	B	N	B	N	B	B	N

Key: N = normal; B = borderline; A = abnormal

DISCUSSION

The primary aim of the present study was to determine the extent to which SLT can improve the expressive language skills of secondary school-aged students with LD and behavioural difficulties. A secondary aim was to establish the extent to which SLT can improve behaviour. The intervention was not disorder-based (i.e. it did not specifically target sentence structure), but focused on more functional aspects of language: creating oral narratives and using appropriate language in social situations. Standardised language and behaviour measures were used to evaluate the intervention. Pre-intervention data demonstrated that participants had deficits in both receptive and expressive language. There was no statistically significant difference between the two groups on any of the pre- or post- intervention measures. Pre-intervention SDQ scores showed the different perceptions of the participants' behaviour held by teachers, parents and participants themselves. As a group, statistically significant improvements were only identified on one expressive language measure, the CELF-3[UK] formulated sentences subtest and one receptive language measure, the CELF-3[UK] concepts and directions subtest. Although improvements across the other measures were identified, particularly the listening to paragraphs subtest, these were not statistically significant. The improvements in performance were most obvious at sentence and conversation level, rather than word level. The focus of the activities was to develop narrative and the experience gained was mainly at sentence level, with the individual contributing to a group-generated narrative. Only a small amount of new vocabulary was introduced and this was not done with a level of frequency that would have facilitated learning (Windfuhr, Faragher & Conti-Ramsden, 2002). This is reflected in the lack of progress on the vocabulary measures. The participants were also encouraged to watch videos of themselves and others and comment reflectively on the content and effectiveness of the communication. The syntactic structure of sentences was not analysed or discussed. As the group progressed there were instances of the boys coaching each other's narrative contributions by providing models of appropriate language to use in that situation.

Post hoc examination of the video recordings of the intervention revealed that the specific skills practised by the participants included: listening to and remembering information in a sequential manner, and formulating sentences to conform to a semantic and syntactic framework congruent with the narrative being created by the group or the role play being enacted. These skills particularly support improvement in the CELF-3[UK] subtests concepts and directions, and formulating sentences. However, eight of the participants improved their performance on the listening to paragraphs subtest. The remaining two participants did not show any improvement, gaining lower post-intervention than pre-intervention scores. The listening to paragraphs subtest required the participants to integrate the skills mentioned in order to interpret a short narrative and answer questions about it. This is a particularly important skill for classroom learning. Several studies have considered the positive effect of teaching narrative skills on expressive language skills (Klecan-Aker,

1993; Hayward & Schneider, 2000) and reading achievement, including reading comprehension (Klecan-Aker & Caraway, 1997) but none has investigated the effect of narrative skill development on the comprehension of spoken language. Further investigation in this area is required, but the outcome of this study would suggest that narrative skill intervention may facilitate verbal comprehension. It was not possible to demonstrate an effect of the intervention on the participants' behaviour, other than some positive anecdotal reports from teachers. However, that 50% of the boys rated their own behaviour as *worse* following the intervention is an interesting and surprising finding. During the group sessions the SLTs talked openly about the type of behaviour that the participants exhibited and the reasons why it might be unacceptable to adults and peers. For many of the participants it was the first time they had considered the consequences of their behaviour from another person's viewpoint. Incidents such as swearing at teachers, answering back and refusing to do things when directed, were all discussed in a way that showed the participant how these events were viewed from the adult's perspective. Care was taken to do this in an objective way, without labelling them as 'naughty'. The post-intervention SDQ score for some of the participants may therefore be a reflection of their greater understanding of how behaviour is viewed in context, rather than an actual deterioration.

CONCLUSIONS

This study shows that adolescents with LD and behaviour difficulties can continue to benefit from appropriately targeted and structured SLT intervention. Significant improvement in expressive and receptive language can be achieved with a relatively small amount of input (seven hours). Furthermore, it is not necessary for participants to be sitting still and quietly for them to be able to attend to and benefit from activities, assuming an appropriate level of engagement and motivation. Further research is required to evaluate the effect of SLT intervention on behaviour.

REFERENCES

Baker, L. & Cantwell, D. P. (1983). Developmental, social and behavioural characteristics of speech and language disordered children. *Annual Progress in Child Psychiatry and Child Development*, 205–216.

Beitchman, J. H., Brownlie, E. B. & Wilson, B. (1996). Linguistic impairment and psychiatric disorder: pathways to outcome. In J. H. Beitchman, N. J. Cohen, M. M. Konstantareas & R. Tannock (Eds), *Language, Learning and Behaviour Disorders: Developmental, Biological and Clinical Perspectives* (pp. 493–515). Cambridge: University Press.

Bishop, D. V. M. & Adams, C. (1990). A Prospective Study of the Relationship between Specific Language Impairment and Reading Retardation. *Journal of Child Psychology and Psychiatry*, **31**, 1027–1050.

Goodman, R. (1997). *The Strengths and Difficulties Questionnaire*. Retrieved 3 January, 2003, from www.sdqinfo.com

Hayward, D. & Schneider, P. (2000). Effectiveness of teaching story grammar knowledge to pre-school children with language impairment. An exploratory study. *Child Language Teaching and Therapy*, **16**, 255–283.

Hutchings, S., Comins, J. & Offiler, J. (1991). *The social skills handbook*. Oxford: Winslow Press.

Kavale, K. A., Mathur, S. R., Forness, S. R., Rutherford, R. B., & Quinn, M. M. (1997). Effectiveness of social skills training for students with behaviour disorders: A meta-analysis. *Advances in Learning and Behavioural Disabilities*, **11**, 1–26.

Kelly, A. (2001). *TALKABOUT*. Bicester: Speechmark Publishing.

Klecan-Aker, J. S. (1993). A treatment programme for improving story-telling ability: a case study. *Child Language Teaching and Therapy*, **9**, 105–115.

Klecan-Aker, J. S. & Caraway, T. H. (1997). A study of the relationship of storytelling ability and reading comprehension in fourth and sixth grade African-American children. *European Journal of Disorders of Communication*, **32**, 109–125.

Leahy, M. & Dodd, B. (2002). Why should secondary schools come second? *Royal College of Speech and Language Therapists Bulletin*, May, 11–13.

Lindsay, G., Soloff, N., Law, J., Band, S., Peacey, N., Gascoigne, M. & Radford, J. (2002). Speech and language therapy services to education in England and Wales. *International Journal of Language and Communication Disorders*, **37**, 273–288.

McAndrew, E. (1999). The relationship between self-esteem and language disordered children. *Child Language Teaching and Therapy*, **15**, 219–232.

Michelson, L., Sugai, D. P., Wood, R. P. & Kazdin, A. E. (1983).*Social Skill Assessment and Training with Children*. New York: Plenium Press.

Nelson, N. W. (1993). *Childhood language disorders in context*. New York: Merrill.

Raven, J. C. (1962).*Coloured progressive matrices*. London: H.K. Lewis.

Rustin, L. & Kuhr, A. (1999). *Social skills and the speech impaired*. London: Whurr.

Semel, E., Wiig, E. H. & Secord, W. A. (2000). *Clinical Evaluation of Language Fundamentals Third Edition UK Standardisation*. London: The Psychological Corporation.

Stothard, S. E., Snowling, M., Bishop, D. V. M., Chipchase, B. B. & Kaplan, C. A. (1998). Language impaired pre-schoolers: A follow-up into adolescence. *Journal of Speech, Language and Hearing Research*, **41**, 407–418.

Tomblin, J. B., Zhang, X., Buckwalter, P. & Catts, H. (2000). The association of reading disability, behavioural disorders and language impairment among second-grade children. *Journal of Child Psychology and Psychiatry*, **41**, 473–482.

Webster-Stratton, C., Reid, J. & Hammond, M. (2001). Social skills and problem solving training for children with early onset conduct problems: who benefits? *Journal of Child Psychology and Psychiatry*, **42**, 943–952.

Westby, C. (1999). Assessment of pragmatic competence in children with psychiatric disorders. In D. Rogers-Adkinson & P. Griffith (Eds.), *Communication disorders and children with psychiatric and behavioural disorders* (pp. 177–258). San Diego: Singular Publishing Group.

Wiig, E. H. & Secord, W. A. (1992). *Test of Word Knowledge (TOWK)*. New York: The Psychological Corporation.

Windfuhr, K. L., Faragher, B. & Conti-Ramsden, G. (2002). Lexical learning skills in young children with specific language impairment (SLI). *International Journal of Language and Communication Disorders*, **37**, 415–432.

9.7 Enhancing Language and Communication in Language-impaired Secondary School-aged Children

VICTORIA JOFFE

Department of Language and Communication Science, City University

INTRODUCTION

BACKGROUND

Research into language development and disorders has routinely focused on preschool and primary children. However, while most children have acquired basic linguistic regularities by the age of 3 years (Rice, 2004), they continue to develop the understanding and use of increasingly complex and abstract language throughout older childhood and adolescence (Berman, 2004; Nippold, 1998). As Berman (2004) concluded from recent investigations of language development in older typically developing children, 'becoming a *native* speaker is a rapid and highly efficient process, but becoming a *proficient* speaker takes a long time' (p. 10). Even though significant changes occur in language during adolescence, Nippold (1998) points out that it is still assumed that language development is complete by then. For example, Lennenberg (1967) argues for a critical period for language acquisition between the ages of 2 and 12 years. This is not to say that there is no language development after puberty; Lennenberg himself reports some linguistic changes in adolescence. The early years should thus be seen as the period of primary language acquisition with subsequent language development being a more gradual and protracted process (Nippold, 1998). It may be, of course, that language development is more difficult to observe during this period, which may be one reason there are relatively few studies reporting typical linguistic development in adolescence.

Adolescents experience fundamental changes in cognitive, social and educational development; when they move from primary to secondary education, their orientation typically becomes increasingly peer-focused (Moshman, 1999). At secondary school, adolescents are required to integrate their linguistic, cognitive

Language and Social Disadvantage: Theory into Practice Edited by J. Clegg and J. Ginsborg
© 2006 John Wiley & Sons, Ltd

and social skills into coherent meaningful discourse. During this period, they enter Piaget's formal operational stage of development, becoming capable of sophisti-cated reasoning and higher-level logical and abstract cognitive processing. These changes pose significant challenges for young people using language to meet social and educational demands.

Not only is there relatively little research on language development in adoles-cence, there is also relatively little clinical research with language-impaired adoles-cents. This reflects the shortage of speech and language therapy (SLT) provision for this population, reported in Britain (Law, Lindsay, Peacey et al., 2000; Leahy & Dodd, 2002) and beyond (Larson, McKinley & Boley, 1993; McKinley & Larson, 1989; Paul, 2001). A significant proportion of secondary school-aged students have profound language and communication impairments, which impede access to the national curriculum. Few currently receive any SLT provision, despite strong evidence for the long-term effects of speech, language and communication impair-ments into adolescence and adulthood (Clegg, Hollis, Mawhood & Rutter, 2005; Conti-Ramsden, Botting, Simkin & Knox, 2001; Johnson, Beitchman, Young et al., 1999; Stothard, Snowling, Bishop, Chipchase & Kaplan, 1998).

The long-term nature of language and communication impairments and the rigorous demands of secondary school justify increasing SLT provision in this context. Limited resources are one stumbling block. Furthermore, awareness of the need for evidence-based practice in health care is increasing (Pring, 2004), while it could be argued that the SLT profession, generally, still lacks a robust evidence base (Reilly, 2004). However, there is some evidence that intervention with secondary school-aged children can be effective (Larson et al., 1993; Leahy & Dodd, 2002; Chapter 9.6, this volume). The present research attempted to address this gap in service provision through an exploratory pilot study, funded by Afasic (a national UK charity for children with speech and language difficulties), investigating the effectiveness of two interventions designed to enhance the language and commu-nication abilities of secondary school-aged children. One involved narrative, the other vocabulary enrichment.

Improving narrative ability has been found to be effective with younger children (Davies, Shanks & Davies, 2004). Storytelling is an integral part of our everyday lives. It is universal and forms part of our common humanity. Narrative ability is required in the school context as well as in social settings as a means of gaining peer group acceptance. At Key Stages 3 and 4, the National Curriculum places great emphasis on speaking fluently and appropriately in different contexts and adapting language for a range of purposes and audiences. Storytelling makes heavy demands on children's receptive and expressive language ability, requiring more complex syntax and semantics, abstract and imaginative thinking, general knowledge, a range of pragmatic and discourse skills as well as drawing on a set of internal organ-isational rules. It is thus unsurprising that individuals with language impairments have been found consistently to have significant difficulties with storytelling (Liles, 1993). There is, however, very little research exploring the role of narrative in SLT provision and evaluating its effectiveness. Yet improving narrative ability is highly relevant to both the school and social context, has great ecological validity, can be undertaken in a very structured way and targets a range of receptive and expressive linguistic skills.

The growth of vocabulary has been identified as an important aspect of development during the adolescent period (Nippold, 1998, 2004). It entails the ability to retrieve words with speed and accuracy (Dockrell & Messer, 2004), use increased numbers of complex and low frequency words and elaborate semantic networks to facilitate literacy (Ravid, 2004), and the ability to define complex vocabulary (Nippold, Hegel, Sohlberg & Schwartz, 1999). The development of vocabulary knowledge has a central role in cognitive development, particularly in the development of literacy (Cunningham & Stanovich, 1997). Vocabulary enrichment is thus an important objective in SLT considering that, during the school years, children encounter new words of increasing complexity and abstractness with little direct time devoted to vocabulary instruction in school (Dockrell & Messer, 2004).

AIMS

The study aimed to determine the extent to which SLT can help secondary school-aged children with language and communication impairments, given their age and the pervasiveness of their impairments. Limited SLT resources meant that the chosen intervention programmes had to be as ecologically valid and cost-effective as possible, so the children were treated at school, in groups. Two interventions were undertaken, so that their relative effectiveness could be assessed: narrative and vocabulary enrichment.

METHOD

PARTICIPANTS

Fifty-four secondary school-aged children (47 boys and 7 girls) with language and communication impairments took part in the study. Their mean age was 12;8 years (range 10;0 years to 15;3 years). They were referred by an outer London borough SLT Service or by Special Educational Needs Coordinators (SENCOs) from participating schools and, except for one child, were not receiving SLT. The children presented with severe and complex difficulties in language and communication, consistently scoring one or more standard deviations below the mean on a range of receptive and expressive language assessments (see Table 9.7.1). The children were randomly assigned to one of the two intervention groups.

MATERIALS

As shown in Table 9.7.1 a battery of assessments was administered pre- and post-intervention exploring non-verbal intelligence, receptive and expressive language abilities, literacy and narrative skills.

Therapy materials were drawn from topics in the National Curriculum. The narrative approach was based on the resources and tasks used by Shanks (2000;

Table 9.7.1. Pre- and post-intervention assessments

Intelligence
Picture Completion and Block Design subtests of the Wechsler Intelligence Scale for Children (Wechsler, 1992a)*
Receptive and expressive language
British Picture Vocabulary Scale (BPVS) (Dunn, Dunn, Whetton & Burley, 1997).
Test for Reception Of Grammar – 2 (TROG 2) (Bishop, 2003)
Clinical Evaluation of Language Fundamentals UK – 3 (CELF-3[UK]) (Semel, Wiig & Secord, 2000), five subtests as follows:
– Word classes
– Formulated sentences
– Word associations
– Recalling sentences
– Listening to paragraphs
Assessment of Comprehension and Expression 6-11 (ACE) (Adams, Cooke, Crutchley, Hesketh & Reeves, 2001), four subtests as follows:
– Naming
– Expressive narrative
– Inferential comprehension
– Non-literal comprehension
Expression, Reception and Recall of Narrative Instrument (ERRNI) (Bishop, 2004)
Literacy
Wechsler Objective Reading Dimensions (WORD) (Wechsler, 1992b), subtests of:
– Basic reading
– Spelling
– Reading comprehension

---

* Not administered post-intervention

Shanks & Rippon, 2003) with school-aged children, and story grammar cue cards recommended by Montague, Graves and Leavell (1991). Vocabulary enrichment was curriculum-based (Paul, 2001; Law et al., 2000), and taught the use of dictionary and thesaurus. A post-intervention questionnaire, administered by the student SLTs, was used to evaluate the children's perceptions of its effectiveness.

PROCEDURE

Pre-intervention assessments were carried out first. The assessments and intervention programmes were administered by student SLTs, although they did not assess the children with whom they carried out the intervention. As shown in Table 9.7.2, there were no significant differences between the performance of the two groups on the two subtests of intelligence.

Each intervention programme took place over a six-week period with two sessions, per week, each lasting about 50 minutes. Detailed guidelines, instructions, session plans and materials were provided.

The narrative approach incorporated the understanding and telling of stories with a focus on story structure, story description and inferential understanding. The

Table 9.7.2. Mean scaled scores on measures of intelligence

WISC	Group	n	Pre-intervention	Mean difference
Block design	Vocabulary	27	5.00 (3.4)	$F(1,53) = 1.03, p > 0.05$
	Narrative	27	6.11 (4.8)	
Picture completion	Vocabulary	27	6.07 (3.8)	$F(1,53) = 0.47, p > 0.05$
	Narrative	27	6.78 (3.8)	

intervention introduced the children to storytelling: the basic components of a story (who, when, where, why and its climax) and story structure (beginning, middle and end). At each session, children listened and told stories using a story planner (Shanks, 2000). The therapy focused on encouraging the children to think beyond the literal interpretation and infer information from the context. The children were encouraged to use paralinguistic features to make their stories more interesting. The children were required to answer questions about the stories they heard and were encouraged to critically evaluate the stories using the narrative features discussed in the sessions.

The vocabulary enrichment programme involved the teaching of key concepts and vocabulary through word associations, mind-mapping and word-building. Topic areas relevant to this age group were used including current affairs, famous people, employment-seeking, exam preparation and the media. Specific vocabulary items from National Curriculum subjects were targeted including geography, mathematics, history, information technology and science. The children were encouraged to categorise new vocabulary into related groups through the use of brainstorming and word webs to help them remember new words more easily. The children were encouraged to use synonyms, antonyms, multiple meanings, definitions and categorisation and classification games to explore word meanings and boundaries.

Four months after the pre-intervention assessments, post-intervention assessments were administered and the children were asked to complete the questionnaire. This required them to describe and evaluate the intervention programme they had received, its specific benefits in the classroom, at home and with friends, and how they thought it could have been improved. Their responses were recorded by the student SLTs.

RESULTS

As shown in Table 9.7.3, below, there were no significant differences between the performance of the two groups on any of the tests. For the group as a whole, there were significant improvements, however, following both types of intervention, on measures of receptive vocabulary (BPVS), recalling sentences (CELF-3) and non-literal comprehension (ACE). Differences in performance on tests of word classes (CELF) and receptive grammar (TROG-2) just failed to reach significance. Gains

Table 9.7.3. Mean-pre intervention and post-intervention standard scores and standard deviations (SD)

Measure	Group	Pre-intervention	n	Post-intervention	n	ANOVA
Receptive language						
BPVS	Vocabulary	67.3 (14.1)	23	70.0 (13.0)	23	Time: $F(1,47) = 6.09$, $p = .017$
	Narrative	74.8 (16.1)	26	78.7 (18.8)	26	
TROG-2	Vocabulary	70.0 (14.1)	26	76.3 (15.7)	26	Time: $F(1,51) = 3.56$, ns
	Narrative	73.9 (23.0)	27	77.5 (22.1)	27	
Word classes (CELF-3[UK])	Vocabulary	4.1 (1.4)	23	4.6 (1.7)	23	Time: $F(1,46) = 3.29$, ns
	Narrative	4.2 (2.0)	25	4.8 (2.6)	25	
Non-literal comprehension (ACE*)	Vocabulary	5.1 (2.7)	26	5.6 (2.9)	26	Time: $F(1,51) = 7.51$, $p = .008$
	Narrative	5.3 (2.5)	27	6.7 (3.4)	27	
Expressive language						
Recalling sentences (CELF-3[UK])	Vocabulary	3.9 (1.5)	26	4.7 (2.0)	26	Time: $F(1,50) = 4.65$, $p = .036$
	Narrative	4.9 (2.7)	26	5.0 (2.8)	26	
ERNNI mean length utterance	Vocabulary	84.9 (25.5)	18	72.1 (28.1)	18	Time: $F(1,36) = 10.8$, $p = .002$
	Narrative	100.0 (18.9)	20	77.8 (29.7)	20	

ACE* = standard score for 11.11 years was used for all children above age of 11.11 years (36 of the children in total)

in pre- and post-intervention mean scores were observed on the ACE narrative task and the reading comprehension subtest of the WORD for the narrative group compared to the vocabulary group but these did not reach significance. The vocabulary group made more gains than the narrative group on the TROG-2, recalling sentences subtest of the CELF and the naming subtest of the ACE. However, these improvements did not reach significance. Curiously, the group as a whole performed worse post-intervention on mean length of utterance using the matched story tasks of the ERNNI.

According to the questionnaires, 74% of the children believed that 'their' programme had helped them with talking and understanding. More than half of them (56%) reported that it helped with their reading and writing, 54% said it helped them in the classroom and in getting on with friends and 33% said it helped them make new friends. A total of 41% felt they would like to have more of these lessons. Thus, the majority of children reported some important benefits from the intervention.

DISCUSSION

The levels of language and literacy skills of the children in the current study raise considerable concern. These children, despite being identified by teaching and therapy staff as having language difficulties, are being educated in a mainstream setting with little or no specialist support. Secondary school-aged children are typically faced with the increasingly rigorous demands of the National Curriculum, which draw on complex higher-level linguistic processing. Their significant language and literacy impairments severely restrict their ability to access successfully the curriculum and place them at increased risk for difficulties in communication, socialisation, self-esteem and employment in adulthood. This situation is made worse by the lack of SLT and specialist education resources with this population.

Low scores were obtained on the two non-verbal subtests of the WISC (Wechsler, 1992a), suggesting that this cohort shows a more general language learning disability than specific language impairment. The developmental nature of non-verbal IQ over time has been discussed elsewhere (Chapter 2, this volume). It is, however, important to note that both groups of children, that is those with specific and non-specific language impairment, require specialist support according to the relative strengths of the individual.

We have to be cautious in explaining the observed improvements on some of the language measures in the absence of a control group, as we cannot be certain that they result from the intervention. Nevertheless, given the pervasiveness and severity of the children's language impairments, and the fact that reported changes in assessment scores following intervention for this age group are often small (Nippold, 1998), it is pleasing to note this improvement on a range of language measures over a relatively short period of time. Certainly these results are encouraging and we shall therefore be undertaking further studies to explore the potential benefits of therapy with this group.

A number of methodological issues arise from the study. There was an obvious need for a no-treatment control group, but this raises ethical considerations. In fact we would not have received support for the study if we had included a no treatment control group. A cross-over design, whereby the children are all given therapy at different times and hence act as their own controls, could be used avoiding the problem of denying therapy to some of the children. Children with very different language skills participated in this study and therefore the intervention was broad. This may explain why we did not find significant differences between groups on the post-intervention measures. Therapy aimed to benefit groups of children with similar needs might have produced better results. Future research will address this by using a more focused narrative programme with smaller groups of children who have specific language impairments. The question of what outcome measures to use to monitor change is another important issue to consider. It may well be that standardised assessments are not sufficiently sensitive to pick up more subtle changes in performance. We are exploring the use of more descriptive qualitative profiles and checklists to assess any additional changes in performance.

CONCLUSIONS

This study reported an intervention study with language-impaired secondary school-aged children, educated in mainstream settings. They had significant language and communication impairments, but were receiving little or no specialist support. The results indicate that adolescents with language and communication impairments can show improvements in their language abilities after relatively short periods of therapy.

ACKNOWLEDGMENTS

Thanks to the Toyne Baby Triathlon and Afasic for funding the study, and to the children, schools, parents, therapists and SLT students who agreed to participate in the study. The intervention was devised by the author in collaboration with three SLT students at City University: Kendall Bright, Lorraine Finn and Linzi Green.

REFERENCES

Adams, C., Cooke, R., Crutchley, A., Hesketh, A. & Reeves, D. (2001). *Assessment of Comprehension and Expression 6–11*. Berkshire: NFER-NELSON.
Berman, R. (2004). Between emergence and mastery: the long developmental route of language acquisition. In R. A. Berman (Ed.), *Language development across childhood and adolescence*. Amsterdam: John Benjamins.

Bishop, D. V. M. (2003). *Test for Reception of Grammar – version 2*. London: The Psychological Corporation.

Bishop, D. V. M. (2004). *Expression, Reception and Recall of Narrative Instrument*. London: Harcourt Assessment.

Clegg, J., Hollis, C., Mawhood, L. & Rutter, M. (2005) Developmental language disorders a follow-up in later adult life. Cognitive, language and psychosocial outcomes *Journal of Child Psychology and Psychiatry*, **46**(2), 128–149.

Conti-Ramsden, G., Botting, N., Simkin, Z. & Knox, E. (2001). Follow-up of children attending infant language units: outcomes at 11 years of age. *International Journal of Language and Communication Disorders*, **36**, 207–219.

Cunningham, A. & Stanovich, K. (1997). Early reading acquisition and its relation to reading experience and ability ten years later. *Developmental Psychology*, **33**(6), 934–945.

Davies, P., Shanks, B. & Davies, K. (2004). Improving narrative skills in young children with delayed language development. *Educational Review*, **56**(3), 271–286.

Dockrell, J. & Messer, D. (2004). Lexical Acquisition in the early school years. In R. A. Berman (Ed.), *Language development across childhood and adolescence*. Amsterdam: John Benjamins.

Dunn, L. M., Dunn, L. M., Whetton, C. & Burley, J. (1997). *British Picture Vocabulary Scale* (2nd edn). Windsor: NFER-Nelson.

Johnson, C. J., Beitchman, J. H., Young, A., Escobar, M., Atkinson, L., Brownlie, E. B., Douglas, L., Taback, N., Lam, I. & Wang, M. (1999). Fourteen-year follow-up of children with and without speech/language impairments: speech/language stability and outcomes. *Journal of Speech, Language and Hearing Research*, **42**, 744–761.

Larson, V., McKinley, N. & Boley, D. (1993). Clinical forum: adolescent language. Service delivery models for adolescents with language disorders. *Language Speech and Hearing Services in Schools*, **24**, 36–42.

Law, J., Lindsay, G., Peacey, N., Gascoigne, M., Soloff, N., Radford, J. & Band, S. (2000). *Provision for children with speech and language needs in England and Wales: Facilitating communication between education and health services*. London: DfEE/DoH.

Leahy, M. & Dodd, B. (2002). Why should secondary schools come second? *RCSLT Bulletin*, **60**, 11–13.

Legler, D. (1991). *Don't take it so literally*. Youngtown, AZ, USA: ECL Publications.

Lennenberg, E. (1967). *Biological foundations of language*. New York: John Wiley.

Liles, B. (1993). Narrative discourse in children with language disorders and children with normal language: a critical review of the literature. *Journal of Speech and Hearing Research*, **36**, 868–882.

McKinley, N. & Larson, V. (1989). Students who can't communicate: speech-language services at the secondary level. *National Association of Secondary School Principals Curriculum Report*, **19**, 1–8.

Montague, M., Graves, A. & Leavell, A. (1991). Planning, procedural facilitation, and narrative composition of junior high students with learning disabilities. *Learning Disabilities Research and Practice*, **6**, 219–224.

Moshman, D. (1999). *Adolescent psychological development. Rationality, morality and identity*. Mahwah, NJ: LEA Publishers.

Nippold, M. (1998). *Later language development. The school-age and adolescent years*. Austin, TX: Pro-ed.

Nippold, M. (2004). Research on later language development: international perspectives. In R. A. Berman (Ed.), *Language development across childhood and adolescence*. Amsterdam: John Benjamins.

Nippold, M., Hegel, S., Sohlberg, M. & Schwartz, I. (1999). Defining abstract entities: development in preadolescents, adolescents and young adults. *Journal of Speech, Language and Hearing Research*, **42**, 473–481.

Paul, R. (2001). *Language disorders from infancy through adolescence. Assessment and intervention*. St Louis, MO: Mosby.

Pring, T. (2004). Ask a silly question: two decades of troublesome trials. *International Journal of Language and Communication Disorders*, **39**(3), 285–302.

Ravid, D. (2004). Derivational morphology revisited: later lexical development in Hebrew. In R. A. Berman (Ed.), *Language development across childhood and adolescence*. Amsterdam: John Benjamins.

Reilly, S. (2004). The move to evidence-based practice within speech pathology. In S. Reilly, J. Douglas & J. Oates (Eds.), *Evidence based practice in speech pathology*. London: Whurr.

Rice, M. (2004). Growth models of developmental language disorders. In M. L. Rice and S. F. Warren (Eds.), *Developmental language disorders: from phenotype to etiologies*. Mahwah, NJ: Lawrence Erlbaum Associates.

Semel, E., Wiig, E. & Secord, W. (2000). *Clinical Evaluation of Language Fundamentals UK* (3rd edn). London: The Psychological Corporation.

Shanks B. (2000). Telling tales. *The Royal College of Speech and Language Therapists Bulletin*, **583**, 9–10.

Shanks, B. & Rippon, H. (2003). *Speaking and listening through narrative*. Keighley: Blacksheep Press with Stockport NHS Trust & Stockport PCT.

Stothard, S., Snowling, M., Bishop, D., Chipchase, B. & Kaplan, C. (1998). Language-impaired preschoolers: a follow-up into adolescence. *Journal of Speech, Language and Hearing Research*, **41**, 407–418.

Wechsler, D. (1992a). *Wechsler Intelligence Scale for Children* (3rd edn). Sidcup: The Psychological Corporation.

Wechsler, D. (1992b). *The Wechsler Objective Reading Dimensions*. Sidcup: The Psychological Corporation.

Afterword

ANN LOCKE
Education and Language Consultant

This book provides clear evidence that socio-economic disadvantage can lead to significant differences, if not deficits, in children's spoken language (Ginsborg, Chapter 1). These differences may in turn impact on their educational progress well into the primary years, if not beyond. The link between spoken language and reading development is well documented and the potential links between spoken language and writing and numeracy also cannot be ignored (Doherty and Landells, Chapter 3). Moreover, evidence from long-term studies of children with specific language impairments and learning difficulties shows that poor spoken language also restricts children's cognitive development (Botting, Chapter 2), social and emotional understanding (Farmer, Chapter 5), social behaviour (Stringer and Clegg, Chapter 6), social inclusion (Bray, Chapter 7) and later life chances (Clegg, Chapter 4). While we need to be cautious in arguing from this research to cases where language delay seems to be due to environmental factors, strong relationships have also been demonstrated between language development and cognitive and social development in typically developing children. It is, at the very least, a reasonable hypothesis that the poor spoken language of children growing up in poverty will have a significant impact on their educational progress in both the short and the long term. It may well be a major factor in the 'tail of underachievement' that is currently the cause of so much concern.

In the USA, attempts over many years to promote the communication skills of socially-disadvantaged children have had varying results, the most successful being those that have addressed the needs of parents as well as their children (Law and Harris, Chapter 8). Since the mid-1990s, there has been a growing awareness by politicians in this country of the need to fund similar projects, and substantial amounts of money have been directed to community initiatives providing support to families with young children. The results of these initiatives are beginning to be analysed, though the time-span so far, often no more than five years, is probably too short to establish significant differences in the families concerned.

In the meantime, the problem of delayed development of spoken language in children entering nurseries has become so acute in areas of social disadvantage that a number of local projects to promote language have been set up by health and

Language and Social Disadvantage: Theory into Practice Edited by J. Clegg and J. Ginsborg
© 2006 John Wiley & Sons, Ltd

education support services, and it is encouraging to see that these interventions can make a difference, not just with younger children (Research Reports 9.1 to 9.5) but also with children of secondary age (Research Reports 9.6 and 9.7). But valuable though this work is, it still only scratches the surface of the problem. These are, of necessity, small-scale studies of focused intervention with a few selected children, showing modest, short-term gains. Longer term gains are more difficult to establish, both in the sense that they are more difficult to generate, especially from short-term intervention, and in the sense that they are more expensive and time-consuming to demonstrate.

The problem of children from disadvantaged backgrounds underachieving in school because of inadequate spoken language is urgent, growing and insufficiently recognised. To deal with it we need to address three interlocking issues.

The first is the need for much greater awareness of the issues, among policy-makers and politicians and in schools and nurseries. Until the problems are recognised by the policy-makers we will not get the changes that are needed in the early education of children in disadvantaged areas. While the importance of language has always been acknowledged, it is almost always written language that gets attention, in education policy, the curriculum and classroom intervention. Ask anyone why spoken language matters and the answer will usually be a vague reference to the value of communication. Yet adequate spoken language is an essential underpinning for all teaching and learning, as well as for promoting children's confidence, social and emotional development and thinking skills. More crucially, a good grasp of spoken language is essential for literacy. Children have to be able to say it before they will read it or write it. An understanding of spoken language is the basis of reading comprehension; coherent talk is the basis of coherent writing. Children who have difficulty with one will always struggle with the other. Yet for all the attention and funding given to literacy in recent years, this fundamental point is not widely recognised. Children are pressured into literacy without ensuring that the essential prerequisites are in place. As a result, the literacy strategy is failing to impact where it is needed most, among the most disadvantaged children.

Schools in deprived areas are well aware of children whose spoken language is inadequate for the demands of the national curriculum. But they too may not be fully aware of how badly delayed many of these children are, what the impact on their later development may be, or, indeed, what to do about it. Staff are not trained in the development of children's spoken language or its importance for literacy, learning and social development. Such guidance as there is in 'speaking and listening' is complex, diffuse and inappropriate for these children. Staff do not know what to teach, how to teach it or how to identify the children who need specific support. Indeed, without some background knowledge of language development, there is a danger that staff working in areas where most children have poor language skills will lower their expectations of what children of that age are capable of, and will actually compound the problem.

The second issue is the need for more information, both about the impact of social disadvantage on children's spoken language and about the impact of language delay on their progress in school and other development. The evidence so far is that many more children are delayed in their spoken language, and their language is much more impoverished, than we might think. We also need to know more about the effect of this delay on their wider development, rather than relying on evidence from studies of children with specific language impairments or learning difficulties. Without strong evidence we are unlikely to change the mind-set of policy makers, focused as it is on written rather than spoken language, or to affect what actually happens in classrooms and nurseries. Politicians, in particular, tend to be more interested in quick fixes than long-term effects. They may need to be shown not just the long-term educational impact of inadequate spoken language in children entering school or nurseries, but also how deep-rooted and persistent the problems of social disadvantage are.

There is, however, something of a vicious circle here. Good research, especially the long-term research needed to establish long-term effects, requires funding, and funding is subject to fashion and the interests and priorities of policy-makers. We need to get the evidence if we are to make policy-makers and funding bodies more aware of the issues; but we also need to make them more aware of the issues if we are to get the evidence. To break into this circle, professionals need to exert pressure on both sides at once: they need to stress the role of spoken language in children's development in general and for literacy in particular, and to promote as strongly as they can the research evidence we do have, and the need for more.

The final issue is the need to affect educational practice. This is unlikely to happen without direction from educational policy-makers, which in turn will depend on evidence of the extent and depth of the problem. But it will not be enough that politicians and policy-makers recognise and understand the problem of spoken language and social disadvantage; they will also need to be convinced that there are practicable and affordable ways of doing something about it. It is not clear, for example, that the type of project reported here can provide an effective model for intervention on the wider scale that is needed. These projects rely on specialist support, and work with only a small number of children. It is unrealistic to expect that the resources needed for this type of intervention can ever be made available for all the children and in all the schools that need it.

If we are to have a real impact on the problem, schools in disadvantaged areas are going to need a whole-class whole-school approach that is manageable with existing staff, within existing resources and on top of the existing curriculum. This will not be easy. In schools and nurseries a limited number of staff have to deal with a large number of children. The natural language-learning environment where one or two adults talk and play with one or two children cannot easily be reproduced in the mainstream classroom. Moreover, the amount of vocabulary and the range of language skills that children from advantaged backgrounds have developed by the time they enter school or nursery is enormous, and we cannot expect classroom teachers to assess, teach and monitor all these skills in all the children in their class.

Instead of the developmental model of intensive, one-to-one intervention, we need an educational or curriculum model where spoken language is promoted for all children through normal classroom teaching and activities and the normal school curriculum. We need to be able to identify the spoken language skills that are most important for progress in school, and especially – since literacy is currently the measure of educational success – for progress in literacy. We need to establish how these skills can best be taught in classroom settings. And we need to train teachers both in what to teach and how to teach it.

Language does not develop in a vacuum and any aspect of the school curriculum can and should provide a starting point for language teaching and learning. But teachers need a degree of structure if they are to know which skills to teach, and they need an understanding of normal language learning if they are to provide the modelling, reinforcement and repetition that young children need. We also need to highlight the importance of allowing children to talk in the classroom. Talk, like other skills, improves with practice, but in too many classrooms it is teachers, not children, who do most of the talking. More crucially, we cannot expect significant long-term improvements in children's spoken language unless we also improve the knowledge and skills of teaching staff, so they can provide the systematic intervention that these children need.

The studies in this volume contribute to our understanding of the importance of spoken language for children's development and educational progress. But if we are to have a significant effect on the tail of underachievement and the problem of children growing up in poverty, we also need radically to rethink what we are doing in our schools.

Index

Language and Social Disadvantage: Theory into Practice Edited by J. Clegg and J. Ginsborg
© 2006 John Wiley & Sons, Ltd